M000313030

THE JAPANESE AMERICAN STORY

THE JAPANESE AMERICAN STORY

As Told Through a Collection of Speeches and Articles

S. FLOYD MORI

YorkshirePublishing
www.yorkshirepublishing.com
Write Now.

ISBN: 978-1-947247-36-9
The Japanese American Story
Copyright © 2014 - Republished 2017 by S. Floyd Mori

For permission requests, write to the publisher at the address below.

Yorkshire Publishing
3207 South Norwood Avenue
Tulsa, Oklahoma 74135
www.YorkshirePublishing.com
918.394.2665

Dedicated to the *Issei* Pioneers,
the *Nisei* Trailblazers,
and *ALL* who suffered
from World War II

Issei: First generation immigrants from Japan

Nisei: Second generation Americans born in the
United States of Japanese immigrant parents

ACKNOWLEDGMENTS

Appreciation is given to Stan Kanzaki for his helpful suggestions and kind words of encouragement, to John Tagami for his useful recommendations, and to those who believed in the concept of this book. Thanks to Irene Mori and Cheryl Mori for their work in bringing this project to fruition.

CONTENTS

PREFACE

Although a number of books have been written about the Japanese American experience of World War II when one hundred twenty thousand persons of Japanese heritage were forcibly evacuated from their West Coast homes and incarcerated in America's concentration camps, it seems to be a story of which much of the population is not aware. This is an attempt to share some of that story, so that the public may know of this period in history when the Constitution did not protect innocent Americans and immigrants of Japanese ancestry because of racial prejudice, war hysteria, and a lack of competent government leadership. The main purpose in sharing this information is to tell about these experiences to, hopefully, ensure that no other people will ever have to endure such mistreatment and injustice as were inflicted upon Japanese Americans during World War II.

THE JAPANESE AMERICAN STORY BACKGROUND

The Japanese American story is a collective tale of courage, sacrifice, faith, hope, and determination in the face of hardship, discrimination, and persecution from which significant success was eventually achieved. It is a complex and interwoven narrative whose main thread is the community's treatment during, and response to, the challenges they faced during World War II. It is a story with tragic elements, but ultimately one of triumph and overcoming which showed a high degree of perseverance, strength, loyalty, and patriotism. This is an attempt to tell some of the Japanese American story and is semi-autobiographical in relating personal experiences from Floyd Mori's own life as an American of Japanese heritage.

Japanese immigrants started arriving in the United States during the late 1800s with larger numbers coming in the early part of the 1900s. Most of the earliest immigrants were young, single men. They arrived on these shores largely for economic reasons, as America was seen as the *land of opportunity*, and they came as laborers willing to work. Many of the men married women from Japan (some of whom were called "picture brides"). Some of the immigrant men, who arrived later, wed Japanese American women.

The people, who came from Japan, were called the *Issei* or first generation. They were pioneers who paved the way for others who came later. Their children born in America were the *Nisei* or second generation and were the first Americans of Japanese descent. They were trailblazers who worked hard to make life better. Subsequent generations are the *Sansei* (third generation), *Yonsei* (fourth generation), and *Gosei* (fifth generation). As the Japanese people in the United States began to establish families, farms, and small businesses with some limited degree of success, they were often looked upon as a threat by the general population. Having distinctly different physical characteristics from Americans and immigrants who had come from Europe, they found themselves treated with disdain, distrust, prejudice, and outright racism. By 1925, further immigration from Japan had been curtailed.

Leaders within the Japanese American community started a national organization, the Japanese American Citizens League (JACL), in 1929 to advocate for civil rights. Several local Japanese American community organizations were already in existence, but the JACL became the main voice for Japanese Americans on a national level. The JACL was founded with the mission to secure and uphold the civil rights of Americans of Japanese ancestry, to preserve the cultural heritage and values of Japanese Americans, and to combat social injustice against all people regardless of race or circumstances.

A dark period in history for Japanese Americans and the entire nation came during World War II after Japan bombed Pearl Harbor on December 7, 1941. American citizens and immigrants of Japanese ancestry were immediately looked upon as the enemy. Many leaders within the community were arrested and imprisoned. President Franklin D. Roosevelt signed Executive Order 9066 (EO 9066) on February 19, 1942, which gave the military commander the authority to remove any person from certain designated areas.

People, who were of Japanese heritage, were first requested to leave the West Coast of the United States voluntarily and move to inland states, which a small number of people did. The rest of the Japanese population living on the West Coast of the mainland United States were forcibly removed from their homes with little notice and incarcerated in hastily constructed camps in remote and desolate areas of the country. They were taken to temporary assembly centers at fairgrounds and race tracks until the camps were ready for occupancy. The government went to considerable expense to build the barracks and other buildings and to staff the ten camps that housed the people who were ethnic Japanese.

The Japanese Americans and immigrants from Japan suffered greatly after the bombing of Pearl Harbor, particularly those who lived on the West Coast. Leaders within the community were arrested and put in prison. A curfew was enforced restricting them to travel only within five miles of their homes. They lost their jobs and businesses. Their bank accounts were frozen, imposing serious financial hardship. Some of the children could not go to school because of the hardships they faced. Fear and uncertainly permeated throughout the community.

Then EO 9066 was signed which allowed the forced evacuation and unwarranted incarceration. This caused tremendous harm and suffering for the one hundred twenty thousand American citizens and immigrants affected by the order. Many suffered the effects of incarceration throughout their entire lives. Some people became ill and died in the camps or soon after being released at the war's end. It is hard to believe that such a thing could happen in the United States of America to its own citizens and legal resident alien immigrants due to racial prejudice and war hysteria.

The Western Defense Command under the direction of Lt. Gen. John L. DeWitt implemented EO 9066 against the Japanese people living in the West Coast states. The order was used only against those who were of Japanese ancestry although it could have been enacted against people of German and Italian heritage as well. Lt. Gen. Delos Emmons, commanding general in Hawaii (which was then a United States territory), determined it was not necessary to implement the order in the islands. The Japanese Americans living in Hawaii were largely spared the same treatment although there were some camps in Hawaii such as Sand Island and Honouliuli where leaders and others from within the Japanese American and Japanese immigrant communities were held as prisoners. A large scale evacuation would not have been feasible in Hawaii because the Japanese people made up such a large part of the population and were vital to the economy.

In addition to DeWitt, other government officials, who were in part responsible for the incarceration and who also expressed racist thoughts were Col. Karl R. Bendetsen, who stated that he wanted all with even "one drop of Japanese blood" to be imprisoned (later changed to 1/32 of Japanese blood), and Assistant Secretary of War, John J. McCloy, who is said to have stated in effect that in time of war the Constitution is just a piece of paper.

There was no logical reason for the evacuation and incarceration of Japanese Americans during World War II, as stated many times by political and military leaders since the war ended. The West Coast was the area over which Lt. Gen DeWitt had command, and he chose to enforce the order. It was enacted in the states of California, Oregon, and Washington, where the majority of the Japanese American population lived. There were local and state leaders in California opposed to the Japanese. People in the agricultural area were vehemently against the Japanese farmers who were their competition. California newspapers printed articles against those of Japanese ancestry and advocated for their evacuation.

Government records indicate that there were approximately 127,000 people of Japanese ancestry living in the continental United States at the time of Pearl Harbor. Hawaii had around 150,000 persons who were ethnically Japanese, and they made up about one third of the population of the islands.

The government used the excuse that those living on the West Coast were more likely to be spies for Japan as they were closer in proximity to the enemy. It was a huge undertaking with just the three states affected and would have been difficult to enact in the entire country. Although there were around 10,000 other Japanese Americans living in the United States, they were scattered throughout several states so they understandably had little influence in their areas and did not seem to be considered a threat. A commission later determined that the act of the evacuation and incarceration was a racist and discriminatory measure illegally used against the people of Japanese heritage.

Most of those directly affected by EO 9066 were incarcerated for the duration of the war, with the majority being American citizens born in the United States. The basic freedoms which should be guaranteed by the Constitution to all citizens were stripped away. They were imprisoned in chain link and barbed wire enclosed camps in bleak and isolated regions of the country through no fault of their own and only because of their ethnic heritage. People who were of Japanese ancestry and living in other parts of the country were not directly and personally impacted by EO 9066, but they suffered difficulties and hatred as well because they were also viewed by many as the enemy.

Even before the war began, unjust laws were adopted targeting Japanese Americans and the immigrants from Japan, such as laws against property ownership and intermarriage as well as the provision against further immigration from Japan. The early JACL leaders fought against the unfair laws in order to make a better life for themselves, their parents, their children, and future generations. Though many of the leaders of the Japanese American community were placed in the camps or other prisons during the war years, the JACL had work to do. The JACL headquarters was moved temporarily from California to Salt Lake City, Utah.

The JACL counts only a small portion of the Japanese American population as its members, but it plays a significant role in advocating for the civil rights of all Americans. The majority of Japanese Americans have assimilated fairly well into the mainstream American society since World War II, and many are likely unaware of the work being done by the National JACL.

Throughout these writings, the camps are referred to as "American concentration camps" or "illegal detention centers" where citizens and immigrants of Japanese descent were incarcerated within makeshift prisons of barbed wire enclosures with searchlights and armed guards with guns pointed inward. This was done to American citizens by their own country without any due process.

The camps have previously also been referred to as "internment camps." The JACL has encouraged a *power of words* campaign to use stronger terms than the euphemisms formerly used. Those who tried to protest the ill treatment of Japanese Americans were arrested and sent to federal prisons or to one of the camps, many to Tule Lake which became designated as the place for troublemakers. Years later these individuals were pardoned and honored for the courageous stand they took.

These illegal detention centers or American concentration camps should be distinguished from the harsh realities and horror of the concentration camps of Europe and other areas where innocent people experienced death and torture during times of war. The Japanese Americans were not physically tortured, but they were held captive as prisoners within the camps. They suffered in ways many of us cannot imagine, including the loss of almost all their material possessions and loss of their dignity and freedom. They endured hardship, pain, shame, illness, and even death. The emotional, physical, social, and psychological ramifications of the unjust evacuation and incarceration were suffered for years and, for many, throughout their entire lives.

In 1980, Congress established the Commission on Wartime Relocation and Internment of Civilians (CWRIC) to study the issue of the evacuation and incarceration of Japanese Americans during World War II. The CWRIC determined that the forced evacuation and incarceration were: "…the result of race prejudice, war hysteria, and a failure of political leadership." Redress for the wrongs committed by the government was sought and achieved through the passage of the Civil Liberties Act of 1988 (the Redress Bill) signed by President Ronald Reagan. Redress is explained further throughout this book.

There were some Japanese people who were incarcerated in Canada and Australia, and Japanese Peruvians were deported and sent to be incarcerated in the United States. The Peruvian government cooperated with the US government and used the Japanese Peruvians as an exchange for American civilians held by the Japanese government. The JACL has been involved with trying to assist the Latin Japanese in gaining redress.

This is a small portion of the stories and experiences of Japanese Americans and of the JACL as told through selected speeches and articles prepared and presented by Floyd Mori during periods of time when he served as the JACL's National Executive Director/CEO (2006–2012), Director of Public Policy (2005–2006), and National President (2000–2004).

This book attempts to share important aspects of the experiences of the Japanese American community. It encompasses a critical part of history when the Constitution did not protect innocent persons, even the country's own citizens. Also included are some of Floyd's personal experiences as well as stories and examples which illustrate a portion of the subsequent success and triumph achieved by some Japanese Americans.

Although much of this work focuses on the treatment of Japanese Americans during World War II and the struggle for civil rights by the JACL, it is not a book about life in the camps. Since Floyd was born and raised in Utah, he and his family were not among those who were forcibly removed from their homes and incarcerated. Books have been written by people who were prisoners in the camps, and their stories are available to those who may be interested in learning more about the actual experience of living in the American concentration camps of World War II.

The JACL and other groups regularly gather on or around February 19 of each year at Day of Remembrance (DOR) events which center around the experiences resulting from the passage on February 19, 1942, and the rescinding on February 19, 1976, of EO 9066. These events are held to remember this period in history and to celebrate the ultimate success attained by many Japanese American people.

The Japanese American story needs to be told and retold in order to hopefully avoid a repeat of this travesty of justice. It is a story about the Constitution and freedom. The purpose in telling about these experiences is to inform the general public, which includes all people, and to prevent such a thing from ever happening again to anyone else in this great nation. It is surprising that many people are not aware of this mistreatment of Japanese Americans which occurred during World War II. It has been found that little about the Japanese American experiences during that period in history is included in most of the history books used in schools. It is important to teach about the Constitution by making known the unique aspects of the Japanese American story. Sharing some of the achievements which followed shows how the community overcame many of their trials.

Floyd has frequently been asked to speak to groups about the Japanese American and Asian American story. He generally delivers his speeches from his head and memory using handwritten notes or a sheet of key words typed on the computer. He prefers to "talk" with groups rather than to "read" a speech. When he began to be asked for copies of his speeches, he wrote them out with increased regularity although he did not always stick with the words as written. Some of the speeches were partially reconstructed from notes or transcribed from tapes. Most of the articles were originally written for the JACL membership with some being in the third person.

Various people within the Japanese American community have spoken at schools and to other groups about the Japanese American experiences during World War II. Most of these speakers were young adults, teenagers or children (as was Floyd) at the time of World War II. Many of their contemporaries and most of the older generation could never speak about those war years publicly (and often even privately) because it was too difficult and painful to talk about those hurtful experiences which had such an effect on their lives.

Because the audiences for the speeches were varied, there is naturally repetition. In addition to the recollections from Floyd's own life and the lives of people whom he has known, included are stories derived from research, study, personal knowledge, and experience. All are believed to be accurate, but they are not intended to be nor do they claim to be, a comprehensive study of the actual historical facts of the Japanese American story. Most of the historical information and quotes presented can be verified on the Internet. If there are errors, they may be attributed to honest mistakes. Apologies are given in advance to any who may find fault or take issue with anything written here.

There are matters and events of importance to the Japanese American community and the JACL which are not covered here. Many other speeches were presented and numerous articles were written which have not been included. Floyd has also spoken to groups at Brigham Young University, Howard University, Harvard University, the University of California Merced, the University of California Santa Barbara, and various government agencies and nonprofit organizations. The speeches which are included were all given in a public setting to various groups as indicated. The articles were printed previously in the JACL newspaper, *The Pacific Citizen*, and/or other media outlets as noted. The "review" item on the CWRIC hearings in Los Angeles was done specifically for this book. The speeches and articles are presented mostly in chronological order as presented or written. Each speech and article was prepared as a stand-alone piece which accounts for the repetition of certain aspects of the story.

This section and some other portions, including comments throughout the book, were written by Irene Mori, who compiled the speeches and articles.

THE JAPANESE AMERICAN CITIZENS LEAGUE (JACL) BACKGROUND

The Japanese American Citizens League (JACL) was founded in 1929 by young Japanese American leaders who felt the need for a national organization to benefit their fellow Americans of Japanese descent who faced discrimination and prejudice on a regular basis.

There were many anti-Japanese and anti-Asian laws on the books at that time which the JACL leaders wanted to have removed. The JACL continues to monitor and respond to issues related to civil rights of all Americans with particular emphasis on Japanese Americans and other Asian and Pacific Islander Americans. The JACL is the oldest and largest Asian American civil and human rights organization in the United States.

Striving to tell the Japanese American story, which includes the forced removal from the West Coast states of people of Japanese ancestry, is important for the JACL and Japanese Americans. It was later determined that the evacuation and incarceration denied Japanese Americans their constitutional rights and were the result of racial prejudice, war hysteria, and a failure of political leadership at that time.

The JACL has a teacher training program and provides teacher workshops to assist educators in bringing information about this period in history to students. Educators may contact any JACL office for information about the program and curriculum guide to teach about this chapter in our nation's history.

Along with other groups, numerous individuals, and members of Congress, the JACL worked to secure redress for those wrongs. The passage of the Civil Liberties Act of 1988 (the Redress Bill) signed by President Ronald Reagan was the culmination of over fifteen years of dedicated effort to bring some sense of justice to the wrongs of the forced evacuation. Leaders within the JACL want to ensure that the unfortunate experience of the incarceration of innocent Japanese Americans and immigrants from Japan during World War II will not be repeated against any other people.

With a headquarters building in San Francisco and a Washington DC Legislative and Advocacy office, the JACL also has four regional offices located in Chicago, Los Angeles, San Francisco, and Seattle with a regional director in each of those areas. The JACL has been a membership-driven organization and has more than one hundred chapters located throughout the United States including Alaska and Hawaii. It also has a chapter in Japan. The JACL strives to be inclusive and is open to interested persons regardless of ethnicity. Many of the leaders, who have served or who currently serve on the National Board of the JACL, such as David Lin, Chip Larouche, and David Unruhe, are not of Japanese descent.

The JACL now has corporate partners that provide financial sponsorships to sustain the organization and its programs. Some of those which have given financial support are: AARP, AMGEN, Annie E. Casey Foundation, Aratani Foundation, AT&T, Caesar's, Cole Chemical, Comcast, Eli Lilly, Embassy of Japan, Ford Motor, GEICO, IW Group, JACL Insurance Services, Japan Commerce Association of Washington,

McDonald's, MGM Grand, Mitsubishi, National Association of Broadcasters, National Education Association, National JACL Credit Union, Nissan, Nitto Tire, Paramount Pictures, Pfizer, Red Cross, SONY, Southwest Airlines, State Farm, Toyota, Union Bank, UPS Foundation, US Navy, Verizon, Walmart, and various others including government agencies, nonprofits, and individuals.

The national organization and the local chapters of the JACL promote values of and opportunities for cultural, educational, social, civic, service, and leadership aspects of life. Advocacy work in the civil rights area is a vital function of the JACL, and preserving the Japanese American history is important to the organization. More information on the JACL may be found at: www.jacl.org.

Anyone interested in learning more about the Japanese American story and history may check out densho.org and JANM.org. Densho is a nonprofit organization in Seattle, Washington, which documents and preserves oral histories of Japanese Americans who were incarcerated during World War II. JANM is the Japanese American National Museum in Los Angeles, California, which is dedicated to sharing the stories of Americans of Japanese ancestry.

JACL NATIONAL PRESIDENTS

(updated as of 2013)

1929-30	Clarence Arai
1931-32	Dr. George Y. Takeyama
1933-34	Dr. Terry T. Hayashi
1935-36	Dr. Thomas T. Yatabe
1937-38	Jimmie Y. Sakamoto
1939-40	Walter T. Tsukamoto
1941-46	Saburo Kido
1946-50	Hito Okada
1950-52	Dr. Randolph Sakada
1952-56	George J. Inagaki
1956-58	Dr. Roy N. Nishikawa
1958-60	Shigeo Wakamatsu
1960-62	Frank F. Chuman
1962-64	K. Patrick Okura
1964-66	Kumeo A. Yoshinari
1966-70	Jerry J. Enomoto
1970-72	Raymond S. Uno
1972-74	Henry T. Tanaka
1974-76	Shigeki Sugiyama
1976-78	James F. Murakami
1978-80	Dr. Clifford I. Uyeda
1980-82	Dr. James K. Tsujimura
1982-84	Floyd D. Shimomura

1984-86	Frank Sato
1986-88	Harry Kajihara
1988-92	Cressey Nakagawa
1992-94	Lillian Kimura
1994-96	Denny Yasuhara
1996-00	Helen Kawagoe
2000-04	S. Floyd Mori
2004-06	Kenneth K. Inouye
2006-10	T. Larry Oda
2010-12	David H. Kawamoto
2012-	David T. Lin

S. FLOYD MORI BIO

Shiro Floyd Mori was born in Murray, Utah, outside of Salt Lake City on May 30, 1939. His parents (Shigenobu Mori and Kusa Kaminishikawara Mori) were immigrants to the United States from Kagoshima, Japan. He is the seventh of eight children (Miyeko "Meg," Shigeru "Shig," Nobuo "Nob," Tsutomu "Tom," Yukiko "Kik," Setsuko "Selma," Shiro "Floyd," and Steven Hiroyuki). When he was a small child, the family bought a farm in Sandy, Utah, where Floyd attended school. Active in sports, he became an All State High School Baseball Player. After graduation from Jordan High School, he served for six months on active duty at Fort Ord, California, with the United States Army Reserves.

Floyd entered college at the University of Southern California (USC). He interrupted his college studies to serve a two year mission to Hawaii for the Church of Jesus Christ of Latter-day Saints (Mormon). He attended Brigham Young University (BYU) from which he received a Bachelors degree with a dual major in Economics and Asian Studies. He received a Masters degree in Economics and Political Science from BYU. He has attended fellowship programs at Stanford University and UCLA.

Upon completion of college, Floyd taught Economics at Chabot College in Hayward, California, for ten years. He was on the Faculty Senate, was a member of the credit committee for the college credit union, taught religious education classes, was advisor of student clubs, and was a member of several professional organizations.

In 1972, he was elected city councilman of the City of Pleasanton, California, was mayor pro tem, and later served as mayor. Floyd was elected to the California State Assembly in March 1975 and served for six years in that capacity as one of the first two Japanese Americans to serve in the State Assembly. He was later director of the Office of International Trade for the State of California. He has worked in various business ventures as an international business consultant and president of Mori-Silva International and Mori International, where he and his partners were instrumental in taking Subway Sandwiches and Pennzoil to Japan. He has also been part owner of a golf business.

Floyd has held various local and national positions for the Japanese American Citizens League (JACL), the nation's oldest and largest Asian American civil and human rights organization, including four years as national president and four years as vice president. He joined the JACL staff in 2005 and was director of public policy (formerly called Washington, DC Rep), followed by the appointment to become the national executive director/CEO of the JACL. He retired from that position on June 1, 2012, and received the title of executive director emeritus of the JACL. He later became the president/CEO of the Asian Pacific American Institute for Congressional Studies (APAICS).

He is a member and supporter of many civil rights and community organizations. He served on the Executive Council of the Leadership Conference on Civil and Human Rights (LCCR) and was chair of the National Council of Asian Pacific Americans (NCAPA). He serves on the Diversity Council for Comcast and has served on various boards of organizations, including the National JACL Credit Union, Alpine Country Club, Independent Voters Project, and the Japanese American National Museum (JANM).

He has received awards for his work in community service including an Outstanding Citizen Achievement Award from OCA National, Community Leadership Award from the Asian Pacific American Institute for Congressional Studies (APAICS), Coalition Building Award from the Sikh American Legal Defense and Education Fund (SALDEF), Community Leadership Award from Asian Pacific Islanders for Professional and Community Advancement (APCA), Voices of Courage Award from the Islamic Cultural Center of Fresno, the Distinguished Citizenship and Patriotism Award from Pan Pacific American Leaders and Mentors (PPALM), and the Order of the Rising Sun, Gold Rays with Rosette Award from the Government of Japan, which was recommended by former Ambassador Ichiro Fujisaki and presented by Ambassador Kenichiro Sasae

Floyd has been chairman of conventions, gala dinners, golf tournaments, conferences, and various events for the JACL and other community groups. He started a Nihon Matsuri (Japan Festival) in Salt Lake City. He initiated the National JACL Gala Dinner in the nation's capital. He fostered corporate partnerships for the JACL and developed Fellowships. He started the JACL DC Digest to inform members and friends of JACL happenings through weekly emails. He was chairman of the 2013 National JACL Convention held in Washington, DC, which commemorated the twenty-five-year anniversary of the passage of the Civil Liberties Act of 1988.

He has held many church and civic volunteer positions including in youth sports, the Boy Scouts, church leadership positions, and inner city service work. He is a sports fan and an avid golfer.

Floyd and his wife, Irene Mano Mori, have five children, Brent, Cheryl (Chris Warner), Julia (Michael Larsen), Paul (Mayumi), Marcia (David Frost), and eleven grandchildren, Garrett, Christiaan, Maiya, Danielle, Mira, Tristin, Kitt, Andrew, Dylan, Ashlee, and Mandy.

MAP AND PHOTOS

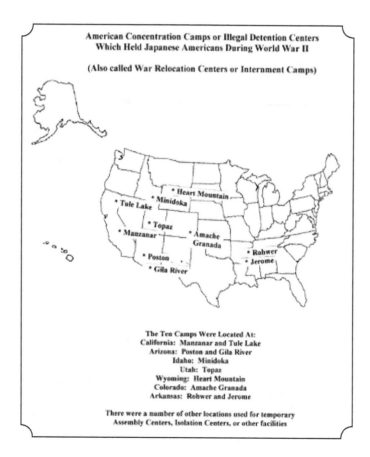

American Concentration Camps or Illegal Detention Centers
Which Held Japanese Americans During World War II

(Also called War Relocation Centers or Internment Camps)

* Heart Mountain
* Minidoka
* Tule Lake
* Topaz
* Manzanar
* Amache Granada
* Poston
* Gila River
* Rohwer
* Jerome

The Ten Camps Were Located At:
California: Manzanar and Tule Lake
Arizona: Poston and Gila River
Idaho: Minidoka
Utah: Topaz
Wyoming: Heart Mountain
Colorado: Amache Granada
Arkansas: Rohwer and Jerome

There were a number of other locations used for temporary
Assembly Centers, Isolation Centers, or other facilities

WESTERN DEFENSE COMMAND AND FOURTH ARMY
WARTIME CIVIL CONTROL ADMINISTRATION
Presidio of San Francisco, California
April 1, 1942

INSTRUCTIONS
TO ALL PERSONS OF
JAPANESE
ANCESTRY
Living in the Following Area:

All that portion of the City and County of San Francisco, State of California, lying generally west of the north-south line established by Junipero Serra Boulevard, Worchester Avenue, and Nineteenth Avenue, and lying generally north of the east-west line established by California Street, to the intersection of Market Street, and thence on Market Street to San Francisco Bay.

All Japanese persons, both alien and non-alien, will be evacuated from the above designated area by 12:00 o'clock noon Tuesday, April 7, 1942.

No Japanese person will be permitted to enter or leave the above described area after 8:00 a. m., Thursday, April 2, 1942, without obtaining special permission from the Provost Marshal at the Civil Control Station located at:

1701 Van Ness Avenue
San Francisco, California

The Civil Control Station is equipped to assist the Japanese population affected by this evacuation in the following ways:

1. Give advice and instructions on the evacuation.
2. Provide services with respect to the management, leasing, sale, storage or other disposition of most kinds of property including: real estate, business and professional equipment, buildings, household goods, boats, automobiles, livestock, etc.
3. Provide temporary residence elsewhere for all Japanese in family groups.
4. Transport persons and a limited amount of clothing and equipment to their new residence, as specified below.

The Following Instructions Must Be Observed:

1. A responsible member of each family, preferably the head of the family, or the person in whose name most of the property is held, and each individual living alone, will report to the Civil Control Station to receive further instructions. This must be done between 8:00 a. m. and 5:00 p. m., Thursday, April 2, 1942, or between 8:00 a. m. and 5:00 p. m., Friday, April 3, 1942.

Notices were placed on telephone poles in 1942

Leaving Bainbridge Island on March 30, 1942

Being taken to an American concentration camp in 1942

America's Concentration Camps
Which Held Japanese Americans Captive
During World War II

Amache/Granada, Colorado
Opened: August 24, 1942
Closed: October 15, 1945
Peak population: 7,318

Gila River, Arizona
Opened: July 20, 1942
Closed: November 10, 1945
Peak population: 13,348

Heart Mountain, Wyoming
Opened: August 12, 1942
Closed: November 10, 1945
Peak population: 10,767

Jerome, Arkansas
Opened: October 6, 1942
Closed: June 30, 1944
Peak population: 8,497

Manzanar, California
Opened: March 21, 1942
Closed: November 21, 1945
Peak population: 10,046

Minidoka, Idaho
Opened: August 10, 1942
Closed: October 28, 1945
Peak population: 9,397

Poston, Arizona
Opened: May 8, 1942
Closed: November 28, 1945
Peak population: 17,814

Rohwer, Arkansas
Opened: September 18, 1942
Closed: November 30, 1945
Peak population: 8,475

Topaz, Utah
Opened: September 11, 1942
Closed: October 31, 1945
Peak population: 8,130

Tule Lake, California
Opened: May 27, 1942
Closed: March 20, 1946
Peak population: 18,789

Floyd Mori speaking at the National JACL Convention in 2010

Floyd Mori speaking at a National JACL event in 2010

Jean Shiraki, Irene Mori, Floyd Mori,
Phillip Ozaki, JACL DC Office 2010

Floyd Mori in an ad for AARP 2012

Convention Chairman Mori

Welcome Fellow JACLer's

It is often said at these conventions that the future of JACL will pass to a new generation of leaders. However, as the Convention Committee chose a theme for this year, we had feelings that included recognition of the past and present as well. Values, principles, leadership, and understanding are not in the exclusive realm of any one generation. We exist today because of strengths in the past. When the past is forgotten or ignored, the future will be dim. Therefore, let us celebrate the 'Legacy of Generations' with the recognition that all of us, no matter what age or where we live, have and will continue to be the total heartbeat of JACL.

It is a great pleasure to have you attend the 33rd Biennial JACL Convention here in Salt Lake City. The Convention Committee has spent four years in working and planning for this week to be successful. Committee members have done much more than asked. That is the kind of dedication that JACL requires to be a strong viable force in the future.

Sincerely,
S. Floyd Mori

Letter from the 1994 National JACL Convention Booklet

JAPANESE AMERICANS IN UTAH AND THE UNITED STATES

Speaking to High School Students
at Juab High School
Nephi, Utah, February 20, 2002

Thank you for the opportunity to meet with you today to share some of the history of Japanese Americans in Utah and the United States.

Probably none of you have heard of the Iwakura Mission, which was likely the first time Japanese people were in Utah. More than one hundred Japanese government officials, students, and others were traveling the world on a trip initiated in 1871. It was a Japanese diplomatic journey headed by Sionii Tomomi Iwakura, Japan's Deputy Prime Minister. They were on a mission to search for methods to position Japan among the most powerful nations in the world. It was possibly the most important venture for the modernization of Japan after a long period of isolation from the western world.

The delegation arrived in Salt Lake City in February 1872 for what was intended to be a very short stopover. Because they were delayed from leaving the state due to heavy snowstorms which prevented the trains from running, the delegation spent nearly three weeks in Utah. During this time they forged friendships with Utah government leaders and officials of the Church of Jesus Christ of Latter-day Saints (Mormons). Utah accepted these Japanese visitors and recognized them as a highly cultured and well-mannered group. However, the visit was largely ignored by the national media, and for a century little was known and reported about the mission's stay in Utah.

My own family has a long history in Utah. My father, Shigenobu Mori, came to the United States from the southern part of Japan early in the 1900s because he wanted to help his family financially. His hometown was a place called Kagoshima on the Japanese island of Kyushu. He came as a young man around the age that you students are now. He stopped in Hawaii and worked to save some money and then was able to come to the mainland. He worked at a restaurant in California and then got a job with the railroad laying track in the desert of Nevada.

After saving enough money and because he was injured while working on the railroad, my father made his way to Utah where he settled on a farm in Cache County near the Utah-Idaho border. There were many struggles as he tried to make a living at farming. After some time, he went back to Japan to marry my mother, Kusa, who was from the same area in Japan. He returned to the United States with his bride, fully intending to return to live in Japan after earning enough money. They moved south to Gunnison, Utah, where they lived in what they later described as like a log cabin. Then the Depression struck which caused huge financial trials. They moved to the Salt Lake Valley to the town of Murray where I was born, and they were later able to purchase a farm in nearby Sandy. There were eventually eight children in the family, of which I was number seven. All of us helped with the work on the farm.

Utah's Japanese people worked largely in farming when they were able to get some land. Some of the men also worked in mining and on the railroads. There was a Japantown established in Salt Lake City on First South Street where there were a number of Japanese stores, barber shops, cleaners, hotels, restaurants, and churches. They catered to the Japanese population, who would come from various parts of the city and outlying towns to purchase goods and patronize the businesses. It was also a place to meet and make friends.

The Japanese people in Utah and throughout the United States often faced discrimination and prejudice from the outside world, but they basically lived peaceful lives while working hard. They occasionally got together for picnics held by Japanese groups where they could socialize with each other. The Japantown in Salt Lake City no longer exists, having been displaced when the Salt Palace Convention Center was built there in the 1960s. There are two Japanese American churches which remain on the same block in the area, but all the businesses were gone long ago although a few may have relocated to other parts of the city.

The Japanese American Citizens League (JACL), of which I am currently the national president, was organized in 1929 by young adult Japanese Americans trying to make a better life for their families and others. By 1925, further immigration from Japan had been banned. The Japanese immigrants already in the United States and American citizens of Asian descent were directly affected by anti-Asian laws. The laws against the Japanese and Chinese immigrants at the time included that they were not allowed to become citizens of the United States; they could not own land in California where most of them lived; and they were forbidden to marry outside their race in many areas.

Utah had an anti-miscegenation law which prohibited interracial marriages as did many states. In 1956, a Japanese American man and a Caucasian woman, who were friends of mine, could not marry in Utah so they drove to Colorado to be wed. The Supreme Court made a decision in 1967 which deemed that anti-miscegenation laws were unconstitutional, with many states choosing to legalize interracial marriage before then.

The JACL worked to repeal the biased and unfair laws. Mike Masaoka, who was born in California but whose father moved the family to Salt Lake City where he was allowed to buy property, spent some of his growing up years in Salt Lake City. Mike was a graduate of West High School and the University of Utah where he was a champion debater. Mike became an early leader in the JACL. He is credited with most of the work that the JACL accomplished to repeal those discriminatory laws. Mike was working as national field secretary for the JACL when the war broke out. He has said that he was the only paid administrative staff person with two secretaries. He and the JACL were instrumental in working with the government to set up the segregated Japanese American unit in the United States Army, the 442nd Regimental Combat Team during World War II which was joined with the 100th Battalion which consisted of Japanese American soldiers from Hawaii. Mike joined the army and served his country in the 442nd along with his three brothers, one of whom was killed in the war.

Mike, along with Saburo Kido, who was an attorney and the national president, had to make important decisions affecting a lot of people. They were very young, but they sought the advice of others. The JACL headquarters was moved to Salt Lake City during the war when all the Japanese people had to evacuate from the West Coast states. A National JACL Credit Union was formed to help Japanese Americans, who could not get loans from commercial banks which would not do business with them because of their race. The National JACL Credit Union remained in Salt Lake City and is operating there to this day, but the JACL headquarters moved out of Utah after the war to San Francisco where they have owned a building since the 1970s.

By the time the Imperial Navy of Japan bombed Pearl Harbor in Hawaii on December 7, 1941, many of the Japanese immigrants had established families. Some had farms and businesses. Some ran hotels and stores. Their American-born children, the second generation, were growing up. Education was stressed by the immigrant parents. Many of the young people were attending college or had graduated, but it was difficult for Japanese Americans to get hired at good jobs in their field of study even after earning a college degree. They regularly experienced prejudice and discrimination which quickly escalated at the war's outset as all the people of Japanese descent, including citizens of the United States, were immediately looked upon as the enemy.

They were suspected of being spies for the government of Japan even though most of them had never been to Japan. Their freedom was in jeopardy and indeed was taken away for a large portion of the Japanese Americans who were incarcerated in the camps. The majority were citizens of the United States, having been born in this country.

Utah had a number of Japanese immigrants, along with their Japanese American children and some young grandchildren, living in the state such as my family did at that time. The major populations of ethnic Japanese people lived in California, and relatively large numbers lived in Oregon and Washington. Those who lived on the West Coast were affected by the war more so than the Japanese people who lived in the inland states like Utah. President Franklin D. Roosevelt signed Executive Order 9066 (EO 9066) on February 19, 1942, which gave the military commander the authority to remove any people from certain designated areas. It was enacted only against those who were of Japanese ancestry.

The areas affected by EO 9066 were described to be all of California, Alaska, and Hawaii, the southern part of Arizona, and the western halves of Oregon and Washington. The military commander in Hawaii stated that it was not necessary to enact the order in Hawaii because anyone potentially dangerous had already been picked up and the others were not a threat. It would have been nearly impossible to enforce the order in Hawaii, where Japanese people were such a large part of the population that they were arguably the backbone of the economy.

The order could have been used with the German and Italian Americans and immigrants as well, but it was aimed at the Japanese people and was only used against those of Japanese heritage. There was almost no one who would speak out for the Japanese Americans at that time although the American Friends Committee members (Quakers) were helpful. Some few people were supportive, but most turned their backs on the Japanese Americans. They were suspected of being spies who were capable of espionage. Most newspapers printed articles in favor of the evacuation.

Realizing the enormous task of trying to move approximately one hundred and twenty thousand people from the West Coast states, the government leaders initially sought to have what was called a "voluntary evacuation." Some people had moved inland by the deadline in March. The others who had been living on the West Coast were removed from their homes and put in temporary assembly centers.

Milton Eisenhower headed the War Relocation Authority (WRA) which was established on March 18, 1942. He envisioned that the Japanese Americans could be disbursed to inland states where they could resume a normal life after being forced out of their homes on the West Coast. The governors, attorneys general, and other state officials of the inland western states were called to Salt Lake City in April 1942 where they were asked to accept Japanese Americans to live in their areas. The officials protested strongly with extreme opposition toward the Japanese Americans.

With the exception of one, the governors protested that they did not want the Japanese people to come to their states since the people were considered a threat. Some of the governors expressed outright hatred for the Japanese, and all spoke of their distaste for the idea. This reaction caused the WRA to pursue the building of the concentration camps to house the people of Japanese ancestry. Milton Eisenhower was disturbed by the attitudes and hostility. He felt that what was being done to the Japanese Americans was wrong, and he resigned from his position with the WRA because he said he could not sleep at night.

The one governor who was the exception was Gov. Ralph Carr of Colorado. He was a Republican governor who stated that the persons of Japanese ancestry had done nothing wrong and had every legal right to live where they pleased. He said they would be welcome in his state. He further stated that every citizen should be guaranteed the right to move freely, including those of Japanese ancestry. Governor Carr had made a brave and courageous move to attempt to treat the Japanese people with kindness and fairness. Many of the citizens of his state, however, disagreed with him and were angry that he would welcome anyone who was Japanese into Colorado. The decision likely ended his political career as he was defeated in a subsequent campaign for the US Senate.

Governor Carr was drafted to run for governor again in 1950, and he continued to defend the constitutional rights of the Japanese Americans and all American citizens. Civil rights advocate and JACL leader, Minoru Yasui, served as the head of the "*Nisei* Committee for Ralph L. Carr for Governor." After winning the primary, Carr died of a heart attack or complications associated with diabetes at age 62.

Most of those evacuated from the West Coast lost virtually everything they had owned as they were only allowed to take with them what they could carry. They were given just a short period of time, days or a week or two, to dispose of their material possessions and be ready to leave. People (even complete strangers) came to their doors asking if they could buy or have their furniture and goods. The Japanese people were offered only minimal amounts for their possessions. Of course, it was well known that they would have to accept almost nothing for their personal property if they wanted to receive anything at all. Some would-be buyers told the Japanese people that they could accept the price offered or they would come back and take their possessions the next week after they had evacuated. Some people stored items in community buildings, churches, or with neighbors, but most returned after the war to find nothing remained. Some few were fortunate that good neighbors took care of their possessions in their absence.

Although Japanese immigrants were not allowed to own land in California at that time, some had been able to purchase property in the names of their adult children who had been born in America and were citizens. Most of the Japanese residents of the West Coast states had likely been living in rented homes and on farms or property they did not own.

Before the deadline for the forced incarceration arrived, some Japanese people had taken the option of a "voluntary evacuation." If they voluntarily left the West Coast, they could avoid going to the camps and would have some measure of freedom. They were allowed to leave if they had someone who lived inland sign for them, vouching they would help with housing for the evacuees. Since my family lived in Utah, we had several families of relatives come from California to our home to live with us or to stay until housing could be found. They lived in Utah for the duration of the war and then were able to return to live in California after the war ended.

My wife, Irene, was living a comfortable life with her family in the Los Angeles area at the outbreak of the war. She was a toddler with one older brother called Kenny. Her mother, Michi, a Japanese American who had been born in Utah, was pregnant with their third child. My wife's father, Eisaku Mano, had come from Japan and was familiar with Utah as he had worked years earlier at the Bingham Copper Mine near Salt Lake City before his cousin summoned him to move to California to join him in his business. The cousin later returned to Japan so Irene's father was the sole owner of the successful produce market in Hollywood. When the war started, most of their customers immediately stopped patronizing the market. They had a few loyal customers for a short period before they had to close the business. Because the family had relatives living in Ogden, Utah, who signed for them, they were able to move to Utah instead of being imprisoned in one of the camps.

Irene's parents loaded as much of their earthly possessions as they could on the back of the truck which had been used for their business. They had sold their new car at a great loss, had burned priceless mementoes from Japan, had sold what household items they could for pennies on the dollar, had given away items, and had left Christmas decorations on the closet shelf of their rented home. Her mother said later that she did not think they would ever need Christmas decorations again. The future looked extremely bleak.

After driving across Nevada to Utah, they arrived in Salt Lake City and stopped at a restaurant, hungry and tired. After sitting for some time without receiving service, they were told that the restaurant would not serve their kind. After suffering this humiliation, the family moved into a small space in the town of Layton. Their new home had been a chicken coop that the owners fixed up just enough to rent to the new occupants. People who lived in those areas made money by renting formerly uninhabitable farm buildings to the Japanese people who arrived from California. Irene's father was able to work at odd jobs, but money was tight.

The family could not afford to return to California after the war ended, so they remained in Utah. They never regained the financial stature they had before the war, but my mother-in-law considered herself fortunate, in spite of everything, to have moved back to the state of her birth because the family later joined the Mormon Church. When she was six years old and living in Utah, Michi's mother died, so the family left Utah and moved to Seattle where they had relatives who would help with the children while her father worked as a porter for the Union Pacific Railroad. She was later sent to Japan to live with an aunt and uncle while going to school until she graduated from high school. Some time after she returned to the United States, she met and married her husband who had immigrated from Japan years earlier.

Although they had heard that the camps might be a possibility, most of the ethnic Japanese on the West Coast never expected the forced evacuation and incarceration in the camps to become a reality, especially for those who were American citizens.

When the evacuation took place, people were rounded up and taken to assembly centers which housed them temporarily until the camps were ready for occupancy. These were usually horse stalls at racetracks and fairgrounds where the smell remained of the animals formerly housed there. If you were especially fortunate, you might have been assigned to a building instead of a horse stall for your living quarters. The people were given a metal cot and a mattress cover which they filled with straw for their bed. They were told that they were being locked away for their own protection because the Japanese Americans were suspected of being spies and people were hostile toward them. It was an invalid excuse for this horrible treatment of innocent people.

Ten camps were set up in desolate regions of the country in unpopulated areas which were generally accessible by train. The government built rows and rows of army type barracks to house the incarcerated persons. Two camps were placed in California and were called Tule Lake and Manzanar. One was in Idaho at Minidoka. Two in Arizona were Poston and Gila River, which are on Indian reservations. The Heart Mountain Camp was in Wyoming, and in Colorado was Amache Granada. Rohwer and Jerome were in Arkansas. Utah had a camp called Topaz near Topaz Mountain and the town of Delta, just down the road a bit south from where your school is located.

The American concentration camps became like small cities of around eight to ten thousand people each, with one large camp of around eighteen thousand. The Japanese immigrants along with the Japanese Americans were basically stripped of their freedoms and locked up. They lived in hastily constructed barracks which let in the severe cold in the winter, the extreme heat in the summer, and the constant dust from windstorms which were a regular occurrence in most of the camps. There were mess halls and community latrines with little or no privacy.

Living conditions were far from ideal and were, in fact, extremely difficult and crowded. Most of the people had been living in comfortable homes. They tried to make the best they could of a bad situation. Whole families lived in one or two rooms. The parents were relieved that the family was at least kept together because there had been rumors that the children would be taken to a different camp than their parents. However, it was very difficult to maintain a healthy family lifestyle, and family units suffered.

After the war began, some Japanese American young men immediately tried to enlist in the United States Army. They wanted to show their patriotism, but they found that they had been reclassified as enemy aliens and were rejected. In 1943, the United States Army announced its plans to create a segregated unit which would be made up of Japanese Americans. The government leaders expected volunteers to rush from the camps to demonstrate their loyalty to the United States by enlisting to fight for what the government now admitted was their country after having considered them to be noncitizens or enemy aliens at the start of the war. Most of them lived in the camps by then. Some did sign up voluntarily, and others were drafted.

The War Department and the War Relocation Authority issued a questionnaire which was purportedly to be used for obtaining travel permission which became known as the "loyalty questionnaire." It was required to be answered by all those incarcerated who were over the age of seventeen. The people in the camps would be determined to be loyal or disloyal to the United States based on their answers.

Two questions caused confusion and controversy. Question 27 asked: "Are you willing to serve in the armed forces of the United States on combat duty, wherever ordered?" Most, including women and the elderly, answered yes that they would be willing to serve if necessary.

Question 28 asked: "Will you swear unqualified allegiance to the United States of America and faithfully defend the United States from any or all attack by foreign or domestic forces, and foreswear any form of allegiance to the Japanese Emperor or any other foreign government, power, or organization?"

They were being asked to foreswear allegiance to Japan although most were American citizens and had no allegiance whatsoever to the Japanese Emperor. It was problematic for the immigrants from Japan who were prevented by law from becoming naturalized citizens of the United States although it had been their home for many years. They were worried that they could become people with no country if they were to lose their citizenship in Japan because of their answer and then later be removed from the United States. They felt they had to answer yes to keep their families together.

It is said that some camp authorities told people that they would receive a $10,000 fine and a prison term of twenty years if they refused to answer the questions. It was confusing and difficult, but most citizens and immigrants alike answered yes to both questions in order to prove their loyalty and to avoid further problems.

There was a group in the camps called the Resisters of Conscience. They answered yes to the two questions but qualified it that they would serve only if their families were released from imprisonment. The questionnaire did not allow conditional answers or written comments so those responses were disregarded and considered as a no. This act of protest got the Resisters arrested with many being sent to the Tule Lake camp which became designated as being the place for the troublemakers. Others were sent to federal prisons. These were young men loyal to the United States but who were not willing to serve while they and their families were incarcerated. It was a brave stand to take in the face of hardship.

Frank Emi, a leader of one of the groups which resisted being drafted while incarcerated, was even married and a father who was exempt from the draft. He was protesting and fighting for the rights to freedom for all those who were incarcerated. After the war ended, the Resisters received a full pardon for their stand from President Harry S. Truman. Some did later serve in the military in other wars and years which followed.

Another group of men were called the No No Boys because they answered no to Questions 27 and 28. They felt that the country was treating them so badly that it did not deserve their loyalty. They were labeled as disloyal, and some were sent to Japan or to prison.

The young men from the camps who volunteered or were drafted into the US Army, became part of the segregated unit of Japanese Americans who made up the 442nd Regimental Combat Team. The mainland group was joined by the 100th Battalion which was comprised of Japanese American soldiers from Hawaii. Other Japanese American young men who lived inland from the West Coast in relative freedom also joined the army or were drafted. The 442nd/100th fought in the European theater and became the most highly decorated unit in the history of the United States Army for its size and length of service.

Other Japanese Americans served in the military intelligence service (MIS) for the US Army and were mostly sent to the Pacific theater to serve as translators to intercept Japanese messages. Their work was kept secret for many years. My oldest brother was one of those. He was serving in Japan with the occupation when he died in the crash of a US military airplane after the end of the war. I was a young boy at the time, but I remember my family's anguish upon hearing of his death.

Some Japanese American men and women were allowed to serve in other branches of the armed forces instead of just the segregated Japanese American unit.

The Japanese Americans who were living in Utah and other inland areas at the time of the war faced discrimination and prejudice, but they were able to continue to live in their homes. Their lives were not disrupted to the extent that was experienced by those living on the West Coast. Some of the Japanese Americans who now live in Utah settled here after being incarcerated in the camps at Topaz or at Heart Mountain, Wyoming. The people were given few options as they left the camps after the war ended. They were asked where they wanted to go and were given $25 and were provided with a train ride or bus fare. Some could not afford to go back to the West Coast although that would have been their preference. They had no place to go and little money, so they stayed in the closest place available which was for some, Salt Lake City or Ogden, Utah.

Many of those who were forcibly removed from their homes suffered greatly throughout their entire lifetimes from the effects of the incarceration. Years after the war, the JACL, along with some other groups, individuals, and members of Congress, worked to redress the wrongs committed by the government against Japanese Americans during World War II. Although EO 9066 which was signed by President Franklin D. Roosevelt on February 19, 1942, was rescinded in 1976 by President Gerald R. Ford, the efforts to gain redress had been largely unsuccessful. In 1978, at a National JACL Convention in Salt Lake City, members passed a resolution to earnestly seek redress with monetary compensation for the forced removal of Japanese Americans from their homes.

A main purpose of continuing this effort was to educate the public and have the government admit that the Constitution was not upheld at that time. The JACL leaders and others wanted to ensure that the same thing never happens to anyone else in this country. After more than a decade of hard work by the JACL, other Japanese American organizations, the four Japanese American members who were serving in Congress, numerous individuals, and with support from other civil rights groups, Congress passed the Civil Liberties Act of 1988 which resulted in a letter of apology from the President of the United States and reparations for the evacuees who were still living. These included all those who were forced to leave their homes on the West Coast after the start of World War II. Congress apologized for these wrongs of the past.

It took a great deal of work to get the bill passed. The majority of Democrats in the Congress voted for the bill, and the majority of Republicans voted against it with some members not voting. Although initially not in favor of the bill asking for monetary compensation, President Ronald Reagan signed the Civil Liberties Act of 1988 into law and said: *"What is most important in this bill has less to do with property than with honor. For here, we admit a wrong. Here we affirm our commitment as a nation to equal justice under the law."*

The first redress checks of $20,000 were presented at a ceremony on October 9, 1990, to nine elderly people of Japanese heritage. The formal apology letter signed by President George Bush stated: *"In enacting a law calling for restitution and offering a sincere apology, your fellow Americans have…renewed their commitment to the ideals of freedom, equality, and justice."* A total of 82,219 people received redress which was accomplished from 1991 to 1993.

As history has shown, EO 9066 proved to be a terrible mistake in which the constitutional rights of citizens were not upheld. American citizens were deprived of their freedoms and were denied equal protection under the law. The incarceration of innocent Japanese Americans who had done no wrong was later deemed to be the result of racism, war hysteria, and a lack of competent political leadership at that time.

As you can see, Utah has played an important and significant role for Japanese Americans and the JACL.

Last year our nation had the unfortunate experience of 9–11 when terrorists flew planes into the World Trade Center in New York City and the Pentagon in Washington, DC along with other horrific acts of violence. Of course, we do not condone any of these appalling acts of terrorism against our country, but we must be vigilant in defending the Constitution. We should be careful not to vilify and condemn innocent Americans and immigrants simply because of their ethnicity or physical appearance as was done during World War II against Japanese Americans. Although all people of Japanese heritage were looked upon as the enemy and suspected of being spies, it was later determined that there were no acts of espionage ever committed by Japanese Americans during World War II.

Immediately after 9–11, the JACL issued a press release admonishing people to not make the same mistake that was done to Japanese Americans during World War II. American Muslims and others who may have similar physical characteristics to the terrorists of 9–11 were being persecuted after 9–11. This should not happen to innocent people simply because of their ethnic background or appearance. Secretary Norman Mineta is a Japanese American who was a young boy when he was incarcerated at Heart Mountain, Wyoming, with his family and thousands of other Japanese Americans during World War II. He is the US Secretary of Transportation. Secretary Mineta was on television right after 9-11 asking people to remember World War II and to avoid punishing and persecuting innocent people simply for how they look.

As young people, you have a bright future ahead of you. There are so many wonderful technological advancements in the world today which were not available a few years ago. You have many opportunities which will help you find success and happiness in life. You can go far and achieve much. I encourage you to get as much education as you can and to keep learning.

Thank you for allowing me to join you today to speak about the Japanese American story and experience, particularly in Utah. I commend you for your willingness to learn about the history of others and of this nation. I admonish you to do your part to protect and preserve the freedoms which we enjoy in the United States of America. I ask that you make compassion, caring, and understanding a vital part of your lives in order to make this a better world for all.

This is a great country, and we are all blessed to live here.

Floyd Mori was asked to make a presentation to high school students about the people of Japanese ancestry in Utah and the Japanese American experience of World War II. He was the national president of the JACL during that time. This presentation was at the request of a teacher at a local high school in Utah where Floyd was born and raised and where he was living at that time.

EXPLANATION OF THE RESISTERS OF CONSCIENCE

Soon after the beginning of World War II, President Franklin D. Roosevelt signed Executive Order 9066 on February 19, 1942, which gave the military commander the authority to remove any person from specified areas of the country. Lt. Gen. John L. DeWitt of the Western Defense Command ordered the removal of all people of Japanese ancestry from their West Coast homes. They were later placed in concentration camps in desolate, remote areas of the country.

After it was decided to allow and require Japanese American young men to serve in the United States Army, the government issued a mandatory questionnaire in 1943 that all those incarcerated persons over the age of seventeen, including women and the older generation who had been born in Japan, had to complete. It was called a "Questionnaire for Leave Clearance," but it seemed to be basically a hunt for anyone who could be considered disloyal to the United States government. It became known as the "loyalty questionnaire."

Two questions which caused problems were Questions 27 and 28. Question 27 was: Are you willing to serve in the Armed Forces of the United States on combat duty wherever ordered? Question 28 was: Will you swear unqualified allegiance to the United States from any and all attack by foreign or domestic forces, and foreswear any form of allegiance or obedience to the Japanese Emperor, to any other foreign government, power, or organization?

Most answered yes to both questions. A group which answered no became known as the No No Boys. They did not believe they had to be loyal to a government which locked them and their families up and treated them so badly by taking away their freedom. It is said that some caused trouble within the camps.

The Resisters of Conscience were different than the No No Boys. They were a group of young men who answered yes to the two questions with the qualification that they would willingly serve in the military if their families were first released from the camps and given their full constitutional rights. They protested by refusing to serve under the present conditions. The government did not allow qualified answers and considered them as a no. These young men showed great courage in trying to have the government uphold the Constitution. They were protesting the fact that they and their families were incarcerated in the camps with no due cause.

When not enough Japanese American young men volunteered for the army as had been expected, the government later set up the Selective Service which meant that the men would then be drafted into the army. Frank Emi was at the Heart Mountain Camp in Wyoming when he and six others formed the Heart Mountain Fair Play Committee. It was an organized challenge to the drafting of the inmates of the concentration camps. They encouraged others to refuse to serve in the military until their full citizenship rights were restored. The seven leaders of the committee were convicted of conspiracy to violate the Selective Service Act. Emi served 18 months at the US Penitentiary at Leavenworth, Kansas, despite being exempt from military service because he was married and was a father at the time. He did it for the sake of the other Japanese Americans who were incarcerated. A federal appeals court overturned the convictions in December 1945.

After the end of the war when President Harry S. Truman paid tribute to the Japanese American veterans for their sacrifices during World War II, he also acknowledged the Resisters of Conscience for their principled stand for civil rights. They were granted a full pardon in 1947. Many had brothers who served in the army during World War II, and many later served in the US military, including during the Korean War. They were not unpatriotic people.

The JACL leadership at the time of the war encouraged cooperation with the government and was critical of the Resisters. Many years later at the urging of Andy Noguchi of the Florin JACL Chapter and others, the JACL passed a resolution at its national convention in July, 2000, to offer an apology to the Resisters of Conscience for not acknowledging their stand of protesting the denial of constitutional rights and for the pain and bitterness this caused within the Japanese American community for many years. The National JACL was mandated by the national council at its 2000 national convention to recognize and apologize to the Resisters of Conscience at an appropriate public ceremony during 2000–2002 before the next convention which would be held in the summer of 2002. The resolution gained the ire of many Japanese American veterans of World War II who were unhappy with the JACL's decision and expressed the feeling that the Resisters did not deserve an apology. Some of the veterans felt it was an affront to their service and patriotism to honor the actions of the Resisters, while the veterans had risked their lives and many of their fellow servicemen had died in service to their country.

The public ceremony was held in San Francisco, California, on May 11, 2002. It was planned by the JACL Resisters Ceremony Committee with co-chairs Andy Noguchi and Alan Teruya. Some of the Resisters of Conscience were present and participated in the ceremony including Frank Emi. Floyd Mori was the national president of the JACL at the time. He wrote and offered the apology speech to the Resisters on behalf of the National JACL. In addition to apologizing to the Resisters, Floyd honored the veterans of World War II and encouraged the JACL membership to accept the rights and actions of the Resisters, to respect the sacrifices made by each other, and to recognize the shared goals of all.

THE RESISTERS OF CONSCIENCE CEREMONY

Apology Speech from the National JACL
At the Japanese Cultural and Community
Center of Northern California
San Francisco, California, May 11, 2002

Most of you know that I was born and raised on a farm near Salt Lake City, Utah. I was a toddler when the war began, and I have only faint glimpses of memory of the beginning of the war. I do remember clearly that relatives from California came to live with us and near us during that time, and I also remember their talk of "camp." I had no idea of what camp was, so I did not pay much attention.

I do remember clearly the days when two of my older brothers left home and went into the United States Army. My oldest brother Shigeru, who was the model son, never came back alive. I remember the anguish of my family, particularly my mother, when the telegram arrived and when the casket was brought home. Although I did not have the experience of camp, my family did experience the sorrows of war.

My wife was also a very young child during the evacuation and traveled to Utah from Los Angeles with her father, mother, and brother to live. They voluntarily evacuated because her mother had been born in Utah and had relatives in Ogden, Utah, who would sign for them to come. Her father had a good business in California before the war, but they lost nearly everything.

My youth was a time when I was introduced to the Japanese American Citizens League or JACL through my older siblings. In recent months, I have often mentioned the various stages that I feel the JACL has experienced over the years. I have said that the postwar years were a time when the JACL provided a major social function for our communities. The sports like baseball, basketball, and bowling, along with dances and picnics, were important in bringing the disrupted lives of Japanese Americans back together. My older brothers and sisters participated in these social activities, and I, as a child, was taken along to attend sports events and picnics. I looked forward to the day when I would grow up and be able to participate more fully in the fun. During this stage of the JACL in that local area, the focus did not include a lot of civil rights issues. The National JACL, however, was working toward removal of the discriminatory laws against the Japanese Americans and their parents.

During the era of protest, the JACL focused on redress as its goal. We spent a decade and a half mobilizing our chapters into political action committees. We were dedicated and successful in our efforts, and many of you here were part of that protest movement. During this stage of the JACL, the social function was neglected, and we have lost many of the programs that brought us together socially after the war.

So what of the war years? What did the JACL do during that time?

It was a time of great stress and uncertainty. For decades prior to the war, the nation had been engaged in some very strong anti-Japanese sentiment that had a major impact on the feelings of Japanese Americans as citizens and as human beings. There was a vast empty feeling of fear as the war escalated, and camp became a reality for most people of Japanese ancestry who lived on the

West Coast. There were many conflicting feelings, thoughts, and ideas that flowed through the minds and hearts of our community at this time.

Many were torn between the ideals of patriotism and justice. Unfortunate incidents that occurred within the Japanese American community were fraught with misinformation and to some, panic. We can look back by listening to the stories of those who were there, but I think it is difficult for those of us who were not directly involved to actually feel what they felt nor can we fully understand why they did what they did.

I think we can understand a little about the deep sense of obligation that was felt by family members at that time. We did not want to shame our family name, and we wanted to do the right thing. Our government, however, had placed our people in a no-win situation. Japanese Americans had experienced racial bigotry, and the fear of reprisal was always in our minds. So the focus of the JACL during this stage of our past was patriotism. The need to show a patriotic front became the activity that engulfed the actions of the JACL and many of its leaders.

Like in other stages of our organization when we emphasize only one aspect of our mission, other areas may be neglected. At that time, we did not recognize, and we neglected to respect, the right of protest and civil disobedience expressed by some who were in the camps. These people felt deeply that the injustice of incarceration needed to be rectified before they could, in good conscience, answer the call to patriotism. This neglect has caused years of mental and social anguish to those who felt strongly that a correction of injustice was essential before they could express patriotism toward the government that held them and their families captive behind barbed wire. In fact, their resistance was a means to emphasize the importance of the Constitution under which the laws of the country were designed to protect their individual rights.

Although we may never fully right the wrongs of the past nor may we fully understand the emotional reasons for their occurrence, the National Council of the JACL in our last convention in Monterey, recognized this neglect. It was their vote that established this event.

Today's ceremony is a clear recognition that the JACL neglected to support the Resisters of Conscience in their protest against injustice. They were brave souls who dared to stand up for their rights and who were trying to protest the incarceration of so many innocent people. In passing this resolution at our last national convention, the JACL offers a sincere apology for the painful experiences and memories caused by this neglect. I know that words cannot sufficiently restore that which was lost nor erase the suffering that has occurred, but it is my hope that we can all share in a sense of pride and honor for having been here today. May all of us remember these events as a lesson that will improve our understanding and increase our resolve to forgive and move on to the next stages of our lives.

Now I know that there are those who have expressed major concern that the JACL would take the actions we have just taken. I challenge their assumption that all Resisters were cowards, troublemakers, and hooligans. We recognize those who were guided by the moral dictates of their conscience to protest injustice. We do not condone any of the physical and mental harassment that was perpetrated by some who called themselves Resisters nor does today's ceremony apply to them.

For those who served in the United States Armed Forces at that time, we are proud of the legacy that they left us. We honor them today as we have in many local and national events in the past. Their service and valor, in large measure, are responsible for the positive image with which we in the Japanese American community are blessed today. Many of the Resisters of Conscience later served in the Armed Forces as well, and we commend them.

Let us today resolve to recognize that we must have a change in heart. Let me paraphrase the thoughts of a modern Zen author, Les Kaye, who admonishes us to see each other through new eyes. Our emotional priorities should be reoriented from self to others. This is when fighting stops and compassion awakens.

May we as individuals and as an organization strive to develop understanding and its accompanying virtue of compassion. The terrorists of today cannot find it within themselves to express compassion in any form. The legacy of wrongs in the past has festered into the horrible blisters of terrorism that we witness today. May we learn from their folly in reasoning.

Let us leave any wrongs that have occurred in the past where they belong and from where we can learn. Then let us bring in the future looking through a more selfless set of eyes that seek for understanding and a heart that has the capacity for expressing compassion to our fellow men and women.

The JACL is grateful for your attendance today. We thank the committee that planned and worked hard to execute today's ceremony. Thank you to the Resisters of Conscience for your courage and conviction to uphold the Constitution and seek justice. The JACL apologizes for not supporting your efforts to restore constitutional rights to Japanese Americans and for the pain caused over the years.

May all of us here today be blessed to be a catalyst that will bring peace of mind and mutual respect to all who have suffered the pains of war and injustice.

Thank you.

BEYOND THE GOOD TIMES OF TODAY

Seventy-Fifth Anniversary of the JACL
Article Originally Written for
the JACL Membership
2004

It is not a long time in the scheme of things, but the past seventy-five years have been the core of the historical legacy of the Japanese American community. During this time we were rejected, ostracized, demeaned, and vilified. Yet the cultural will and determination that Japanese Americans had inherited proved strong enough to bring an era of acceptance, accomplishment, and in some areas admiration, while at the same time maintaining a sense of community and ethnic pride.

The Japanese American Citizens League (JACL) was formed in 1929 when Japanese Americans and their immigrant parents were facing extreme discrimination. There were negative actions against them by the government and their neighbors. The Japanese American young adults who established this organization fought hard for the civil rights of their families and friends. This was twelve years before the start of World War II at which time the harmful feelings against them escalated. After the bombing of Pearl Harbor by the Imperial Navy of Japan, all

American citizens and immigrants who were of Japanese ancestry were immediately looked upon as the enemy and were suspected of being spies for Japan. The JACL continued to be important during the war as well as after it ended, and it still works today to ensure the human and civil rights of all people.

I was born and nurtured in the midst of this struggle for survival and acceptance. When I was aware of being a person, the war raged in the Pacific and the fathers and sons of many of my neighbors went off to fight in the war. It was not long before two of my older brothers put on US Army uniforms, the older one serving in the Pacific as a counter intelligence officer and the other being sent off later to the European front. Although I was at the time a small child, I remember each of them returning home for his final visit before being shipped off. They had been the target of racial bigotry and discrimination, but they felt that they had a duty to serve our country, the land of their birth.

The European war ended while the younger of these two brothers, Tom, was on a ship going to Germany as a replacement for the 442nd Regimental Combat Team/100th Battalion, the segregated unit of Japanese Americans. He returned safe and sound to continue his life, marry, have a family, and pursue his accounting career in California. My other brother, Shig, was involved in a terrible crash of a military airplane while stationed in Japan with the Military Intelligence Service (MIS) during the occupation after the war had ended. We expected him to come home and return to college when this tragedy occurred. Although I was a young child at the time, the events of the return of his casket to our home and the funeral are still vivid in my mind. What a sacrifice to pay for a sense of duty. Yet many did it.

Although I had heard references to "camp" from the adult conversations around me during the war, I had no understanding at that time of what the camps were. Having been born and raised in Utah, our family was not required to go to camp and be incarcerated as were the families from the West Coast who were forcibly uprooted from their homes. Some of our relatives took the option of the "voluntary evacuation" before the camps became a reality. They came to live near us in Utah, and one family lived on our farm during this time. The one bright spot was that I got to know relatives that I would not have come to know as well. I came to appreciate family and the joy that comes with family gatherings. Although the feelings could have been buried for a time, I believe the sense of community and cultural heritage became ingrained in my being.

However, not a lot of things were positive for Japanese Americans at that time. As a child, I received my share of racial slurs and intolerance. There was a time when as a child I used to wonder why I had to be Japanese in the midst of a white society. Those feelings actually lingered on into my later childhood and teenage years as well. This was a time when I did not like being of Japanese heritage, and I was embarrassed that my parents did not speak English like the rest of the parents and that we ate unusual food rather than the typical "meat and potatoes" meals of my friends. My parents did not participate in the regular community and school activities that my friends' parents did. There was a cultural gap that was amplified by ongoing racial bigotry.

Now, as we fast-forward through two or three generations of the Japanese American community, the reality of assimilation has occurred to a large degree. We still have pockets of racial bigotry that we must continually battle. The war against discrimination will always go on because of human imperfections. However, the battles are less costly to our community and are fewer in number than previously. There are indeed other minority communities who continue to face the kinds of problems that I and other Japanese Americans faced as children. Today they need our help and support.

For the next seventy-five years, the struggle will continue as we strive to claim our fair share of the democracy which we have worked to create and where lives were sacrificed to preserve. It is a time when we must assert our political and economic strength to become more equal as citizens in this great country. Glass ceilings and "good ole boy" barriers continue to exist in corporate and legislative America. The workplace continues to serve the majority and often skips over the ethnic minorities. We are at a time when most of society understands civil rights and at least gives lip service to the concept. The next seventy five years will be the time for us to implement the reality of civil rights beyond mere lip service. The JACL will continue to have an important role in this effort.

Today, there are many aspects in the Japanese American community for which we can be very proud. As I understand more each day of the great values and commitment of those who bridged that cultural and civil rights gap in the early days of the JACL, the more I appreciate them for the work they did to create the life we are able to enjoy today. It was not an easy task, and there were mountains to conquer, but they did their part to make a better world. It is our job to assure that this Japanese American pride, commitment to excellence, and sense of duty to each other continues for the next seventy-five years and beyond.

THE MODEL MINORITY MYTH

Speech to an Ethnic Minority Student Group
American University
Washington, DC, Spring 2006

Thank you for inviting me to speak with you today about Asian Americans, and the so-called model minority myth. Many years ago I taught Economics at a community college in California, and I always enjoy associating with college students. You are to be commended for your interest in the heritage, culture, and history of Asian Americans which may include the stories of your own families.

As you know, I am the director of public policy of the Japanese American Citizens League known as the JACL. Most of you are probably not that familiar with the JACL, so I will tell you a little bit about our organization, but first I will start with some background about the Japanese and Chinese people who were early immigrants to the United States which will explain why the JACL was formed.

The first Asian immigrants to the United States were the Chinese who began to arrive in the 18th century. The earliest Chinese immigrants were reportedly well received by the Americans. They were wealthy, successful merchants, along with artisans, fishermen, and owners of hotels and restaurants. They became known for their hard work and dependability. By the mid-1800s, however, many unskilled Chinese immigrants came to this country as laborers, and American views of the Chinese started to change. The Chinese people formed ethnic enclaves called "Chinatowns" in various parts of the country. Drugs and crime began to creep into the communities, which contributed to the American attitudes toward them becoming negative and hostile.

The Chinese mined for gold in California and took on jobs as cooks, peddlers, and storekeepers. Many accepted jobs that nobody else wanted, or that were considered dirty. During the 1860s, ten thousand Chinese workers were involved in the building of the railroad. As they grew larger in number and influence, resentment increased against the Chinese. The government responded by passing the Chinese Exclusion Act of 1882 which restricted immigration of Chinese into the United States.

Japanese immigrant young men started to come to the United States mainly as laborers to Hawaii in the late 1800s with larger numbers arriving in the early 1900s to the mainland West Coast states. They came to this country for economic opportunities and big dreams of prosperity. The customs and language of their new home were unfamiliar to them, but they worked hard at various types of work. They found that the country was not entirely welcoming of them, and many laws were enacted that restricted their progress. As the Japanese immigrants began to establish themselves with families and some measure of success in farming, mining, or small businesses, they faced more discrimination and even hatred from the mainstream American population.

The Japanese immigrants stressed education to their children, and the Japanese American young people were attending college in large numbers. However, they often found that no one would hire them after they received their college degrees. The students were told that they were wasting their time because they would not find a job after they graduated. Some with teaching degrees worked in restaurants. College graduates worked in the fields as farm laborers. Professionals routinely could get almost no clients or patients except others of Japanese descent.

Because there was rampant discrimination against the Japanese Americans and their immigrant parents, some young leaders within the Japanese American community decided they needed a national organization which could work for their civil rights. Several local organizations were operating in various locations. Some leaders from these groups banded together to form the Japanese American Citizens League (JACL) in 1929. Although it was a small organization with limited resources, they started the work to repeal the discriminatory laws against them. They held their first convention in Seattle, Washington, in August 1930. Their early victories were to restore US citizenship to American women of Japanese ancestry, who were married to Japanese nationals, and to provide citizenship for US Army veterans of Asian ancestry. In 1936 they established the JACL Endowment Fund to provide a funding source for programs for Americans of Japanese ancestry.

When Japan bombed Pearl Harbor in Hawaii on December 7, 1941, it was a huge shock to the Japanese Americans and their parents. Most of them probably had never heard of Pearl Harbor. It was a Sunday when people were going to church or participating in social activities with family or friends. The people of Japanese ancestry living in the United States were immediately suspected of being spies for Japan. Fear and apprehension became part of their daily lives. By that time, the majority were American citizens since they had been born here, and they had never even been to Japan.

There had been rumors of war, and the United States government had been doing research for some time on leaders within the Japanese American community including the Japanese immigrants. On the very day and evening of December 7, 1941, and in the days that followed, many Japanese immigrants and Japanese American men were taken from their homes by the FBI and put into prison. Sometimes the families did not know where they were for weeks or months. Some were separated from their families for years.

Then the unthinkable happened. President Franklin D. Roosevelt signed Executive Order 9066 on February 19, 1942. This meant that people could be forcibly removed from their homes at the orders of the military. The order affected around one hundred twenty thousand people of Japanese heritage who were living on the West Coast of the mainland United States. They were placed in American concentration camps with armed guards in sentry towers looking over them. They were imprisoned in barbed wire compounds constructed in remote and desolate regions of the country. Most who were incarcerated remained there for the entirety of the war years. Because they were rounded up before the camps were ready for occupancy, they were first housed in horse stalls at racetracks and fairgrounds. It was a horrible experience for many people from which some never recovered. They lost almost everything they had including their dignity, self respect, and freedom.

Yet they persevered and did what they needed to do to continue living after the war ended. Many, miraculously, since they were given only $25 and a train ride or bus fare when the camps closed, were able to return to their previous cities of residence on the West Coast. They generally returned to find nothing of their former homes and belongings, but they started to work hard to rebuild their lives.

The war ended in 1945. For two decades after that, the Japanese Americans were busy rebuilding and reconstructing their former lives. Most of the Japanese immigrants were never able to regain the financial stature they had before the war. Even though some of them were not that old after the war ended, they may have been broken in spirit from the experience of incarceration and evacuation. The second generation, the Japanese Americans who were mainly teenagers or young adults during the war years, was able to rebound. Although it was not easy and most of them never spoke of the camp experience to even their families until they were forced to face the issue during the period of seeking redress, they quietly lived their lives. They earned college degrees and began to have successful careers. They married and raised families. Some people, however, have stated that they have felt like second class citizens and have suffered from an inferiority complex which they attribute to the treatment they received during World War II.

In the 1970s and 1980s, the JACL and others pushed for redress for the actions of the government against Japanese Americans during World War II. With the passage of the Civil Liberties Act of 1988 (the Redress Bill), some measure of recompense was achieved. Those who were evacuated from their homes received an apology letter from the President of the United States along with a token payment of $20,000 (which was determined to be a miniscule amount compared with what they had lost). It was an effort to ensure that no one else would ever have to suffer the experience of undue incarceration inflicted upon innocent Japanese Americans through no fault of their own.

Years after the end of World War II, the Japanese Americans and other Asian Americans who had achieved some success in life became known as what has been called *the model minority*. These were people who had done well in achieving *the American Dream* of getting a good education, working at a good job, and earning a good living. They had high incomes and low crime among their populations. They were largely in the middle or upper middle class, so they were held up to others as a "model minority" whose example other groups were admonished to follow.

There was a feeling in the general public that Asian Americans can and did help themselves to achieve. They were not in need of government or social help from the outside. They were regarded as minorities who did not need to be provided with anything because they could do it on their own. Indeed, Asian Americans have achieved a lot because they were willing to work for it. They did not want to bother others and make waves.

Those who support affirmative action assert that discrimination and racism have caused minorities to be underachievers in the United States, and that affirmative action is needed to correct it. Critics have asked why African Americans and Latinos are being held down by discrimination while Asian Americans are doing well. Asians have been said to migrate to this country with little or nothing, which has definitely been the case of most immigrants. Yet they struggled and worked hard to become more successful than many European Americans. This *model minority myth* suggests to some that the United States does not really discriminate against minorities.

We know that some of the newer immigrant children such as the Vietnamese have done as well or better than Japanese Americans in achieving outstanding success in school. Their parents may have escaped Saigon amid bombs and gunfire. Many came as refugees with a suitcase and piles of worthless Vietnamese cash. They arrived in America along with 700,000 other Vietnamese refugees often to do domestic work as they started life in a strange, new country. Three decades later many are successful entrepreneurs and appear to have achieved the American dream. Others are suffering from isolation in areas of high poverty and persistent crime. Even though they have made some headway, many are far from finding the success they desire.

While African Americans have a long history of repression in the United States from the days of slavery to the present day, some remarkable achievements have been accomplished by African Americans. They have become respected leaders in many fields. Some few are in the top leadership positions within government and the private sector. They are outstanding athletes in the major sports, but those who are successful worked very hard. There is still much of poverty and hardship among many in the minority communities, including African Americans and Asian

Americans. It is well known that it is extremely difficult to break out of generations of poverty. But it can be done.

Anyone who studies corporate America will find that there is still a "glass ceiling" which causes a barrier through which top management can be seen but not reached by Asian Americans who may be considered as passive and not the right material for top management jobs. Although some Asian Americans seem to have "made it" through the glass ceiling, the numbers are very low. The same can be found in the university campuses throughout the land where few Asian Americans reach the top.

It is always a mistake to generalize and assume the same is true for large numbers of people when there are exceptions to every rule. Not all Asian Americans are doing well. There are many among us who need help. They are having financial and emotional struggles.

While many Asian Americans may fit into the mold of the *model minority*, it is still a myth that they have all made it. It is a falsehood, illusion, and untruth that all are doing well. Reports indicate that many Asian Americans are earning good salaries, but statistics paint the picture that they are still not up to the status of their white American counterparts. The data which contend that Asian Americans have higher incomes than the normal average American may be exaggerated and misleading. The success may not be what it seems although Asian Americans as a whole appear to be doing quite well. They work hard and maintain faith in the future. They have a dream which is still there, and hope springs eternal for accomplishments and triumphs to come.

Families can have a great impact on the success a person achieves. When the Japanese Americans were placed in the American concentration camps during World War II, many family units suffered. The teenagers found it more desirable to eat in the mess halls with friends than with families. The children went to school and spent time with friends. Their family generally had one small room which was "home" for up to five people. The children had little desire to spend any more time there than they had to, usually just to sleep. Family life disintegrated. That was one of the many problems which occurred from the camp and incarceration experience of Japanese Americans.

No matter what your family structure is, your family cares about you. They are the ones who should be closest to your ideals and goals. They want to know what they can do to help you. Keep them close in your life and share your dreams with them.

In a speech in 1984 to Asian and Pacific Islander Americans, President Ronald Reagan said, *"America has a rich and diverse heritage. Americans are all descendants of immigrants in search of the 'American Dream.'"* The President was speaking of the accomplishments of Asian Americans at a time when they were starting to be looked at as the *model minority*.

While the model minority issue may be a myth instead of fact, we should all strive to achieve our goals and aspirations. Don't let anyone steal your dreams. Keep building and climbing. Being considered part of what is called a *model minority* may mean that you are doing well. If you are now or if you become successful, consider yourself fortunate and remember to give back.

Be what you were intended to be, and you will go on to bigger and better things.

Thank you and good luck.

INSTITUTE FOR COREAN-AMERICAN STUDIES

Speech for a Korean American
Organization in Philadelphia
2006 Summer Symposium
Montgomery County Community College
Blue Bell, Pennsylvania, August 5, 2006

Thank you for the invitation to meet with you to discuss some of the issues we have as Asian Americans in this country today. I commend you for attending this symposium to learn more about the issues facing you as Korean Americans and as Asian Americans.

Being of Asian heritage several decades ago was extremely difficult for the immigrants who came to the United States in the early 1900s. Some of the Asian immigrants, who have come to this country in recent years, may be suffering some of the same discrimination. There were many laws against immigrants with Asian backgrounds in those early days. They were not allowed to become citizens of the United States because of their race. There were many immigration barriers placed upon them. There were land ownership barriers as they were not allowed to purchase property in some areas of the country. They were not looked upon favorably because they were different in appearance than the mainstream population. Their physical characteristics were not the same as their European counterparts, and they did not speak the English language. They faced prejudice and discrimination at nearly every turn as they tried to earn some money and make a life in this land of opportunity.

This all added up to the Asian immigrants being seen as nonentities. They were not recognized as part of the communities in which they lived. They were ignored in most aspects of the community. There were economic barriers in America to these immigrants who had come to this country with such high hopes of gaining some of the wealth that was promised here. They were shunned and passed up for opportunities for meaningful employment. This continued for many years.

More recent Asian immigrants may have come to this country as refugees, and they should be welcomed as they embrace the freedoms and opportunity offered here. That was not how most of the earliest Asian immigrants were treated. The early Japanese immigrants came to America to find work and earn money. They were generally not from the upper classes of their country where they enjoyed privilege and riches. The immigrant men saw this land as a place where they might be able to experience some financial well-being. As they began to see limited progress in their lives, they faced even more discrimination and prejudice. They began to be seen as a threat and were treated poorly. Later some young men from the upper class in Japan came to the United States as college students to study abroad, but they also often faced discrimination.

Many Japanese immigrants and their American-born children encountered prejudice on a daily basis. As the second generation became young adults, they started to fight the discrimination that they and their parents faced. The Japanese American Citizens League (JACL) was formed in 1929 as a civil rights organization to change the laws and attitudes which were aimed at Japanese Americans to hold them back. The JACL is the oldest and largest Asian American civil and human rights organization in the nation.

After the start of World War II when the Japanese Naval Forces bombed Pearl Harbor in Hawaii, people of Japanese descent living on the West Coast of the United States faced the ultimate humiliation when their liberty and freedoms were taken away. The Constitution did not protect these innocent American citizens and their immigrant parents. They were forced from their homes and incarcerated in camps surrounded by barbed wire and armed guards. Many had no choice but to remain imprisoned for the duration of the war.

The JACL leaders earnestly worked after the war's end on the civil rights issues which were considered in 1929. They were able to get laws which were clearly discriminatory removed from the books. The JACL continues to work today to make a better life for all Asian Americans as well as becoming involved with civil rights for everyone.

There has been recent discussion on the Voting Rights Act, which is an important piece of civil rights legislation. The right to vote without intimidation is the first step to citizenship. Newer immigrants, who have become naturalized and are now citizens of this country, should be sure to register to vote. Becoming informed of the issues and candidates is important. However, the most important matter is actually going to the polls and casting a ballot to vote. Just registering to vote is not enough. Voting is a privilege of which we should all take advantage whenever it comes around.

There are ways for each of us to become a force to bring about good policy in government and in our communities. Participation in an advocacy organization is a good way. Being a member of an organization such as you have here, the Institute for Corean-American Studies, is an important step to becoming involved. Finding organizations which work for the benefit of

Asian immigrants or anything which interests you and becoming active in them is a way to make a difference.

Becoming involved in leadership is important for our community. We need to make our voice heard and show support of the matters of importance to us. Leadership is a way to affect change.

Become involved in issues that concern you. There are many local issues which affect immigrant communities with which we can become involved and participate. There are local issues of zoning, education, utilities, etc. There are state issues of education, infrastructure, and government. There are many national issues affecting our communities such as immigration policies, health care reform, and the Voting Rights Act.

Becoming a policy maker is always helpful to the community. There are various ways which a person could do this, including public service. Running for office and becoming an elected official is a good way, but it is not something that many can or will do. Those who have become successful are paving the way for others to become a bigger influence in the nation and to bring the issues of concern to their communities to the forefront. We can show support for these people by becoming aware of them and possibly giving them financial help for their campaigns.

When I was in my early thirties and teaching Economics at a community college in the Bay Area in California, there was a city council race going on in the city where I lived. On the last day of filing, I threw my hat in the ring. I started to knock on doors in that small city of thirty thousand plus, and I think I knocked on almost every door. I told people I was running for the city council, and consequently, I became the top vote getter in that election out of a field of more than ten candidates. I served on the city council and was made Mayor Pro Tem. I later became Mayor of the City of Pleasanton, California. After that, I was elected to and served in the California State Assembly for six years. It is possible to get involved if one is interested and willing to put in the effort to do so. Elective office is not an easy life and it takes sacrifice, but it is a good way to make a difference and to help your community.

Working in a government job or for a nonprofit organization is a way to be a policy maker. Public policy is an important area of involvement for all Americans. Having our faces in these areas and making decisions which affect us will be beneficial. Becoming a volunteer in public and political arenas can help us shape the future. There is something each of us can do to become involved in policy making.

Empowerment for the Asian American community requires us all to become involved. While there is something which we can all do, we may need to look for it. We need to find what suits us. We should test the system and do our part to make our voices heard.

America is a wonderful place to live, and we should exercise our rights as Americans by becoming more involved in the community and the nation.

Thank you for allowing me to share these thoughts with you.

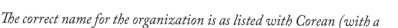

The correct name for the organization is as listed with Corean (with a C) being used for Korean.

BEGINNING A NEW YEAR

Report to the JACL
Article Originally Written for
the JACL Membership
January 20, 2007

Before beginning this report, I would like to say something about John Tateishi, who has very ably served as the national executive director of the JACL for the past seven years and who had taken ill around Thanksgiving. Let me report that John is feeling a lot better. His illness is very serious, and he will not return to work for the JACL, having already tendered his resignation at the National Convention last July. As he continues to recuperate at home, he is up and around, taking daily walks to restore some strength in his body. His mind is as keen as ever, and his typical humor remains, as noticed through an occasional email.

When I was serving as vice president of operations for the JACL some years ago and was given the responsibility of finding a new national executive director, I thought of John. I had known John for some time and was aware that he is a very capable leader so I approached him to see if he would consider serving as the interim director, which he agreed to do. It was fortunate for the JACL that John was willing to take on the job as the permanent national executive director. Our thanks for a job well done and best wishes to John and his wife, Carol. We wish for a complete recovery and hope he will be back to normal soon.

The November 2006 elections not only brought change to
the dynamics of the United States House of Representatives and
the Senate, but we have seen many adjustments and changes in
the Asian American and Pacific Islander (AAPI) community in
Washington, DC. Congratulations to Congresswoman Mazie
Hirono from Hawaii. She is a veteran politician, having served in
the Hawaii State Legislature as well as lieutenant governor. She is
a welcome addition to the Congressional Asian Pacific American
Caucus (CAPAC) of which Congressman Mike Honda remains
chair. Congressman Honda also was given a coveted seat on the
Appropriations Committee. Congressman Xavier Becerra from
California, another member of CAPAC and a good friend of the
JACL, was named assistant to Speaker Nancy Pelosi.

One of the great victories for the JACL was the swift passage of HR 1492, the Camp Preservation Bill, and having the
bill signed into law by President George W. Bush in December
2006. It was one of a few pieces of legislation to pass in the wan-
ing days of the session for Congress, where many gave it little
chance of passage. The major credit for getting this work done
goes to retiring Congressman Bill Thomas (R) of Bakersfield,
California. When the possibility of his carrying the bill was first
discussed, he stated that he would be happy to do it, but it would
have to be done "his way." His way was using his position as
Chairman of the powerful Ways and Means Committee to push
the bill through both houses of Congress and eventually getting
President Bush to sign the bill. It worked out well, and the JACL
sincerely thanks Bill Thomas for his extraordinary efforts in getting the bill signed into law. We express our thanks to all who
worked on the bill and supported it. Funds from the passage of
this bill will help to tell the Japanese American story.

AAPI staffers on the Hill are a key element in our relationship with members of Congress. Esther Kiaiana, who was chief
of staff for former Congressman Ed Case of Hawaii, decided to
return to Hawaii after a very positive career on the Hill. Mark

Keam, who most recently served as Senator Durbin's Judiciary Committee staffer, will move on to the private sector. Howard Moon, who served as Speaker Pelosi's floor staff, will also move to the private sector. The AAPI liaison for Speaker Pelosi will be Carmela Clendening, who has shifted from her position in communications. Carmela replaces Frank Carrillo, who has moved to a committee assignment.

Several of the leaders within the AAPI organizations recently met with Speaker Pelosi's staff to urge the hiring of more AAPI's in order to maintain the face of AAPI's on the Hill. We feel it was a productive meeting.

OCA National, originally known as the Organization of Chinese Americans, has named Michael Lin as its new executive director. Michael, who is a former OCA national president, brings many years of volunteer service and experience to the OCA staff. Lisa Hasegawa was named chairperson of the National Council of Asian Pacific Americans (NCAPA). Lisa, who is the executive director of the National Coalition for Asian Pacific American Community Development (National CAPACD), is a veteran in the AAPI advocacy arena, worked on the White House Initiative, and is a member of the JACL. With the growth of AAPI organizations here in Washington over the past decade, one may find it difficult to remember the acronyms of all the AAPI organizations represented here.

Plans are being made for a major National JACL event in Washington, DC. The first National JACL Gala Awards Dinner, A Salute to Champions, will be held at the J.W. Marriott Hotel Grand Ballroom on Wednesday, September 12, 2007. This promises to be an outstanding event. It would be a good time for any JACL members to plan a vacation to the Washington, DC area to attend the Gala.

Thanks for all the good work of the members of the JACL everywhere, and especially the work being done in the various JACL chapters throughout the nation and our chapter in Japan.

The chapters are the lifeblood of the JACL. Each member is valuable to the organization. I would like to encourage each of you to help increase membership in the JACL by bringing in new members. We all have family members and friends who could benefit by being members of the JACL. There are many people who would join if we told them about the JACL and our experiences in this great organization. Let's help the JACL to remain vital by inviting others to join and being sure to make them feel welcome.

Have a great year.

———⊗⊗⊗———

Many changes have occurred since this was written, including that George Wu became the executive director of OCA followed by Tom Hayashi. Mark Keam has been serving in the Virginia House of Delegates since 2009.

Floyd Mori worked closely with former JACL National Executive Director John Tateishi and regularly worked with former JACL Washington,, DC Representatives, Paul Igasaki, Bob Sakaniwa, Karen Narasaki, and Kristine Minami.

IMMIGRATION REFORM

Speaking at a Press Conference
Washington, DC, May 1, 2007

This is a great Country. I grew up on a small dirt farm in Sandy, Utah, just south of Salt Lake City. My parents spoke little English and had little formal education. Yet their children all obtained an education. Some served our country in the United States Armed Services, with one making the ultimate sacrifice by not returning home alive. Their posterity includes college professors, teachers, elected officials, political activists in the major political parties, bankers, investment professionals, business leaders, health care professionals, entrepreneurs, company presidents, and lawyers. My parents were immigrants who tilled the soil, taught their children the value of hard work, and instructed us to do well in school.

The organization which I represent, the Japanese American Citizens League or JACL, the nation's oldest and largest Asian American civil and human rights organization, was founded in 1929 by Japanese American young adults who were contemporaries of some of my older brothers and sisters. That was almost eighty years ago.

While making a place for themselves in this great nation, these people had to fight anti-Asian immigration laws. They fought for the ability to gain full citizenship in this land of opportunity. Their parents were barred from owning land in many areas as alien land laws crept into the law books. They could not play in the same playgrounds or swim in public swimming pools. They could not work the jobs they were trained to do. Even after obtaining college degrees, many could not find jobs in their field of study. Nobody wanted to hire them. Many leaders of the community were thrown into prisons and labeled enemy aliens during World War II. This was done without allowing them any of the due process of law that should have been guaranteed by the Constitution. Yet they maintained their values of hard work and reverence to family.

The *American Dream* is based on this *Spirit of America* that has been brought here by immigrants for as long as we have existed as a nation. All immigrants were not perfect. Some were even criminals escaping the grasp of the law in their home countries. Yet, all came here to make a better life for themselves and for their families. Most worked to earn the money to bring family members here or to send money back home. Immigrants have been the *Engine of Progress* for this great nation.

Those same traditions that made our country great then are values that make our country great today. Immigrants today toil hard in factory assembly lines, on construction sites, in the leisure industry, in the fields of agriculture, in the food and service industries, and in small businesses. They also teach at our most prestigious universities, are medical professionals, and have been the entrepreneurs behind the development of a new *age* of technology. They have invested both monetary and human capital to make their *American Dream* come true for their families. Some have been waiting for *decades* for the fulfillment of their dream, patiently waiting their turn for family members to be reunited.

But today we are hearing the same cries as of eighty years ago when the Japanese Americans felt they needed a strong national organization to fight discrimination and the view that immigrants are dangerous to our American way of life. The specter of fear and the seeds of mistrust are being sown just as they were eighty years ago against Asians. That needs to stop here and now. Immigration is the lifeblood that has made our nation great.

Present immigration laws have not been serving our nation well. New proposals are aimed at keeping families apart. This is not good for our nation. President George W. Bush recognized the importance of *Comprehensive Immigration Reform* when he said just a month ago, *"It is in our nation's interests to have a comprehensive immigration law, so we can uphold the great values of America."*

It is time for Congress to pass a bill that preserves the great values of family and keeps families together. We need a bill that will assure continuing prosperity to this great nation.

So, *When do we need Comprehensive Immigration Reform? Now! Should families be part of this reform? Yes!*

I urge all of you to make this known to your Representatives in Congress

Thank you.

GEICO PRESENTATION

Speech to a GEICO Asian
American Employees Group
GEICO Headquarters
Chevy Chase, Maryland, May 3, 2007

Asian Pacific American Heritage Month is a great time for all of us to reflect on the past and understand better who we are and why we are an important part of this great nation. I was born and raised in the state of Utah. I am going to refer to my life from time to time today as I am sure many of you may have had similar life experiences.

While I am proud of my Asian heritage today, this was not always the case when I was a child. During World War II as a young boy, I often saw people who looked like me being depicted as the enemy and doing horrible things. The caricatures of the Japanese soldiers made them look diabolical and mean. Being the only family of Asian ancestry in the small farm town where we lived, I was sometimes the object of unkind and not gentle words. So as a child and even as a teenager, I often asked myself why I had to be Japanese. This was probably the case with some of your parents or grandparents, who had to endure the racism that war brings to the forefront—be it on the battlefield or in the economic realm. I say the economic world because the war for jobs and economic well-being creates scapegoats and so-called enemies for Asian Americans, particularly if the competition comes from Asia.

Most of the earliest immigrants, who arrived on the shores of the United States from Japan and other parts of Asia, were young adult men or even teenage boys who were seeking a better life in America, the land of opportunity. They were willing to leave their homelands and families to improve their way of life in an unknown world. They often tried to earn money to send back to their families in their home country as well.

Some Filipino men jumped ship and landed in New Orleans in the late 1700s. The earliest Chinese immigrants are said to have arrived in the late 1700s and early 1800s. Chinese men were recruited as laborers for the railroads and mines in the West where bachelor communities were created. Contract laborers from Japan arrived in Hawaii in 1868. The Japanese began to come to the mainland of the United States in the late 1800s and in larger numbers in the early 1900s.

Their dreams of finding and obtaining a degree of prosperity in this new land, for these early immigrants, were largely unfulfilled. They found a hard life full of difficulties and backbreaking labor. The language barrier they faced because they did not have a command of the English language brought more hardship to their lives. Because their physical characteristics were different than the mainstream American population, they were viewed with suspicion. They regularly faced discrimination and prejudice.

The work they found was largely on railroads, in mines, or on farms and occasionally menial tasks such as washing dishes in a restaurant and domestic work. This was much the same as newer immigrants are finding as they arrive in the United States even today.

However, these early Asian immigrants worked tirelessly and believed in the American dream. They endured years of struggle burdened with afflictions and misfortune. They had enough faith and courage to continue on when life was dark and hope was dim. As they began to establish themselves, bigotry raised its ugly head in the name of laws that prohibited further immigration; thus, keeping families apart or from forming. There were alien land laws that prohibited Asians from owning land with some of these laws on the books until the 1960s and beyond. They were not allowed to become American citizens, and laws prohibited them from marrying outside their race.

By the late 1930s, the Asian immigrants were finally finding some success in their new home. Life was beginning to look slightly more promising for these immigrants from across the Pacific Ocean. Some had businesses, and some owned land in states where it was allowed. Many of the men had married and with their wives, mostly brought over from their native countries, had children and families. Some of their American-born children were college graduates by this time although most found it difficult to find good jobs in their field of study even after they had earned a degree. Their parents had stressed education, but generally, almost no one would hire these graduates.

As some of the Asian immigrants began to experience more financial well-being, they faced even more discrimination. Sometimes envy by their neighbors and associates became displayed in outright acts of racism. The immigrants often found comfort among their friends, who were also from Asia as they were, but their children were generally out in the larger community as they were becoming educated. People, who were born in Japan, were not allowed to own property in the State of California, but some were able to buy land in the names of their children, who were at least twenty-one years old and were American citizens. Life seemed to be getting somewhat better with some conditions improving, but it was not an easy life for the Japanese Americans.

Many of the children of the Japanese immigrants were by then young adults, the second generation, American citizens by birth. They had begun to get involved in the political process to try and make life better for their generation, their parents, and their children. The Japanese American Citizens League (JACL), which is the oldest and largest Asian American civil and human rights organization in the nation, was actually established in 1929, quite some time before World War II began. Although there were other local organizations which had been formed by Japanese Americans, the JACL was the first national organization to represent them. When Japan bombed Pearl Harbor on December 7, 1941, and the United States entered the war with Japan, life became even more difficult for the people of Japanese heritage. Leaders within the JACL tried to step up and help.

Prejudice and discrimination against the Japanese people became more rampant. Wartime hysteria was manifest in an order to put all the people of Japanese ancestry along the West Coast of the United States in concentration camps in remote locations of the country. Most evacuees lost virtually everything they had as they were hastily removed from their homes in California, Oregon, and Washington with little notice or time to prepare.

During the early days of the horrific acts of World War II, many Asian American young men, mostly Japanese, Chinese, and Filipino at that time, volunteered to serve in the United States military. Most were rejected. The famed 442nd Regimental Combat Team/100th Battalion, which was made up of Japanese Americans, many from the concentration camps, was a segregated unit established in 1943. This group of mainland and Hawaii-born Japanese Americans became the most highly decorated unit for its size and length of service in the history of the US Army. They were sent to the European theater and suffered an inordinate amount of casualties for which they received many Purple Heart Awards, but discrimination prevented them from receiving the highest honors. The top rank they could attain at that time was that of Major of which there were four. When they came back to the United States even while wearing their US Army uniforms, the Japanese American soldiers were sometimes spat upon, called names, and denied access to basic commercial services such as taxi rides and haircuts.

After the war ended and it was widely recognized that Japanese Americans were loyal and patriotic Americans, they were finally able to begin to break into mainstream American life. Although there were doctors, lawyers, and other professional people among their ranks before the war, they were largely discriminated against and were often unable to practice their professions or had only Japanese American and Japanese immigrant clients and patients. It has taken many years, but some of the children and grandchildren of the early Asian immigrants have attained remarkable success in a variety of fields. New immigrants today are also making their mark on American society as well.

Remember, I mentioned economic wars? During the late 1970s when I served as a California State Assemblyman, there were proposals to prohibit Japanese nationals from buying property in the State of California. This was during the Japanese boom period when they were buying some very visible and desirable property in the United States. People did not want to allow that to continue. Nothing was said about the European conglomerates that were doing the same thing at that time. It was a matter of prejudice, and these were fairly recent times.

During the early years of various anti-Asian laws, there was nobody here in Washington, DC to speak on behalf of the Asian American community. The JACL was the only national Asian American advocacy organization for many years. The JACL fought against anti-immigration and anti-citizenship laws and was instrumental in the repealing of these laws. OCA National (originally known as the Organization of Chinese Americans), was formed in the 1970s and joined the JACL as a national advocacy organization. Today, there are over twenty-five national Asian American nonprofit organizations in the nation's capital that advocate for the various needs of the Asian American communities.

Asian Americans are now contributing to every aspect of American life. Even in the political arena we are seeing an Asian American face here and there being elected to various offices throughout the country where there were only a handful previously. There are a few leaders of corporations who are of Asian background.

Sen. Daniel K. Inouye, who lost his right arm during casualties in the Second World War as a member of the 100th Battalion/442nd Regimental Combat Team in the US Army, has been a United States senator for many years and was a member of the House of Representatives for his home state of Hawaii when it became a state. The senator has often stated, *"If you are not at the table, you will be on the table,"* meaning that if we are not part and parcel of the political process, we are simply set aside and forgotten.

The Honorable Norman Y. Mineta, who spent part of his boyhood years in an American concentration camp located at Heart Mountain, Wyoming, became the first Asian American mayor of a major city, San Jose, California, in the 1970s. He later was a United States congressman for many years followed by being Secretary of Commerce under President Bill Clinton and Secretary of Transportation under President George W. Bush.

George Takei and Pat Morita, children of Japanese immigrants, are among Asian Americans who became successful fairly early on in the entertainment industry in Hollywood. Now there are many others.

Although less well known, many Asian Americans have attained notable success as leaders or presidents of corporations such as in the fashion industry where the Kawakami sisters from Utah, Marilyn and Smiley, were influential. Marilyn was president of Ralph Lauren Women's Wear and Anne Klein. Their mother, Mary Kawakami, who is now in her nineties, was an early leader in business as owner of Mary's Beauty College in Provo, Utah, which she owned for forty-two years. Asian American men and women have become leaders in other fields and at universities throughout the land. Many Asian Americans have been and are owners of their own companies and are leaders in various professional arenas. Yet the percentages are low.

Most Asian Americans, who have achieved success, merely live quiet lives, not unlike their counterparts of every race and creed within the United States. They have families that they enjoy. They seek education and the better things of life to bring peace and happiness. They belong to church and community groups. They find ways to give service and help their fellowmen.

We cannot generalize and say that everyone in the so-called model minority, which is often referred to as the Asian American community, has done well. There are great successes within our communities in the United States. However, there are great difficulties as well. We all know that everyone is not well-off and successful even if their families have been here for several generations, and new immigrants continue to face some of the same barriers that were faced by earlier Asian immigrants.

Today as I speak, there are proposals being discussed that would continue to keep Asian American families apart and further delay any hope for family reunification through immigration procedures. There are discussions to limit language access to government services. There are proposals to bar children of immigrants from a full educational opportunity.

There is no room for complacency. Some in our society have achieved success and attained greatness. Others have lived lonely lives of despair and heartache. The recent horrific tragedy at Virginia Tech showed us all that there are people among us in our Asian American communities who often suffer in silence until some force within them bursts into a violent act with drastic consequences. It behooves us all to be more mindful of our fellowmen and to try to help those who cry out in need or perhaps suffer in silence.

So in the end, what is it that the Asian Pacific American community has brought and contributed to American society? While we have visible individuals who work tirelessly on our behalf in some public aspect, it may be the values within the Asian Pacific American cultures that have most greatly benefitted America.

The values of love and respect for family are of great worth. The admonition of my parents to not tarnish our good family name still rings clear in my mind. In Japanese, we say *"Kodomo no Tame."* We do it for the sake and good of our children.

The Asian Pacific American culture of hard work and industriousness adds to the competitive nature of our great economy and our nation. We are willing to earn our day's pay by giving more than a day's worth of work.

The talents of creativeness and vision in the Asian Pacific American mind continue to fuel the entrepreneurial sectors of our economy. High tech and the arts are filled with talented Asian Americans who make our society better and more productive. The sports world has some Asian Americans who excel in their fields.

The *Character* and the *Integrity* of the Asian Pacific American are like a beacon on a hill. History has shown that Asian Americans can claim to be loyal and committed to the freedoms and responsibilities embodied in our Constitution. I commend all of you for your contribution to the fabric of this great country and challenge you to do more. Our work will never be finished. We all need to take part.

Thank you.

"THE KID FROM NEBRASKA: BEN KUROKI"

Speech to an Employee Group at Freddie Mac
Freddie Mac Offices
Washington, DC, May 10, 2007

Yesterday I had the honor of meeting a gentleman by the name of *Ben Kuroki*. I am sure that most of you have never heard of Ben. To me, he is the *The Kid from Nebraska*, as I was given a book by that title back when I graduated from high school about a century ago. He became one of my heroes, so what a treat it was for me to meet him and to hear of his life experiences. Let me tell you a little bit about this man who turns ninety years old next week.

Ben's dad immigrated to the United States from the same province in Southern Japan from where my father came. His father, like mine, worked on the railroad when he came to America and later began farming in rural America, his in Nebraska and mine in Utah. Ben was one of ten siblings; I was one of eight. He learned the value of hard work and of upholding and honoring the family name just as my parents taught.

Ben and some of his family's Japanese American farming friends were at a meeting to form a new chapter of the Japanese American Citizens League (JACL), the organization which

I represent, in North Platte, Nebraska, on Sunday, December 7, 1941. The speaker was a young man by the name of Mike Masaoka, who was then working for the JACL. Incidentally, Mike (who passed away in 1991) is Norman Mineta's brother-in-law. Right in the middle of Mike's presentation, two white men dressed in suits came into the meeting and whisked Mike away to jail because he was a leader in the Japanese American community. The gathering quickly dispersed, and then they discovered that Pearl Harbor had been bombed by Japan.

That day was the beginning of much mental and social turmoil in the Japanese American communities throughout the nation. The government had already identified prominent persons of Japanese ancestry and many, like Mike Masaoka, were immediately arrested by the FBI and placed in jail although Mike was soon released. A few months later, the people who were of Japanese heritage who lived in the West Coast states were ordered to be removed from their homes and incarcerated in detention centers or American concentration camps scattered throughout desolate regions of America. This was done without any due process which should be guaranteed by the Constitution for citizens of this country.

Although Hawaii was then a territory of the United States and was part of the area where the executive order could have been used, it was determined to be unnecessary by the military commander who said that any potentially dangerous people had already been rounded up. The order would likely have been difficult to execute in Hawaii because of the large number of Japanese Americans and Japanese immigrants who lived there and were important to the economy.

The day after the events of December 7 occurred, Ben and his younger brother Fred went to enlist in the United States Army. They were refused acceptance because they and all Japanese Americans had been immediately reclassified as enemy aliens or noncitizens. Remember, they were born in Nebraska and were

American citizens. A few weeks later, Ben heard that the Air Corps was recruiting in a city about one hundred fifty miles away. Before traveling that distance, he phoned the recruiting sergeant to make sure that he would not get rejected again. The sergeant indicated that he was getting paid $2 per recruit, so he said to come ahead. Ben and Fred traveled there and were allowed to enlist, which they did with the blessing of their father.

Ben and his brother went to basic training, but Fred was later washed out to some ditch digging engineer unit. For some reason, Ben was permitted to stay on and was transferred to the next level of training. He was assigned permanent KP duty which he would rather do than to have the same fate as his brother. So he worked hard and kept his nose clean. When one crew needed a replacement, Ben was assigned to an actual unit. However, when the time came to go to the battlefield, Ben was the only one ordered somewhere else. He persisted with the commander and begged to stay with his unit. The commander was moved and allowed Ben to be shipped with his unit to a US Base in England where he again was pushed aside and grounded in a menial job.

As the B-24 flights were sent out one of the crews needed a gunner so Ben trained for two weeks as a gunner and joined that crew. The average number of flights that a crew survived was nine missions. Ben completed the maximum duty of twenty-five missions over Europe and Northern Africa and then extended to do five more. He was given a much-deserved furlough to Santa Monica, California. On his way there, while in Southern California he tried to hail a taxi but was rebuffed, given racial slurs, and told to go back where he came from even though he was wearing a US Air Corps uniform at the time.

Because of this kind of reception, he felt he had to go further to "prove that he and his fellow Japanese Americans were loyal citizens," so he volunteered to train in a B-29 for the Pacific war. After training, he was refused duty in the Pacific because of a ban in allowing Japanese Americans on aircraft over the Pacific. After much effort and the help of prominent California citizens who petitioned directly to the Secretary of War, Stimpson I believe, he was approved to serve in the Pacific. He flew twenty-eight more missions and never received a scratch. Although he realized that his bombs killed many people and destroyed property in Japan for which he felt bad, he did all of this to prove that Japanese Americans were loyal citizens of the United States of America.

I tell this story, which I read as a young high school student and reheard yesterday, because Ben is what I would classify as a *Leader*. He was *not* concerned about himself, but he stood fast to his values to change the lives of others. Mine is one of them. While it took a few more decades for him to receive the credit he deserved for his service (he received the Distinguished Flying Cross), that was not his objective. He had his family and community in mind when he went to enlist and afterward endured being the target of racial bigotry. He told of flying in the Pacific while his crew had to surround him when they were on base in order to protect him from the other American soldiers. This was while he was in the service of his country. He said he often felt safer on a bombing mission than he did on base among his fellow American soldiers.

There were many other Asian American soldiers during this time in our history who, like Ben, held to their principles and became leaders. My challenge to you is that you provide that same kind of leadership for our future generations. We can all leave some kind of legacy that will benefit the generations of tomorrow.

Ben, along with others like him, made it easier for all Asian Pacific Americans to hold their heads high and move about more easily in today's society. However, the work is not done as there are still barriers with which to contend. It will require *your* leadership. Like Ben, you should not take *no* for an answer when you know the answer should be *yes*. Like Ben, you can go beyond expectations and do thirty missions rather than the maximum of twenty-five. Then do another twenty-eight. Like Ben, we need to value our family heritage.

I hope that the life and story of Ben Kuroki, *The Kid from Nebraska,* will be an example from which we can all model our lives. Thank you for allowing me to share this story with you today.

Now it is my honor and pleasure to introduce one of the great leaders of our time. This is someone who has blazed many trails to make our journey as Asian Americans today much easier. The Honorable Norman Y. Mineta, *The Kid from San Jose,* has been the first Asian Pacific American in many, many arenas of leadership and great importance. In public service and political stature, Mr. Mineta is second to none, having served the people of his neighborhood to serving in the highest counsels that govern this nation.

He is a man who is proud of his heritage and honors the name of his parents. His integrity and character are respected at the highest levels of government throughout the world. In commitment to the Asian American community, there is nobody who can begin to equal his record. He has always been there when asked. He has created institutions that will benefit generations of Asian and Pacific Islander Americans, young and old, for many years to come.

In spite of all that he has already given us, he continues this unselfish role as a leader among leaders. So you can understand a little about Norm's unselfishness, he flew back to Washington just this morning to participate with you today. Mr. Mineta will join Ben Kuroki at the White House later today where some outstanding Asian and Pacific Islander Americans will be honored, including Ben. After our time here, I am going to drop him off at the northeast gate of the White House.

I am proud to have been associated with Norm for the past thirty some odd years, and I am happy to call him a great friend. I give you, Mr. Secretary, The Honorable Norman Y. Mineta.

This speech was presented to an Asian American Pacific Islander employee group at Freddie Mac where Floyd Mori was asked to speak along with the Honorable Norman Y. Mineta, Secretary of Transportation. After the event at Freddie Mac, Secretary Mineta made a phone call to the White House. Instead of dropping the Secretary off at the White House, Floyd was allowed to park his car there and accompany Secretary Mineta to the White House event and to witness the proceedings which honored Ben Kuroki and others.

CIVIL LIBERTIES SYMPOSIUM

Speech at a Symposium
Twin Falls, Idaho, June 22, 2007

It is my privilege to speak to you today regarding the Japanese American experiences of World War II—the forced removal from their homes and incarceration of innocent Americans and immigrants of Japanese descent who were living on the West Coast of the United States after the bombing of Pearl Harbor by the Imperial Navy of Japan on December 7, 1941.

We may be asked, "Of what relevance is the incarceration of Japanese Americans?"

We are told that we cannot live in the past, but we should learn from the past as we live in the present.

In the Japanese American Citizens League (JACL), which is the oldest and largest Asian American civil and human rights organization in the nation, we often find ourselves talking about the "incarceration" when people were forcibly removed from their homes and stripped of their freedoms. We think people should be educated on this part of history in order that it is not repeated against any other group of people. We need to learn from the past.

Some ask: "Why do we keep dwelling on the past?"

Others say: "Our history and heritage are important."

It is my feeling that knowing ourselves gives us a sense of pride and belonging. Let me illustrate by referring to my own childhood. I am a child of World War II. As I was born shortly before the war began, I lived through it as a young child. I started school during that time when the depiction of anyone who was of Japanese heritage was less than flattering. There was a lot of belittling childhood banter against me and anyone like me. I lived in what was then a rural farm area in Utah where we were the only Japanese family or even minority family in the neighborhood.

Because we lived inland from the West Coast, my family was not directly affected by the evacuation and incarceration of Japanese Americans. We were not required to leave our home to be imprisoned in a camp. We did, however, have relatives from California who came to live with us during that time. They had done what was called "voluntarily evacuated" and avoided being placed in a camp by moving to a state which was inland before the American concentration camps became a reality. They could do this because they had relatives living inland who would sign for them and agree to help them get settled.

There was prejudice displayed against me, especially during the war. Because of the treatment I received and the depictions I saw of the Japanese enemies, I developed a dislike toward who I was. I wanted to be white like most of the people around me. As the years went by after the end of World War II, there began to be more acceptance of and regard for Japanese Americans in most areas. However, discrimination by some people was always evident and remains today to some degree. There were only a few other Japanese Americans in my high school and few others of different ethnicities from the mainstream white population so I was always a distinct minority while I was growing up.

After I completed high school, I served for six months on active duty with the United States Army Reserves at Ford Ord, California. Later I went to college in Southern California, where I met other Japanese Americans with whom I became friends. I lived in Hawaii for two years as a Mormon missionary and found that most people whom I met there were of Asian descent. There was little choice in food for me in Hawaii other than Asian food, which I started to enjoy. I began to gain a greater appreciation and understanding of my own heritage and culture as a Japanese American and an Asian American.

Originally, I had been enrolled in engineering, but after switching colleges and majors, I settled on Economics and Asian Studies at Brigham Young University. When I completed a graduate degree, I moved to California where I taught Economics at a new community college in Hayward in the Bay Area, called Chabot College. I taught for ten years and during that time entered politics. I ended up as an International Business Consultant living in Utah and working with companies primarily in Japan and other parts of Asia before joining the staff of the JACL and working in Washington, DC.

It took me a long time to figure out who I was and to gain some pride in my heritage. Although my family was not forced from our home during the war, we still felt the hardship and discrimination of being looked at as the enemy. Most Japanese Americans at that time had similar experiences no matter where they lived.

We know what Executive Order 9066, which was signed by President Franklin D. Roosevelt on February 19, 1942, did to the Japanese American population. There were roughly one hundred twenty thousand people of Japanese ancestry forcibly uprooted from their West Coast homes. They were largely placed in camps which were like whole cities of people being moved to some desolate area of the country. They generally lost virtually everything they owned as they were only allowed to take with them what they could carry. Even those who participated in the so-called "voluntary evacuation" lost most of their earthly belongings and had to start over. Life was difficult as they usually were forced to live in less than desirable, and sometimes primitive, living conditions.

Many of the evacuees who were displaced were immigrants. They were the first generation, who had arrived in this land with high hopes and dreams for a better life. They had worked hard and had established families, homes, and small businesses. However, the majority of those who were incarcerated were citizens of the United States, the immigrants' children who were the second generation with their children who were the third generation. They had been born in the United States and were American citizens. The Constitution did not protect these citizens and resident aliens as it should have done.

There were rumors of all kinds going around before the incarceration became a reality. Most Japanese Americans never believed it would come to fruition. A few people spoke out against the incarceration of Japanese Americans. Francis Biddle, Attorney General of the United States, counseled that the forced removal and incarceration of Japanese persons who were US citizens would be unconstitutional although he later went along with the idea. General Mark Clark and Admiral Harold Stark of the United States military both said that the "evacuation" of Japanese Americans was not necessary.

Leaders within the Japanese communities along the West Coast and also inland were arrested and taken away to prisons immediately on or soon after December 7, 1941. These people included officers of Japanese community organizations and leaders within Japanese American groups, business owners, Japanese language teachers, religious leaders, and others who were thought to have some connections to Japan. Some were picked up that very day without any knowledge to them or their families as to where they were being taken. A curfew order was imposed. The Japanese people were restricted to travel of only five miles from their residence. Windows had to be blackened. The people who were able to "voluntarily evacuate" to other states before the deadline in March of 1942, when further travel was not allowed, apparently believed the rumors about the camps which, unfortunately, did come true.

Almost no one came to the aid of the Japanese Americans during that difficult time, and many encouraged the mistreatment of them. Most civil rights organizations and religious groups (with the notable exception of the American Friends Committee or Quakers) kept quiet on the issue. Few friends could be found, and enemies were especially prevalent and vocal. Newspapers printed hateful articles against the Japanese Americans and immigrants.

Before the concentration camps were ready, the people were housed at temporary assembly centers at racetracks or fairgrounds where many lived in horse stalls which smelled of the animals which had lived there. They were given a cot and a mattress cover which they could fill with straw for a bed. Several months later after the camp buildings were built and ready for occupancy, the people were taken by train to the American concentration camps where they were held as prisoners behind barbed wire. Some told of traveling in the trains with blackened windows. They thought that they were being taken somewhere out in the middle of the desert where they would be removed from the trains and shot.

In the camps, whole families lived in a single room of a barracks. There were guard towers at the camps with armed soldiers holding rifles pointed inward at the occupants who were locked up and denied their freedom. Although some people, mostly young adults, were able to leave the camps before the war ended to attend school at inland universities or if they found outside work away from the West Coast and received permission to leave, most of the people had no place to go and remained in the camps for the duration of the war.

After Japan surrendered and the war ended, the Japanese Americans were released from the camps. Those who returned to the areas on the West Coast where they had previously lived were placed on trains. Others were given a bus ticket. Those who had been incarcerated received $25 and were sent on their way either by train or bus. Some people had stored belongings before the war but returned to find that everything had been stolen. A few people were fortunate to find that trusted neighbors had cared for their possessions. Many of the older people were broken in spirit and in health. It was a devastating experience about which some people who experienced it are still unable to speak because of the huge emotional toll it took on them. Yet the Japanese Americans persevered and overcame huge obstacles to find their place in society after many years.

For a long time after the war was over, those who were incarcerated generally were reluctant to talk of the camps even when asked by family members. They experienced horrible feelings of shame, humiliation, and embarrassment at being forcibly removed from their homes and held as prisoners in the camps. They were distrusted and rejected by their own government. There may have been relative freedom within the camps, but there was little chance to escape to the outside world although there were some exceptions. Through no fault of their own, they were taken from their homes and incarcerated simply because of how they looked. It was clearly a racist issue. Those who had been incarcerated were usually silent about the experience and did not speak to anyone about the experiences of the war years.

When the JACL and other groups pressed forward many years later in the 1970s and 1980s to seek reparations and redress for the wrongs of the World War II incarceration of Japanese Americans (largely to ensure that it would never happen again), Senator Daniel Inouye from Hawaii suggested that a commission should be set up to hear the personal stories of this terrible period in our nation's history. The members of Congress who would vote on the issue needed to know about the actual experiences of those who lived through it. A commission was set up called the Commission on Wartime Relocation and Internment of Civilians (CWRIC). Though most internees had never talked about the issue, Japanese Americans who had been imprisoned finally began to tell of their experiences. Some testified before the CWRIC telling poignant stories of hardship and sadness. They had great feelings of shame and distress when their own government did not trust them and called them noncitizens. Others began to open up to their families and tell of their wartime experiences of being held as prisoners in barbed wire enclosed camps or prisons.

The CWRIC held hearings throughout the country. I was able to testify at the hearing in San Francisco, not as one formerly incarcerated, but as someone representing elected officials speaking about the injustice of the World War II experience of Japanese Americans. I was glad to give my perspective on how the Constitution had not protected these innocent citizens who certainly were deserving of redress.

A report was issued in 1983 by the CWRIC, and Congress became educated on what had happened more than thirty years prior. It was ten years after the redress campaign was officially launched in earnest at a National JACL Convention held in Salt Lake City in 1978 that the Civil Liberties Act of 1988 was passed. It was called the Redress Bill and resulted in a Congressional apology and a letter of apology from the President of the United States with some redress of monetary funds paid to the victims who were still living on August 10, 1988. The nation admitted its mistakes, which started the healing process.

The findings of the CWRIC determined that the incarceration was the result of racial discrimination, wartime hysteria, and political incompetency of the leaders in power at the time. It was always known that racism played the major role although it was, at the time, attributed to military necessity as all people of Japanese background were immediately suspected of being potential spies for Japan. The victims were also told that it was being done for their own safety and protection. Japanese American young men who tried to enlist in the United States military immediately after the war began found that they were rejected because they had been reclassified as enemy aliens or noncitizens. Japanese

Americans were loyal citizens, and there were no cases of espionage ever proven among them during those war years.

These unfortunate experiences which were forced upon the Japanese American community can teach us lessons in sociology, economics, psychology, politics, and, of course, the Constitution. The Japanese Americans were denied due process and deprived of their liberty and property. They did not receive equal protection under the law. They were persecuted simply because of their heritage. It is hard to believe that our government could do such a thing to so many innocent people. It must never be allowed to happen again.

As we look at the issues of the civil rights community today, what are they? Comprehensive immigration reform. Habeas Corpus and the Constitution. Disparities in access to government institutions. Health care problems and disparities.

The lessons of the past can teach us about what we need to do to protect the rights of our citizens in this day. We of the JACL are anxious to tell the story of the Japanese American experiences during World War II in order to prevent such a travesty of justice from ever happening to any other people. We believe that the success of the Redress Movement and the monetary payment help to ensure that it will not happen again. However, the danger exists that it could be repeated. We would like to do our part to protect the rights of American citizens and others who may be wrongly persecuted just for how they look and not for anything they did. We need to be ever vigilant to maintain the freedoms we enjoy.

Thank you.

JAPANESE AMERICANS ON BAINBRIDGE ISLAND

Article Originally Written for
the JACL Membership
September 5, 2007

Reaching Bainbridge Island from Seattle takes slightly over half an hour on a pleasant ferry ride. The ferry holds hundreds of vehicles with many locals staying in their cars for the ride. Tourists leave their cars to wander on the upper deck of the boat to view the scenery from the outside. It is also possible to reach the Island by driving across a bridge at the ends of the Island. Bainbridge Island is a beautiful, lush area with a population of around twenty-two thousand people.

After the bombing of Pearl Harbor by Japan, war hysteria broke out. The Japanese Americans living on the West Coast of the United States were faced with evacuation and incarceration in American concentration camps. Residents of Bainbridge Island became the first group of Japanese ancestry along the Pacific Coast to be forced to leave their homes. They were given six days notice to be ready to leave.

Dr. Frank Y. Kitamoto, DDS, PS, who has a health-centered family dentistry practice on Bainbridge Island, left with that group of 272 Japanese Americans. He was a four-year-old child at the time and is in the photo often used to show the Japanese Americans leaving Bainbridge Island at the former Eagledale Ferry Landing on March 30, 1942. They were taken at gun and bayonet point by order of the military commander who was given authority to remove the people of Japanese descent through Executive Order 9066 signed by President Franklin D. Roosevelt. They boarded the ferry and later a train which left heading south. The occupants did not know where they were going, and there was much apprehension.

After meeting Dr. Kitamoto at the Minidoka pilgrimage, I decided that I would like to visit Bainbridge Island. When the JACL Bi-District Conference in Seattle was completed this July, my wife and I visited the Island. Dr. Kitamoto called together a group of local Japanese Americans and other friends to meet with us at his dental office where they regularly hold meetings to plan for a memorial to honor the Japanese Americans of Bainbridge Island. We were privileged to meet these dedicated individuals who are helping to preserve the Japanese American experience.

Dr. Kitamoto has been president of the Bainbridge Island Japanese American Community (BIJAC) for more than two decades. Clarence Moriwaki chairs the BIJAC committee in charge of the memorial. The million dollar memorial project has raised half of the funds needed for completion, and they are seeking donations. Plans are to place names on the donor wall of those who donate $1,000 or more. The Japanese American community and friends have erected other memorial areas around the Island including a Haiku Noniwa Garden at the grounds of the Library. Their motto is: *Nidoto Nai Yoni, Let It Not Happen Again.* They are also doing oral histories.

At the suggestion of Sheldon Arakaki, vice president of operations on the National Board of the JACL and a resident of the Seattle area, I was able to secure reservations to stay at a quaint Japanese Inn on Bainbridge Island which is a private bed and breakfast called Fuurin-Oka. It is a separate Japanese cottage in a grove of bamboo trees behind the owner's home. It was constructed in 2001 by Ron Konzak, who had traveled extensively in East Asia and who had it built to exacting Japanese standards. Visitors may feel as though they are actually in Japan. The current proprietor continues the tradition of serving breakfast although it is an American breakfast instead of the original Japanese breakfast. It is an appealing place in a peaceful setting on the beautiful island.

Bainbridge Island is just across the Puget Sound from Seattle. In 1942 there were more than two hundred fifty people of Japanese heritage living on Bainbridge Island, which included farmers, businessmen, fishermen, and their families. Japanese immigrants reportedly first arrived on Bainbridge Island in the 1880s, working in sawmills and strawberry harvesting. By the early 1940s, Japanese Americans had become an integral part of the Bainbridge Island community. Supposedly because of the island's proximity to naval bases and because they were suspected of being or becoming spies for Japan, the Japanese people from Bainbridge Island were the first in the country to be removed from their homes under the evacuation order.

After President Franklin D. Roosevelt signed Executive Order 9066 on February 19, 1942, which allowed for the forced removal of all those of Japanese ancestry from their homes on the West Coast, there was much apprehension as people wondered if it would really happen. On March 24, 1942, Lt. Gen. John L. DeWitt, the West Coast commander of the US Army, issued Exclusion Order No. 1, ordering the evacuation of all people of Japanese ancestry from Bainbridge Island. This first evacuation became a model for the subsequent removal of all people of Japanese descent from the West Coast of the United States.

The Bainbridge Islanders affected, which included aliens and non-aliens (as were called the citizens of the United States) were given just six days to register, sell or somehow rent their homes and property, and pack to leave. On the morning of March 30,

1942, at 11:00 a.m., these Japanese Americans and immigrants from Bainbridge Island, under armed guard, were put on the ferry Keholoken to Seattle where they boarded a train which would take them to their new residence. They were not to return to Bainbridge Island for more than four years.

The people were told that they were being instructed to go to a reception center under government supervision and must carry with them the following property, not to exceed that which could be carried by the individual or family members:

a. Blankets and linens for each member of the family
b. Toilet articles for each member of the family
c. Clothing for each member of the family
d. Sufficient knives, forks, spoons, plates, bowls, and cups for each member of the family
e. All items carried will be securely packaged, tied, and plainly marked with the name of the owner and numbered in accordance with instructions received at the Civil Control Office
f. No contraband items may be carried

The editors of the *Bainbridge Review* newspaper, Walt and Milly Woodward, openly opposed the evacuation for the duration of the war (which was unique among West Coast newspapers which generally supported and encouraged the mistreatment of the Japanese Americans).

An editorial in the *Bainbridge Review* on March 26, 1942, stated: *"But we are talking here about 191 AMERICAN CITIZENS! Where, in the face of their fine record since December 7, in the face of their rights of citizenship, in the face of their own relatives being drafted and enlisting in our Army, in the face of American decency, is there any excuse for this high-handed, much-too-short evacuation order?"*

The *Bainbridge Review* printed the following on April 2, 1942: *"The Navy and others who feared the presence here of Japanese aliens and Japanese American citizens breathed easier this week, for the Island was cleared of every last one of its Japanese residents in the nation's first enforced evacuation.*

"There were others, though, who mourned at their departure. They included Caucasians who gathered at the Eagledale dock Monday morning and wept unashamed as their Japanese neighbors obediently boarded the ferry Keholoken for their last trip from the Island for a long time, a ride which was the first step in the Government's forced evacuation to the reception center at Camp Manzanar, high in Owen Valley, California."

This first group of those evacuated and incarcerated in the country was assembled on Bainbridge Island where they were forced to march to the Eagledale ferry landing. The group numbered 272 men, women, and children who were allowed to bring only one suitcase and what they could carry or wear. They eventually were moved to the Mojave Desert in California at the Manzanar Camp, a far cry from their comfortable homes on Bainbridge Island. About half would return to Bainbridge Island after the war to rebuild their lives.

The BIJAC in 1998 partnered with the Bainbridge Island/ North Kitsap Interfaith Council to create the Bainbridge Island World War II Nikkei Internment and Exclusion Memorial Committee. The committee had the intent to construct a memorial to the internees at the former Eagledale ferry landing from which the Japanese Americans were forced to leave Bainbridge Island. The United States House of Representatives unanimously (419–0) passed a bill sponsored by Representative Jay Inslee (D-WA) in 2007 to give National Park status to the memorial site at Bainbridge Island. The legislation would make the site a satellite of the Minidoka Internment National Monument in Idaho, which was designated such by President Bill Clinton. The bill was introduced in the Senate by Senators Maria Cantwell

(D-WA) and Patty Murray (D-WA). It came out of committee but has yet to be voted on by the full Senate.

Although approximately half of the Island's Japanese American residents returned after the war's end, there are fewer people of Japanese heritage living there now than were living on the Island when they were evacuated. Junkoh Harui was a child when the war broke out and is one of those whose family returned. His father owned land and had developed successful businesses on Bainbridge Island before the war. Junkoh has restored a nursery business there which is called Bainbridge Gardens Nursery. It is a five star Environ Stars certified business and is a showcase place to visit on the Island. Besides a thriving nursery business and gift shop surrounded by a forest of trees, there is a tranquil Japanese Garden.

Plans have been in the works for some time to build a memorial near the site where the Japanese Americans left the Island. The park is a fifty acre area with the memorial being on eight acres. On March 30, 2006, a Memorial Blessing and Dedication Ceremony were held at the memorial site. Construction was initiated on April 3, 2006, and some portions have now been completed. Footbridges, entry gates, and a pavilion have been erected. The first gate was built four years ago and placed outside the local Windsor Post Office with an explanation about the Japanese American experience on Bainbridge Island at the time of World War II. The gates are hand built of cedar without metal bolts, fasteners, or brackets. They are wonderful examples of beautiful craftsmanship and materials.

Johnpaul Jones and John Buday have been instrumental in the design and craftsmanship which have graced the memorial thus far. Much of the work and materials have been donated by members of the Timber Framers Guild, a nonprofit organization dedicated to promoting the benefits, beauty, and practicality of timber frame structures. Kevin Coker and Bob Sproul have also contributed time, expertise, skills, and materials.

The memorial is intended to enforce the message of *"Nidoto Nai Yoni,"* or *"Let it not happen again."* It recreates the walk that Japanese American Bainbridge Islanders were forced to take so many years ago. A 272-foot "story wall" containing the names of the 272 Japanese American residents on Bainbridge Island in 1942 leads to a 150-foot pier at the water's edge where the ferry dock once was. Each foot of the pier represents one of the citizens who ultimately returned to Bainbridge Island after the war ended. The site may expand eventually to include other elements such as sculptures and an interpretive center.

In May 2008, President George W. Bush signed into law S 2739, an Omnibus Parks Bill, which among other things, "…expands several national parks." Wording within the bill states: "…adjusts the boundary of the Minidoka National Monument to include the Nidoto Nai Yoni Memorial commemorating the Japanese Americans of Bainbridge Island, Washington, who were the first to be forcibly removed from their homes and relocated to internment camps during World War II."

Members of Congress who were especially helpful in getting this bill passed were Senators Mike Crapo and Larry Craig and Rep. Mike Simpson of Idaho as well as Senators Maria Cantwell and Patty Murray and Reps. Jay Inslee and Jim McDermott of the State of Washington. Dan Sakura, vice president for Government Relations and director of Real Estate for The Conservation Fund, worked hard on the bill as did other individuals and several groups including the JACL.

The Bainbridge Island Japanese American Exclusion Memorial is an outdoor exhibit located on the south shore of Eagle Harbor, where Japanese Americans were loaded on to a ferry as the first of those evacuated from their West Coast homes. The completed memorial was dedicated on August 6, 2011. The photo on page 35 is of the people leaving Bainbridge Island in 1942.

MIAMI DADE GALA

Speech at the Miami Dade County
Asian American Advisory Board Gala
Miami, Florida, September 8, 2007

First, let me add my congratulations on the tenth year anniversary of the Asian American Advisory Board. The work you have done in giving scholarships and community service will have a long lasting impact on many individuals. I am particularly proud of your work in supporting Asian American women who suffer from domestic violence. Thirty some years ago while a California state assemblyman, I authored one of the nation's first laws that was aimed at spousal rape and domestic violence. I know the struggle of those who are the object of this demeaning and violent behavior. Your work to help the victims is truly commendable.

I hope you don't mind if I reflect on a little bit of my life as we look at where Asian Americans find themselves today in the fabric of American society. I was born on the wrong side of the tracks on a tiny vegetable farm near Salt Lake City, Utah. Our farm later became the location of the city sewer plant. We were poor in material goods, but our large family of eight siblings learned to enjoy and appreciate what we had. Since that time, I have had the honor of attending signings in the Oval Office and meeting several Presidents of the United States, I have met with prime ministers and ambassadors of major nations, and I have negotiated business deals with Fortune 500 companies. So, one could say that I have come a long way from the farm. But on the other hand, there are some aspects of my life that still reflect a perception from some in society that, simply because of my physical characteristics and appearance, I may not really be an American.

So how far have we come as an ethnic community? Are we making headway in embracing the American dream?

My father came as an immigrant to the United States just a century ago. His reasons for immigrating from the southern part of Japan were not much different than the reasons new immigrants come to America today. He, being the oldest son, felt an obligation to help support the family of his father who was in ill health. His mother had already passed on. The economics of feeding a family became a stark reality for this sixteen-year-old boy. America provided the opportunity for him to become a major contributor to his family's well-being. He brought to America the values of his Japanese culture. His, like the cultures of your heritage, was a culture of *Respect, Reverence, Industry, and Integrity*. He passed these ideals on to his children. Like immigrants today, he worked hard for the benefit of his children, which is a basic value in the Asian world.

A century ago, Japanese and Chinese immigrants to the United States faced a world that did not have a clue as to who these Asians really were. My father worked side by side with other Asians at physically taxing work on the railroads. Others labored in the mines or fields and in various types of menial work. During this era, Asians came to this country for the same reason for which their counterparts from Europe were coming at the time. The opportunity to earn money to feed and clothe families was the main motivation. Their thrift and hard work allowed many to move into other sectors of the economy such as commerce and agriculture. I don't think that history gives due credit to the Asian laborers who helped build the major infrastructure and primary industries of the industrial age.

This first generation of immigrants with their language difficulties normally struggled to fully assimilate into the mainstream of American society. Yet they withstood various hardships in order for their children to come closer to the full American dream. In Japanese, *"Kodomo No Tame"* or *"For the Sake of the Children"* was the continuing motivation for the Japanese immigrants to work hard, stay focused, live right, and try to be good neighbors.

When the rails were completed and mechanization took over the mines and railroads, Asians were no longer wanted and in fact were often despised. Anti-Asian sentiment grew, and government policy reflected the attitude of that day. Measures were adopted that no longer allowed Asians to immigrate to the United States. Agreements were made and consummated with foreign governments to keep their people in the home country. In many states, anti-Asian land laws were adopted that prevented the Asian immigrants from owning land. Anti-miscegenation laws prevented Asians from marrying outside their race in many states. Some of these laws remained on the books until the 1950s, 1960s, 1970s, and beyond.

This was an extremely difficult era for Asian Americans. Many of the young people began to graduate from colleges; yet they could not find meaningful jobs in their field because no one would hire them. Asian Americans were barred from swimming in public pools except on one day of the week just before the water was going to be changed. Asian Americans were not allowed to participate in bowling leagues. Agricultural organizations opposed any inclusion of Asian American farmers. Asians were not permitted to become naturalized citizens of the United States. And it goes on and on. One would think that things could *not* get worse.

However, with the attack on Pearl Harbor by Japan on December 7, 1941, things did get worse for the immigrants from Japan and their children who were born in the United States. When they heard the report of the attack on the radio, Japanese

Americans were horrified. Most likely had no idea where Pearl Harbor was or why this had happened. They felt immediate fear and anxiety.

Hearings held by a commission years later in the 1980s produced evidence that the incarceration came about because of racism, war hysteria, and the lack of competent political leadership. The ethnic Japanese, mostly citizens of the United States living in states on the West Coast, were given just days or maybe a week to dispose of their goods and pack what they were able to carry, so they could be transported to the ten American concentration camps which were hastily constructed in desolate areas of the country. Even though the camps were not yet ready for occupancy, the people of Japanese descent were taken from their homes and were required to stay temporarily in horse stalls at racetracks and fairgrounds. The horse stalls had been whitewashed to be made ready for the occupants, and they still contained horse hairs and the smell of the animals.

There was no due process. The only evidence presented against them was the color of their skin and other physical features. The courts at that time allowed this forced incarceration. There were some few cases where people tried to resist the treatment, and it was later determined that the Japanese Americans had been denied their rights under the Constitution.

Forty-six years later, in 1988, the nation apologized through legislation and a Presidential apology letter and reparations. It took a lot of hard work for this to happen. The Japanese American Citizens League (JACL) and other groups put in an inordinate amount of effort to bring about the success of the Redress Movement. The four Japanese American members of Congress were key to its passage. It did not just happen because people in leadership decided it was wrong. Redress came about because a dedicated group of Japanese Americans pushed to convince the members of Congress to right the wrong.

One of the important happenings during the war was the unprecedented patriotism shown by men who were incarcerated in these wartime concentration camps. Along with Japanese Americans from Hawaii who comprised the 100th Battalion, a segregated unit, the 442nd Regimental Combat Team of Japanese Americans, was formed. The 442nd became the most highly decorated unit for its size and length of service in the history of the US Army, likely due largely to the high number of Purple Heart awards for injuries sustained and lives lost. Over twenty Congressional Medals of Honor and other awards have been subsequently given to them many years later.

In addition, Japanese Americans served in the Military Intelligence Service, called the MIS, in the Pacific theater. They served under difficult circumstances where they could easily be mistaken for the enemy. Their work was highly classified, so their contribution to America's victory could not be recognized until decades later. Recently, Gen. Colin Powell, former secretary of state, declared that the MIS in the Pacific, by their intelligence work, saved thousands of lives and shortened the war in the Pacific perhaps by as much as two years. Some few other Japanese Americans were allowed to serve in regular units of the armed forces. Japanese American women served in women's units of the army. While many of these heroes came home to the same prejudices that existed when they left to serve their country, their valor eventually opened many doors for postwar Japanese Americans and other Asian Americans.

Thousands of Filipino Americans and other Asian Americans also served with valor in the United States military. Florida's own Frank Fung was part of the Asian American patriotism during World War II that paved the way for a more rapid process of assimilation after the war. Frank was initially turned away from the Army Air Corps because of his race. He persisted and was finally allowed to join. He later became an ace fighter pilot and hero of the war. Even though he was eventually injured, he made a comeback and served in Korea as well as Vietnam.

The loyalty and patriotism shown by the World War II generation of Asian Americans allowed America to see that Asian Americans really were proud and loyal Americans. This is the generation that opened the gates of opportunity for you and me. So, as we moved into the 60s and 70s, the Asian Pacific American community began to have some visibility and gain some respect. When Hawaii became a state in 1959, Congress saw as members the first Asian Americans, Daniel Inouye and Hiram Fong.

In the 60s, 70s, and 80s, we saw more Asian Americans entering the political arena. In California, former congressman and later Secretary of Commerce and Secretary of Transportation, the Honorable Norman Mineta, began his political career on the planning commission and then became mayor of the City of San Jose. Patsy Mink and Spark Matsunaga were elected to the House of Representatives from Hawaii, where Matsunaga went on to become a respected US senator. Bob Matsui was elected to the Sacramento City Council in the early 70s before he was elected to serve in Congress. Tom Kitayama became mayor of Union City, California, a position he held for three decades. Paul Bannai and I were the first Japanese Americans to serve in the California State Assembly. March Fong and Al Song were also early Asian Americans elected to the California legislature. S. I. Hayakawa became a controversial United States senator from California. Many Asian Americans were finally appointed or elected to the bench as judges.

In the following years, there was a wave of new Asian American political figures from California, Hawaii, Utah, and Washington State. We have watched Asian Americans enter state houses in Colorado and Alaska while numerous others hold offices in many corners of the nation, including New York, Massachusetts, Texas, Louisiana, Nebraska, and Minnesota. Yet the percentages of Asian American elected officials are still low.

There are some interesting trends that will bear watching in the next decade. In Congress, some of the initial Asian American members are gone. Matsunaga, Mink, and Matsui have passed away. Mineta has retired from elected public office. Only Senator Inouye remains from the earlier days, with newcomers since that time: Sen. Daniel Akaka and Rep. Mazie Hirono from Hawaii, Rep. Mike Honda and Rep. Doris Matsui from California, and Rep. David Wu from Oregon. The problem is that there are currently few up and comers in the pipeline.

Is it important to have Asian Americans in public office? According to Senator Inouye and Secretary Mineta, because they were there at the political table during the time when critical issues for Asian Americans were discussed and debated, they could not be ignored. When we are not *at* the table, it is as if we and our community do not exist.

There are some in the Asian American and Pacific Islander community who feel that we have arrived and that all is well. There are those with the erroneous security that we are totally assimilated and are part of the American mainstream with full acceptance and without any of the problems of the past.

Let's look at the reality of our assimilation and acceptance. While it is a long way from the tiny truck farm to being invited to the Oval Office and a long way for Secretary Mineta from an American concentration camp in Heart Mountain, Wyoming, to becoming a member of the Cabinet for two Presidents, it is still a much further distance to an equal shot at opportunities for most in our community. For those of us who feel that we have really made it, then it is time for us to begin to give back to that community heritage that allowed us to be in the good station in life that we enjoy. *Kodomo no tame. For the sake of the children.* Let's make sure that we are engaged in preparing the future society for our children and grandchildren, that it is not just a financial fortune but a treasure of social justice and equity.

But let's look at some of the realities of today. We have all heard the derogatory terms that are still used today to refer to our ethnic heritage as Asian Americans. Does it make us feel good when these epitaphs are hurled into our faces or we hear of it being done to others? It normally occurs when one wants to demean or belittle another person.

When a shock jock radio host calls a Chinese restaurant to belittle those who answer, does that make us proud of who we are? When we see degrading stereotypes on the movie screen, what does that do to the public perception of who we really are? When we watch sitcoms and reality shows on television where there is a total absence of the Asian American character, does it make you wonder what reality really is? Reality, to many in the media, is a world without the rich inclusion of the Asian American mind, culture, and presence.

Does it matter that when a drug is tested, only white patients are used when it is known that Asian Americans may react differently to prescribed dosages of that drug? Is it important to know that Asians may be more or less susceptible to certain diseases than the mainstream white American? These disparities can only result in inferior health care of Asian Americans.

While the federal government does set aside some contracts for minority small businesses, is it important to know that Asian American businesses are woefully under represented in doing work for the government? There has been little outreach to the Asian American small business person. Should not Asian Americans be part of this multitrillion dollar business opportunity?

We spoke of the importance of being at the table when government decisions are being made. Well, is it important to know that Asian Americans occupy very few seats on boards of directors in the corporate and banking world? In the entrepreneurial segment of our economy, Asian Americans have shown others how to succeed with small businesses. Yet in the traditional corporate world and in the financial infrastructure of our economy,

Asian Americans are rarely seen. The glass ceiling continues to exist for Asian Americans.

A couple of weeks ago while traveling from Washington, DC to the Pacific Northwest, I had an all too typical experience that points to the fact that Asian Americans may always be seen as aliens or perpetual foreigners and not be considered part of the mainstream by some people. My wife and I boarded an airplane and took our seats in the exit row. I have flown over three million miles and consider myself a seasoned traveler. I normally am given an exit row seat when I am flying coach class as is my wife when she is traveling with me. As I was about to take my seat and had spoken to my wife in my perfect Utah dialect of English, the flight attendant tried to stop us from taking the exit row seats. She said, "You can't sit there because you have to speak English to sit in the exit row." I don't know how she could not have heard me speaking English, but she just assumed that we could not speak English because we were obviously ethnic Asian. It was a clear case of needing diversity training.

European visitors or other white people who do not speak English are not treated as ethnic Asians often are even when we are actually Americans who were born and raised in this country. There were people seated in a nearby exit row who were speaking Russian and did not seem to have a command of the English language. They could answer yes to the standard question that they were willing to assist in an emergency, but they were not questioned further as we were. Diversity training is lacking in many areas.

Across the nation in recent months we have seen violence against Asian Americans perpetrated simply because the people were ethnically Asian. In Minnesota, Chicago, and Sacramento, we have seen what hate can do when innocent people are targeted simply because of their race or appearance. It does not only cause humiliation and embarrassment, but it can result in injury and even a death sentence just because innocent people happened to be Asian or something other than white.

So what I am saying is that, yes, while we have made a great deal of progress as Asian Americans and our stature within society has improved, on the other hand, we have much to do and a long way to go before we can consider ourselves fully vested into the mainstream of America. We continue to face some of what we might consider the social ills of the day. At the same time, Asian Americans may enjoy less of what could be considered the economic benefits of the market economy. We still have barriers to overcome. What we do have to help us along the way are the values instilled in us by our parents and our grandparents—those who came from Asian countries.

The work of the Asian American Advisory Board is critical. The individual involvement of each one of you is essential for *kodomo no tame, for the sake of the children.*

Thank you for the work that you do, and thank you for allowing me to join you today along with my friend and colleague, Karen Narasaki, who is an icon in the Asian American and civil rights community in Washington, DC. It has been a pleasure to share with you some thoughts and observations about our community.

Floyd Mori, national executive director/CEO of the Japanese American Citizens League (JACL), and Karen Narasaki, president/CEO of the Asian American Justice Center (AAJC), were keynote speakers at the Tenth Year Anniversary Dinner Gala of the Miami Dade County Asian American Advisory Board on September 8, 2007, at the Mandarin Oriental Hotel in Miami, Florida.

Dalip Singh Saund was the first South Asian elected as a voting member of the US House of Representatives. He served from 1957 to 1963. Patsy Takemoto Mink was the first woman of color elected to Congress. She was a Democrat from Hawaii elected to the House in 1989 who served from 1990-2002. She won her last election after her death in 2002.

HEART MOUNTAIN INTERPRETIVE LEARNING CENTER

Heart Mountain, Wyoming, Camp
Article Originally Written for
the JACL Membership
April 29, 2008

Some recent visitors to the JACL DC office were Shirley Higuchi and Doug Nelson, board members of the Heart Mountain, Wyoming Foundation (HMWF). This was an opportunity to receive an update on their efforts to raise funds for an Interpretive Learning Center at Heart Mountain. The foundation has been in existence for eleven years and is a nonprofit organization established to memorialize the camp and educate the public about the incarceration of Japanese Americans at Heart Mountain near Powell, Wyoming. Its president is David R. Reetz. The foundation has set and achieved an aggressive agenda of preservation and education. They are currently seeking funds and support to build an interpretive learning center which they expect to open in 2010.

Shirley Higuchi is the assistant executive director of the Legal and Regulatory Affairs of the American Psychological

Association and has served as president and board member for the District of Columbia Bar. Shirley's parents met at Heart Mountain as children and later became reacquainted at the University of California at Berkeley. They have supported the HMWF for many years, and a self-guided walking tour at the Heart Mountain site is named for Shirley's mother, Setsuko Saito Higuchi.

Doug Nelson is president of the Annie E. Casey Foundation in Baltimore, Maryland, which is a leading advocate for children. He became interested in Heart Mountain while attending graduate school at the University of Wyoming. His social history of the World War II relocation of Japanese Americans entitled *Heart Mountain* earned a Pulitzer Prize nomination in 1976. He has taught social history at the University of Wisconsin. The Annie E. Casey Foundation is a financial contributor to the educational efforts of the JACL.

The Honorable Norman Y. Mineta, immediate past secretary of transportation under President George W. Bush, was incarcerated at Heart Mountain as a young boy and has been very active in supporting the HMWF. His close friend, former Wyoming senator Alan Simpson, whom he first met when both were Boy Scouts in Wyoming during Norman's camp incarceration days, has also been involved with Heart Mountain and redress efforts. Retired judge Raymond Uno, a former National JACL president from Salt Lake City, was also incarcerated with his family at Heart Mountain and helps with fundraising. Jeanette Misaka, an active member of the Salt Lake JACL Chapter, an educator, and a former internee at Heart Mountain, works on the project as do many others.

Through the efforts of the Japanese American National Heritage Coalition, the JACL, with the considerable help of former US congressman Bill Thomas (R-CA), Sen. Daniel Inouye (D-HI), and others, Public Law 109–441: Preservation of Japanese American Confinement Sites was passed by the

Congress and signed by President George W. Bush. Congress has not yet appropriated funding for this program, but it is anticipated that matching funds will be available for the camp preservations. The National Parks Service has held hearings on the matter. The HMWF has already secured donations of over $1 million and hopes to raise $2 million to receive matching funds from the appropriations. The project is anticipated to cost $6.2 million.

The Heart Mountain Camp is named for nearby Heart Mountain and is located just north of Cody, Wyoming, sixty miles east of Yellowstone National Park. More than two thousand laborers were employed to work on the camp in June 1942. They enclosed seven hundred forty acres of buffalo grass and sagebrush with a high barbed wire fence and nine guard towers. Under the direction of the US Army Corps of Engineers, they built six hundred fifty military style buildings which included four hundred sixty-eight residential barracks for the incarcerated persons plus administrative, hospital, and support facilities. The camp opened on August 11, 1942, when the Japanese Americans started to arrive by train from the assembly centers at Pomona and Santa Anita, California, and Portland, Oregon. The camp reached its maximum population of 10,767 by January 1, 1943, which made it the third largest community in Wyoming at that time. The camp closed on November 10, 1945, when the last of the Japanese Americans were released. Most of the buildings were sold off to local residents or left to decay. In early 2007, one hundred twenty-four acres of the camp were listed as a National Historic Landmark. The HMWF purchased fifty acres to memorialize the camp's occupants and to interpret the site's historical significance.

Heart Mountain was the site of a resistance movement by Japanese American men who opposed being drafted into the United States Army while they and their families were incarcerated. They were willing to serve if their constitutional rights were restored and Japanese Americans were released from the imprisonment of the camps. They formed the Heart Mountain Fair Play Committee which tried to encourage others to resist the draft. Seven leaders of the committee were convicted of conspiracy against the Selective Service Act, and eighty-five were imprisoned for draft law violation. However, seven hundred ninety-nine Japanese American men who were volunteers and draftees from Heart Mountain served in the US Army. The resisters were later pardoned for the brave stand they took against the unjust incarceration, and some later served in the US military.

Different groups are helping with preservation projects of the various camps. Local community members and those formerly incarcerated and their families are involved. As we commemorate this year the 20th Anniversary of the Civil Liberties Act of 1988 (The Redress Bill), it is a good time for all of us to consider supporting these worthy causes. Thanks to everyone who is working on these camp projects. Remembering the Japanese American history and making it known to the general public is very important. These projects help in that effort.

The Heart Mountain Learning Center held its dedication ceremony in August 2011 and is open for visitors year round during regular visiting hours or by appointment.

A JAPANESE AMERICAN'S PERSPECTIVE

Article Written for and Printed in
the JCAW Memorial Booklet
Washington, DC
June 2008

Having never previously lived on the East Coast, the prospect of moving to Washington, DC in the year 2005 seemed a somewhat exciting adventure. Although I was at an age when many of my friends who were my contemporaries were retiring, and I had actually been semi-retired myself while I was an International Business consultant in Utah for a number of years, I was anxious to accept the position of director of public policy when an opening came up for the Japanese American Citizens League (JACL) in the Washington, DC office. I had some experience with public policy while working in government and had many years of volunteer leadership roles on the local and national levels within the JACL. Founded in 1929, the JACL is the nation's oldest and largest Asian American civil and human rights organization. Leaving family and friends behind, my wife and I pulled up stakes in Utah, where I was born and raised, and moved across the country to work in Washington, DC and live in Virginia.

The job as director of public policy for the JACL was busy, demanding, and stimulating. I found that Washington, DC was a great place to work and live. Although I had anticipated staying for only two years when I began working for the JACL (a job, which at the time was not considered a full-time position for me, although the actual work was more than full time), unforeseen circumstances brought about an opportunity to continue to work for the JACL as the national executive director/CEO when John Tateishi, who held the position previously suddenly became ill while at the office around the end of 2006. John had already given notice of his impending resignation and had agreed to keep working until a replacement was found.

After serving as the interim national executive director, I then took over the regular position with the understanding and stipulation that I would be able to remain with an office in Washington, DC where I feel most of the action takes place for nonprofit organizations such as the JACL. It is important for the JACL to maintain an active presence in the nation's capital. Although the JACL has had a Washington, DC representative for many years, Mike Masaoka, an early leader in the JACL, advocated some fifty years ago that the JACL headquarters should be in Washington, DC with the national executive director housed there. The coalition building aspects and visibility in the nation's capital of having the executive head of the JACL there seem especially beneficial for the JACL although the National JACL headquarters building is located in San Francisco with some staff there. I anticipated living in the Washington, DC area for another few years while serving in the position of the JACL's national executive director.

Many years earlier, not long before the start of World War II, my life began on a small farm just outside of Salt Lake City, Utah, in what was then a rural area. I was born on Memorial Day when May 30 was a national holiday. Although I had been told by my mother that the rain was leaking through the roof on her as she gave birth, my older brother told me many years later that the weather was sunny that day, and my siblings were upset at the time of my birth because it meant they had to miss the annual Memorial Day picnic held by the Japanese community. My mother may have gotten my birth mixed up in her memory with my younger brother Steve who was born in May four years later. My parents were immigrants from Kagoshima, Japan, and I was the seventh of eight children. My father had settled in Utah early on and farmed with the help of all his children.

Because my family lived in an inland state at the outbreak of World War II, we were not forcibly removed from our home as were those of Japanese ancestry, who had been living on the West Coast of the United States, and were incarcerated in the American concentration camps during the war. I do recall that relatives from California came to our home, having "voluntarily evacuated" in order to avoid being locked up in the camps. Being a small boy during the period of the war, I remember hearing people talk about "camp" although I did not understand much about what it actually entailed.

My entire childhood was spent in Utah, but I did experience discrimination and prejudice as did my Japanese American counterparts in other areas of the country. There were some kind neighbors, but there were occasions when people were unkind and hateful toward me and others of Japanese ancestry. I grew up in a white community among people who predominantly belonged to the Church of Jesus Christ of Latter-day Saints (Mormons). I became a Mormon myself when I was an older child, not yet a teenager. Most of my family eventually joined the Mormon Church as well. The discrimination against me and my family came mostly and understandably from people who did not know us personally.

Some of my brothers and sisters were considerably older than me. My oldest brother, Shigeru, was a college student at the University of Utah in Salt Lake City when the war broke out. He was an excellent student and hoped to attend Harvard University at some later time. He joined the United States Army when I was still a young child not yet in school. He was trained in the Military Intelligence Service (MIS) of the United States Army. His unit served in the Pacific as translators and interpreters.

At the war's end, my brother was in Japan for the occupation to help Japan recover from the effects of the war. He wrote a letter to our family while he was stationed in Kobe, Japan, to announce that he would be going to Harvard after his tour in the army was completed, which he expected to be soon. He indicated that he had made the necessary arrangements. However, he never had the chance to return to college as he did not come back alive from the service. He was traveling as a passenger in a US Army plane in Japan when it crashed, and he was killed. I remember when the unfortunate news arrived at our home. It was a horrifying and devastating day for all of us, especially my mother.

Although almost all of my associates and friends from school and church were white, I had some interaction with other people who were of Japanese descent occasionally as my family participated in the picnics and activities held by Japanese people in the community. Since my older brothers and sisters were involved with the JACL, I was able to attend local JACL social and athletic events with them from childhood. This gave me some associations with other Japanese Americans as I grew up. Most of my school days, however, were spent generally as the only ethnic minority until high school where there were a few others.

After graduating from high school, spending six months on active duty with the US Army Reserves, beginning college in California, and serving a two-year mission to Hawaii for the Mormon Church, I entered Brigham Young University (BYU) in Provo, Utah. I had married and had a young child by the time I received my graduate degree after which I embarked on my first real career job at Chabot College in Hayward, California. I taught Economics to college freshmen and sophomores. My wife, son Brent, and I drove to California in our first new car, pulling a trailer containing the sum of our earthly possessions.

I enjoyed teaching college students, and I felt it was a good position at which I fully intended that I might stay until retirement. However, my life has taken many turns since then. Experiences have come to me that I would never have imagined in those early days.

While I was busily involved with teaching and working with college students in 1972, an opportunity came up to run for the city council of Pleasanton, California, where we were living. It was a small town of around thirty thousand at the time with some older areas and lots of new homes. I had been interested in the political arena for some time, mainly since my own college days when a group of economics students conducted political polls with our college advisor, Richard Wirthlin, who later became the pollster and chief strategist for President Ronald Reagan. I decided to throw my hat in the ring. There were about a dozen people running for three seats, but I knocked on doors throughout the small city and campaigned heavily. Although relatively unknown, I became the top vote getter in that election.

After being elected, I was immediately made mayor pro tem and later served as mayor of the City of Pleasanton. That was a period when there were three Japanese American mayors in the Bay Area of California. Norman Y. Mineta was mayor of San Jose (the first Japanese American mayor of a major city), Tom Kitayama was mayor of Union City, and I served as mayor of Pleasanton. Norman Mineta went on to serve in high positions as a US congressman as well as secretary of commerce under President Bill Clinton and secretary of transportation under President George W. Bush. Tom Kitayama was a successful businessman who served as mayor of Union City for over thirty years. I was fortunate to be able to develop lifelong friendships with both of these great Japanese American gentlemen.

At Thanksgiving in 1975, the local California state assembly-man from the area where I lived suddenly passed away after just having been reelected to a position he had held for many years. I decided to run for his seat in the Assembly of what was then the 15th District in California which encompassed the communities of and areas around Hayward, Castro Valley, Pleasanton, Livermore, and Dublin. Although I was given only an extremely slim chance of winning, I again campaigned heavily and knocked on many doors. Some Democrats who were leaders in the community had been planning on running for the seat whenever the assemblyman, who had been in poor health, stepped down. However, I became the Democratic nominee after a primary victory. Then the Democratic Party stepped in to help me. I won the election to become the state assemblyman and was soon immersed in legislation and politics.

Paul Bannai (a Republican Japanese American from Southern California) had just been elected that fall as the first Japanese American in the California State Assembly. He and I were the only Japanese Americans in the Assembly at the time with only a handful of Asian Americans serving in elective office in the State Legislature and throughout the state. I became a friend and advocate for the Japanese American community, for the JACL, and for Japanese and Asian businesses and organizations within the State of California.

During this time I was able to make my first visit to the land of my ancestry, and I thoroughly enjoyed this first trip to Japan. As a television commercial about people visiting the country of their ancestors mentioned at the time, it was something like "going home." It was an emotional time for me as I visited the village of my parents and met relatives I had never known. It was the first of many trips to Japan over the years as my business subsequently has taken me there often during certain periods of my life. I was traveling to Japan nearly once a month at one point. At the current time, I have two sons who live and work in Tokyo.

After serving six years in the State Assembly, I became the director of the Office of International Trade for the State of California, which was a newly formed department at the time which I had actually helped create. This position gave me many more opportunities to interact with executives of various Japanese businesses and other Asian American groups. After serving in that position, I moved back to Utah where I became involved with business, later primarily international business working mostly with Japanese businesses until the move to Washington, DC a few years ago. My partners and I worked on taking Pennzoil and Subway Sandwiches to Japan, among other ventures.

Many friends and contacts, which I had from the past in the California State Assembly in the late 1970s and early 1980s, are now members of the United States House of Representatives or are United States senators. I also had the opportunity to become personally acquainted with some of the members of other state delegations over the years, including my home state of Utah. These friendships and those with the Asian American elected officials have given me strong contacts within Washington, DC. This has been very helpful as I have served the JACL and other Asian American organizations in trying to further the work in which we are engaged.

It has been a distinct privilege and pleasure for me to become personally acquainted with the Honorable Ryozo Kato, ambassador extraordinary and plenipotentiary of Japan to the United States of America, and with other Japan Embassy officials. Over the years, I have had the honor of becoming friends with several consuls general of Japan to the United States and have met with some of Japan's prime ministers. While I was national president of the JACL in 2001, I was able to represent the JACL and Japanese Americans on an A-50 ceremony program in Tokyo with former Prime Minister Koizumi and Dan Quayle, former Vice President of the United States, to commemorate the 50th anniversary of the US, Japan Peace Treaty of 1951. My wife and I arrived home in Utah the night before 9-11 happened.

Working for the JACL in Washington, DC allows me to continue to nurture increased interaction of Japanese nationals and Japanese Americans. Our ancestral heritage can allow Japanese Americans to be key players in the ongoing process of bilateral relations with Japan. Being part of the American society for a century and a half has allowed Japanese Americans to be seen as trusted and productive citizens of the United States. Although the history of Japanese Americans has been tarnished with the experience of being incarcerated in American concentration camps by our own government, we have overcome the difficulties to a large degree. The Japanese American veterans of World War II did much to help the cause of acceptance by showing great dedication and patriotism to our nation.

Japanese Americans have a rich cultural heritage of our Japanese ancestry which is now embraced more fully by the younger generations of Japanese Americans. This mix of positive experiences can be the source of maintaining peaceful and productive bilateral relationships between the two nations. Strong ties can become stronger through our continued and increased involvement with each other.

My past work experience has also afforded me the opportunity to meet many high level people in Japanese businesses in the United States and in Japan. I feel that the future holds good things for Japan's commerce and for the Japanese society in Washington, DC. My advice would be for Japanese business people in the United States to become more involved with Japanese American individuals and groups such as the JACL whenever possible. There is much we can gain from each other, and there can only be benefit derived from our interaction.

The JACL has been a chapter-based organization, and chapters are located throughout the United States including in Washington, DC and with a chapter in Japan. The JACL offers opportunities for social and cultural interaction between the Japanese Americans, Japanese nationals, and any others who are interested in our common goals. The JACL would wholeheartedly welcome the participation of more native Japanese as well as all others into the organization. We can learn much from each other, and the association is sure to be enjoyable.

This article was requested by the Japan Commerce Association of Washington (JCAW) on its 20th Anniversary of Official Incorporation for inclusion in the JCAW 20th Anniversary Memorial Booklet, "Japan-America Relationships Which We Can See Face to Face".

PATRIOTISM IS IMPORTANT

Speaking to a Church Congregation
Arlington, Virginia, July 2008

July is the month of patriotism and remembering our freedoms. We live in a great country with forefathers who were inspired. We could not exist without some form of government, and the framers of the Constitution gave us an ideal government where people can exercise free agency.

What should our government be? We should have free exercise of conscience. We should be able to choose how to live our lives within certain boundaries of the law. We should have the right and control of property. We should have protections which help us live life fully.

This sounds a little like *life, liberty, and the pursuit of happiness*. That is what we want from our government, and we are blessed to live in the United States of America where we can live freely and enjoy life.

Back in the early 1970s when I was a college instructor in Hayward, California, there was an admonition by church leaders to become involved in community affairs. I was busy and had a young family at the time, but I was prompted to run for elective office in the City of Pleasanton, California, where I lived. It was a city of around thirty thousand or more at that time, and I was basically an unknown. I decided at the last minute to throw my hat in the ring for a city council election which was coming up.

There were three seats available. Because I knocked on nearly every door in the town and campaigned heavily, I was able to come out victorious. I had a good support group from mostly my fellow church members and my students at the community college where I taught Economics.

After the election, I became the mayor pro tem and later was mayor of the city. When another opportunity came up to run for the California State Assembly, I once again decided to run. It was a lot different campaigning for a state position, but I was fortunate to win again. It gave me the opportunity to serve a larger group of people and to try to make the world a better place. The State Assembly in California is a full-time job so it did mean that I had to give up my teaching position at Chabot College, which I was somewhat sad to do because I truly enjoyed teaching college students.

Winning the election or even running would not have been possible without the freedoms that we enjoy in this great country. I was one of the first two Japanese Americans to serve in the California State Assembly. It was a breakthrough for me and for Asian Americans. I was also able to represent my church with a few other members who served in the Assembly at that time.

For a great part of my life, I have been involved in some form of government. I was able to teach young students in college, serve in elected offices, and now as the director of public policy for a civil rights organization.

Government is service. In our country, government serves the people. In government as in most of life, there are always at least two sides to most issues. In government, I have found that the caliber of the character of people involved is generally a notch above the general public. People serving in political office often get a bad rap and are blamed for all kinds of bad things. When a scandal hits a political person's life, it is front page news. Yet, most of the people I have met serving in government are dedicated individuals who are trying to serve to the best of their abilities.

We will not agree with everything they do, but we should understand that they are doing what they believe is best for the country.

Generally, there has to be some kind of very *strong commitment to doing good* when one chooses a government career, whether it be an elected position or as a civil servant. There are many challenges to this type of service.

We are often quick to be critical of those in government. We may think things take too much time. That happens in the private sector as well. We may not understand all the ramifications and the processes for getting things done and laws passed.

Sometimes we hear people say that everyone is dishonest in government. Is there dishonesty in the private sector? We should realize that there may be bad apples in every field, but there are extraordinary people serving us in government. Most are working extremely hard, they sacrifice family and personal pursuits, and many are compensated less than they would be in the private sector. People who choose to run for public office put themselves up for all kinds of scrutiny. They must be willing to endure trials and hardships if they want to serve.

There was a time in history when the government did not protect innocent citizens of this country. After Japan bombed Pearl Harbor in Hawaii on December 7, 1941, all the people of Japanese ancestry were immediately looked upon as the enemy. The government did the unthinkable when it forcibly removed one hundred twenty thousand people from their homes on the West Coast of the United States and placed them in American concentration camps which had been hastily constructed in remote and desolate regions of the country. There were ten such camps which each contained around eight to ten thousand or more people. This was a dark period when the Constitution did not protect its citizens because of war hysteria, racial prejudice, and incompetent government leaders at that time. Hopefully, such an experience will never be allowed to happen again to anyone else in this country.

What should government be doing? Some people and teachings say that the function of government is threefold: protection of life, the right to control personal property, and free exercise of conscience.

Government is *not* our moral watchdog. Then who is? *We* are our own watchdog. Morality is up to each one of us. Government is there to assure that we have free agency, but it is up to us individually to make correct choices for our well-being. Government is to provide an atmosphere of peace and liberty to allow us to pursue any worthy goal in life. It has allowed many people to rise out of humble circumstances to achieve greatness.

This is a great country with all the basic elements to allow for the progress of all of us. The basic operating procedures of our government were inspired.

Our material, spiritual, and emotional well-being today and in the future depends on our intelligent and caring involvement in the governmental process. Like all good things, this takes effort and some degree of sacrifice.

May we all do our part to help this country remain great, and may God bless us all.

NATIONAL JACL CONVENTION

Welcome Remarks at the Opening
National Council Session
Salt Lake City, Utah, July 17, 2008

Good Morning. You know, it was just the other day, it seems, that we had a convention here in Salt Lake City. It was fourteen years ago. Yours truly happened to have the privilege of chairing that convention. It was a very, very hot summer, and we had a lot of heat issues that we addressed during that convention. Some of you remember that convention. How many were here then? We had a midnight session, right? After the Sayonara banquet on Saturday night, we had a midnight session to complete the budget process. It wasn't the budget, however, that was the big issue at that time. It was the issue of same-sex marriage which took extra time to discuss, and the JACL was one of the first ethnic organizations to come out in support of same-sex marriage or marriage equality at that convention way back in 1994. The Honorable Norman Mineta, who was then a United States congressman from San Jose, California, spoke for support of the issue.

We can go back some years prior to that. In 1978, there was another JACL convention in Salt Lake City. How many of you were here then? There are a few here who were at that convention. That was the time when the JACL, with the prompting of many community leaders throughout the country made the decision to earnestly take on the issue of redress for the unjust incarceration which Japanese Americans suffered during World War II, asking for monetary reparations as well as an apology from the government.

Here we are back in Salt Lake City thirty years later. It is twenty years since the passage of the Civil Liberties Act of 1988 which provided for redress to the Japanese American community who suffered greatly at the hands of their own government during that dark period in history. We are here to once again get together and resolve the issues facing the JACL today.

I hope that you feel upon your shoulders the responsibility of governance of this great organization. It is not a frivolous thing for us to get together and meet in this way at our conventions. It is very important, and often is a groundbreaking occasion for JACL delegates to join together and make decisions that impact the lives of American people we hope for the better, and to improve our communities. So you have a great responsibility as we deliberate, as we discuss, and as we debate the issues during this week.

You are to be congratulated for your commitment. You are appreciated for taking the time, making the effort, and using your talents to uphold and move forward the objectives and the mission of the JACL. I commend you as delegates and thank you for all that you do.

We want you, during this time, not only to be serious about the issues but to really hopefully get to know some people that you have not previously known. And, particularly, would you pay attention to the young people that are among us this week. You know, this convention is groundbreaking in some sense, that we are having a parallel youth convention going on in the Salt Palace Convention Center next door. We have a very good participation of youth from throughout the country. As we have often spoken of in the past, youth are our future and we need to pay more attention to our young people. We need to listen to what they have to say. Although I think there are times when our young people think we have closed ears and closed minds, I hope some of what they are saying comes through to us. We recognize and respect the vision that our youth and young adults have in moving forward in a different kind of world and a different kind of society today.

Thank you for being here. We expect to get a lot done. We are going to have some plenary sessions that are sure to be very interesting and informative. Hopefully, these sessions will get you excited about some of the things with which we deal in the JACL, not just the mechanics of our constitution and of how we do this and how we do that. We want to get involved in the things that are important in our society today. The plenary sessions are aimed at informing us to get us better acquainted with those issues.

We are especially privileged to have NASA astronaut, Dan Tani, give a keynote speech at the convention. Dan is a third generation Japanese American and Chicago area native who has been an astronaut since 1996. His parents, Rose and Henry Tani, were incarcerated at Topaz, Utah, during World War II. Dan will also speak to schoolchildren while he is in town. He is a great example for all of us.

We know this will be an outstanding convention. So again thank you for being here. We appreciate you and welcome you to the great state of Utah and the great city of Salt Lake.

The Japanese American Citizens League/JACL held a biennial national convention for many years which was changed to an annual convention starting in 2011 instead of holding it every two years. The 2008 convention was held in Salt Lake City, Utah, with the Mount Olympus Chapter (which had previously been Floyd Mori's home chapter) as host chapter assisted by the Salt Lake Chapter and the Wasatch Front North Chapter. Floyd, as national executive director, gave the opening remarks and also a National Executive Director's Report at the opening session of the National Council, which includes

delegates from the various chapters of the JACL who discuss and vote on important issues for the organization. This was Floyd's first convention as national executive director.

After the 2008 National JACL Convention in Salt Lake City was completed, Floyd Mori and Larry Oda, then national president of the JACL, were talking in the Marriott Hotel lobby when Tim Koide came to them and said that President Thomas S. Monson, the leader of the Church of Jesus Christ of Latter-day Saints, was getting his shoes shined close by and no one else was around. They approached President Monson and had a little visit with him before a TV crew, which was covering another event, spotted President Monson and came to film him. The piece about President Monson getting his shoes shined aired on a local television news show on Channel 2 that evening. Tim, Floyd, and Larry appeared briefly in the clip which can be seen on YouTube. [Tim Koide was a staff member of the JACL and belongs to the Church of Jesus Christ of Latter-day Saints as does Floyd Mori.]

The photo and letter on page 42 were taken from the convention booklet of the National JACL Convention held in Salt Lake City in July 1994.

NATIONAL EXECUTIVE DIRECTOR'S REPORT

Speaking at a JACL National
Convention Opening Session
Salt Lake City, Utah, July 17, 2008

I am often asked if I like living in Washington. I always say that we love it in DC. It is not that the place itself is so wonderful, although it is pretty amazing, but it is because I really enjoy the work and the mission of the JACL in which we are engaged. There is great merit in what we do in the JACL, and we do things that improve the lives of people. We do things that help our community members, young and old, to fulfill their life's dreams and aspirations. We strive to educate others about our history and our goals. We also try to assist people of other communities.

The work of the JACL involves a multi-faceted process of identifying issues, developing plans to solve problems, and finding the resources to accomplish our goals. The JACL is a classic model of citizenship in action with results-oriented objectives.

The mission of the JACL tells us that social justice and human rights are critical for our society to function effectively. Our mission also tells us that we place great value on our Japanese heritage. So, all elements of our organization work to the end of preserving both civil rights and the values embodied in our heritage.

The base or foundation of the JACL is built upon individual members who are committed to this mission. Although we do not always agree on all issues, chapters and districts give strength in a unified voice and are able to provide the important social aspect of the JACL. A talented and dedicated staff enables us to implement programs that embody the mission of the JACL.

While we assess the performance of the JACL, it is easy to pick out flaws if we ignore the actual work that we do. Some may say that our foundation of members is getting weak or that we don't have adequate staffing to implement programs. Others may feel that we need to adhere to the organization's design from the past, or that form is more important than performance.

I would propose that our perceived flaws are only opportunities to improve upon who we are and increase our effectiveness in meeting our mission. Let's look at what we are doing and how we are beginning to re-establish the JACL as a major factor in the lives of our community.

We have an effective teacher training program that has helped teachers and students understand the great necessity for a strong Constitution. We know that the Japanese American experience of World War II is a great lesson for our entire citizenry in the United States to understand. Our teacher training and curriculum guide continue to provide teachers with real lessons in patriotism, courage, and citizenship. The teachers, who receive this training, are able to share this knowledge with the young minds in their classrooms throughout the nation.

We are responding to acts of defamation and using these experiences to develop a more tolerant and fair society. Yes, these issues of racism, discrimination, and prejudice still exist. We must be ever vigilant in order to combat them.

We have increased our stride in advocacy by strengthening our coalition partnerships, increasing our visibility in the halls of Congress, and developing legislative relationships from the local to the federal level.

The *"New JACL"* that is emerging is one with a major emphasis on youth programs. Our Leadership and Empowerment Workshops on college campuses, our new Community Awareness Program for high school students, and a Self Awareness Initiative for primary age children are expanding JACL's image among our younger ranks.

Becoming part of a society that desires and works for better health care and more equitable access to health services is a direction in which we have already embarked and which has an attraction to those trying to be healthier and striving to raise a healthy family.

We are working toward new partnerships and joint ventures with other Japanese American organizations in preserving historical artifacts of our past as well as jointly implementing social programs for youth and the elderly. We are weaving new pan-Asian partnerships as we see many issues that we have in common. We are helping those groups which have recent immigrants facing similar problems to what our parents and grandparents faced decades ago. We are forging corporate partnerships in the hope of not only enhancing our financial base but to augment our organizational experiences with those of the business sector to help build a stronger organization that will withstand the pitfalls of social and economic change.

The JACL is unique among most Asian American civil rights organizations. Our membership base with our structure of local chapters gives us the tools to be an effective grassroots advocacy organization. This same structure now allows us to implement new programs that improve our lives as Americans and to help newer immigrant populations avoid the barriers to full citizenship.

Our challenge is to realize how powerful we are and can be as an organization and to take the necessary measures to enable us to continue to be an effective voice for social justice. Change is in the wind. We need to have the insight to ride this surging wave of change to improve what we can do as an organization.

We need to look at our priorities as individuals and use our time and talents to give back to a heritage that has given us so much. We should help the younger generation to feel the pride of their heritage as Japanese Americans. We also want to be welcoming to all those who are interested in our organization who are not of Japanese heritage. The JACL is open to all.

I want to recognize the people who work very hard to give us the capacity to be a great organization, our JACL staff. Thank you also to the local convention committee with chairs, Silvana Watanabe and Reid Tateoka, who worked hard to make this experience valuable and enjoyable.

May I personally thank everyone here today for all you have done for the JACL and for taking the time to attend this National JACL Convention. Thank you for doing what you do best. That is, building better Americans toward a greater America.

Have a great convention!

NIHONMACHI SHOW A BIG HIT AT THE JACL CONVENTION

Article Originally Written for
the JACL Membership
July 23, 2008

Attendees at the national convention of the JACL held in Salt Lake City, Utah, in July, 2008, enjoyed a performance of *Nihonmachi, The Place to Be.* The musical production by *The Grateful Crane Ensemble* of Los Angeles was a big hit at the convention. It is a story about historic Japantowns in America (Nihonmachis), which were once prevalent in many cities and towns in the United States. They were areas where Japanese businesses operated and catered to people of Japanese ancestry.

The Honorable Norman Mineta, former secretary of transportation, was at the convention with his wife Deni, and they attended the performance. Secretary Mineta was asked to give remarks at the conclusion of the show. The audience was moved as he praised the cast and recalled Japantowns of the past, especially in his hometown of San Jose, California, which still has an active Japantown.

Salt Lake City once had a thriving Japantown which was displaced when the Salt Palace Convention Center was built in the 1960s. The businesses were all closed or required to relocate. The only remnants of the original Japantown are the Japanese Church of Christ and the Salt Lake Buddhist Temple on opposite ends and opposite sides of one block on First South Street. A small memorial area has recently been erected in remembrance of the original Japantown. The National JACL convention was held across the street at the Marriott Hotel. Ogden, Utah, also had a Japantown with perhaps a few businesses still operating in the area.

Many Japantowns existed throughout the country. Although some Japanese businesses remain in the areas, the Japantowns have almost disappeared. There are only a few remaining Japantowns which are still in existence and operating. Japantowns or some portions of them remain in San Francisco, Los Angeles, San Jose, Seattle, and some other areas throughout the United States.

This musical journey performance is seen through the eyes of a Japanese American *manju-ya* family, a family in the business of making *manju*, a Japanese rice cake confection and a staple of Japantowns throughout America's history. The story is centered around a Japanese American family in Japantown, but it could be close to home for other cultures and ages which have experienced life in the melting pot of America.

In the *Nihonmachi* play, Alan Iwata, a *Sansei* (third generation Japanese American) is burned out with the business, so he decides to close the family *manju* shop after ninety-nine years in Japantown. Just before Alan closes his doors for good, the spirit of his *Issei* (first generation Japanese immigrant) grandfather returns and takes Alan on a journey back some seventy-seven years to *Nihonmachi* the way it used to be.

"Along the way," said *Sansei* playwright, Soji Kashiwagi, "our character meets his feisty *Issei* grandmother, sees his family business through the Great Depression, the war years during the 40s spent incarcerated in a concentration camp, resettlement after camp, redevelopment in the 50s and 60s, and Asian American civil rights movements of the 70s and 80s. By learning his family history, Alan realizes the tremendous sacrifices and challenges his family overcame to keep the family business going. In the end, he decides it is worth the extra effort to work one more year, so he and the community can celebrate one hundred years of making *manju* together in *Nihonmachi*."

The two act play features both Japanese and American classic songs interspersed throughout the show, some with traditional Japanese instruments. Like in many early American communities, cultural songs in Japantowns inspired hope and strength. This helped the people get through difficult times in their lives.

"These songs can be very emotional for people because the songs are so inspiring and often bring back memories of a parent or grandparent singing similar songs as they were growing up," said Kashiwagi.

Nihonmachi featured a nine member cast, including Kerry Carnahan, Loryce Hashimoto, Yoko Ibuki, Keiko Kawashima, Darrell Kunitomi, Kurt Kuniyoshi, Clutch Kuramoto, Merv Maruyama, and Helen Ota. Musicians included Scott Nagatani (piano), Danny Yamamoto (Taiko, drums, and Japanese flute), and Gordon Bash (bass). The musical was directed by Darrell Kunitomi with musical direction by Scott Nagatani.

The Salt Lake City Japantown, though no longer in existence, remains the location of various cultural events such as a yearly Nihon Matsuri (Japan Festival held in the street) started in April 2004 as a way for the community at large to learn more about the Japanese American culture, the Obon Festival (street dancing) presented each summer by the Salt Lake Buddhist Temple, and the Aki Matsuri (fall festival) hosted by the Japanese Church of Christ. Japantowns were and are an important part of Japanese American history.

Renee Tuck and Cheryl Mori were co-chairs of the *Nihonmachi* event at the JACL convention. The major sponsor was the National JACL Credit Union. A reception was held before the performance and during the intermission. It was an evening well spent for convention delegates, boosters, and local attendees at which they were able to learn and enjoy some of the Japanese American story and history while being entertained.

SOME BACKGROUND ON THE REDRESS MOVEMENT

Article Originally Written for
the JACL Membership
October 14, 2008

The Japanese American Citizens League (JACL) voted at its national convention in Salt Lake City in 1978 to earnestly seek redress for the victims who were incarcerated unjustly during World War II in what have been called "America's Concentration Camps," where people of Japanese heritage were imprisoned without due process and through no fault of their own. It was determined that asking for some token monetary compensation was necessary in order to ensure that the injustice would not happen again to any other people.

The evacuation and incarceration came about as a result of President Franklin D. Roosevelt signing Executive Order 9066 (EO 9066) on February 19, 1942. The order gave the military commander the authority to remove any person from a specified area and affected all the people of Japanese heritage living on the West Coast of the mainland United States.

Years earlier in July 1970, Edison Uno, who seemed to be the main force behind the Redress Movement and was a long time activist within the JACL as well as a lecturer at San Francisco

State University, proposed a redress resolution at the biennial convention of the JACL in Chicago. The resolution passed, but there was not a lot of progress or support from Congress in the years that followed.

The matter of redress was not without contention as some members within the organization were opposed to "rocking the boat" and "bringing up old wounds" at a time when Japanese Americans had gained a measure of well-being in the United States since the war years. They were afraid of the old hatred against them returning and being rekindled because of the Redress Movement. Some opposed asking for money. The war had ended long before, but leaders within the JACL and the Japanese American community were convinced that redress was a worthy and necessary effort because it would cause the government to admit its wrongs and apologize so that, hopefully, no one in this country would again have to suffer the indignities and hardship inflicted upon so many innocent people of Japanese ancestry during World War II.

A Redress Bill was introduced by Representative George Danielson, a Democrat from California, in June of 1974. It did not pass in committee. The National JACL Convention in July 1974 appointed a National Committee for Redress. President Gerald R. Ford formally rescinded Executive Order 9066 in 1976. John Tateishi was named the National JACL Redress chairman in 1978 and served in that capacity until 1987.

The Legislative Education Committee (LEC) was formed in 1982 by the JACL as a 501(c)4 organization intended to act as a lobbying organization on the Japanese American Redress Movement. The LEC, however, did not become really active until 1985 when it was staffed and funded. Grayce Uyehara of Philadelphia became the executive director. Grayce provided information to the grassroots of the JACL as well as contact with Congress and was important in the passage of the redress legislation which was later achieved.

The JACL decided at the national convention in 1978 to seek $25,000 for each person who had been incarcerated and a trust fund set up to benefit Japanese Americans. In January 1979, the JACL National Committee for Redress met with Japanese American members of the United States Senate (Daniel K. Inouye and Spark Matsunaga both of Hawaii) and the House of Representatives (Norman Mineta and Robert Matsui both from California) to develop the best strategy to move forward on redress. Senator Inouye strongly suggested that they needed to get the Japanese American story of incarceration told in order to get their colleagues to vote for redress, and he suggested a commission be formed. Senators Inouye and Matsunaga introduced S 1647 with 110 cosponsors to create the Commission on Wartime Relocation and Internment of Civilians (CWRIC) Act. In September 1979, nine Democrats in the House introduced HR 5499, the companion bill to establish the CWRIC. The bill was signed by President Jimmy Carter.

It was felt that a commission would give the opportunity for the untold stories to be heard. The CWRIC held hearings at various locations throughout the country at which Japanese Americans who had been incarcerated told their heart-wrenching stories of their imprisonment during World War II. Others, including elected leaders and social workers, testified about the reasons for seeking redress and why it was justified. People who were opposed to redress were also given an opportunity to speak at the hearings, and some tried to disrupt the proceedings.

Some groups opposed the formation of a commission and formed another organization to work for redress called the National Council for Japanese American Redress (NCJAR). Other progressive organizations joined together and formed the Nikkei for Civil Rights and Redress (NCRR) to reach out to those who were opposed to the JACL leadership in the redress matter. The American Jewish Committee became the first outside organization to show support for the Redress Movement. Other civil rights groups joined in support later.

The Civil Liberties Act of 1988 (the Redress Bill) would likely not have passed without the efforts of Senator Spark Matsunaga of Hawaii. He is credited with producing a veto proof majority for the authorization bill in the Senate. There was some talk that President Ronald Reagan might veto the bill, but he later became convinced to sign it, largely due to efforts of former Governor Tom Kean of New Jersey and Grant Ujifusa. Former Congressman Mervyn Dymally (D-CA) was also helpful. Sen. Daniel Inouye has often given credit to his fellow senator from his home state for Sen. Matsunaga's tireless efforts in getting the commitment from the other senators to pass the bill. Senator Inouye was instrumental in helping to have the bill become an entitlement rather than having to fight for appropriations every year.

On the House side, Barney Frank, who chaired the Judiciary subcommittee in which the bill had been held up, got the bill on to the House floor after he took over the chairmanship. Reps. Norman Mineta and Robert Matsui worked very hard on the bill for years.

There were thousands within the JACL community and other Japanese Americans who worked on redress who deserve praise and thanks. The Redress Bill, which provided for a Presidential apology and a token payment of $20,000 in reparations to all living evacuees at a certain date, was the result of much dedicated effort.

At the National JACL Gala in Washington, DC held in September 2008, on the 20th anniversary of the passing of the Civil Liberties Act of 1988, some of the "Champions of Redress" were honored. The honorees included: The Honorable Norman Y. Mineta, former congressman from San Jose who worked to get the legislation through Congress; John Tateishi, National Redress chair for the JACL; Grayce Uyehara, executive director of the

JACL's Legislative Education Committee (LEC); The American Jewish Committee (AJC), the first outside organization to support the redress effort; and AT&T, a corporate partner currently supporting the effort to continue to tell the Japanese American story. Senator Inouye had previously been honored at the first JACL Gala in 2007. Senator Matsunaga and Congressman Matsui had passed away.

It was a long uphill battle, but in the end, redress was achieved.

VOTE YES ON AMENDMENT 1 AGAINST ALIEN LAND LAWS

Op Ed Piece for a Newspaper in Miami, Florida
October 16, 2008

The alien land laws adopted in the early 1900s prevented Asian immigrants and other noncitizens from owning land. Throughout the United States, these racially discriminatory and unconstitutional laws have largely been repealed. Most of the alien land laws throughout the country were repealed between 1940 and 1960. New Mexico removed the law from its books finally in 2006. Florida is the last state in the nation to still have an alien land law. Although the law is not applied, it exists today because it has taken so long to find and remove all the racially discriminatory statutes in the state constitution.

When the alien land law was adopted in the early 1900s, eligibility for citizenship was determined by race. It took until 1952 for Asian immigrants to be granted naturalization rights although Asian immigrants have been in this country since the 1800s and possibly earlier. The courts have found the alien land laws to be unconstitutional under the 14th Amendment because they discriminated due to race and violated equal protection under the law.

The alien land laws throughout the country were part of the prevalent racial discrimination against Asian Americans in the early 1900s. This discrimination caused the unjust incarceration into concentration camps in remote areas of the United States of one hundred twenty thousand people of Japanese ancestry, mostly citizens of this country, during World War II. This year is the twentieth anniversary of the passage of the Civil Liberties Act of 1988, which sought to right a wrong by providing for a Presidential apology and a token of monetary reparations to Japanese Americans whose civil rights were violated during that shameful period of history.

Voting Yes on Amendment 1 to repeal the alien land law in Florida will help to correct a historic wrong in the constitution. There is no reason for the law to stay on the books.

TRADITIONS AND CHANGE

Article Originally Written for
the JACL Membership
November 2008

One of my favorite movies is *Fiddler on the Roof.* I believe the music is outstanding, and the acting is superb. I have enjoyed the stage play as well as the movie. Of course, the storyline that pits traditional ways of life against the backdrop of a changing society is a real event in the lives of all who are part of the recent immigrant history in America, which means most of us. We can all "relate" to this conflict in many aspects of our lives. The words and the song about tradition are thought provoking.

Institutionally, the Japanese American Citizens League (JACL) faces the same dilemma about change. The JACL was organized way back in 1929 by young Japanese Americans who wanted to fight discrimination and prejudice. They felt that there were certain laws in the country that needed to be changed because they clearly discriminated against their parents and themselves along with other Asian Americans. They wanted to make this a better world in which they and their families could live productive and satisfying lives.

During the period of World War II, Japanese Americans faced extremely difficult circumstances with persons of Japanese descent, through no fault of their own, being evacuated from their West Coast homes to be incarcerated in hastily constructed camps in remote areas of the United States. Although it was said at the time to be for military necessity, this act was later determined to have been done because of racial prejudice, war hysteria, and the lack of adequate political leadership.

Life was uncomfortable and hard as they were locked up behind barbed wire enclosures under armed guard. Those who were not directly affected with the incarceration still faced difficulty as they regularly endured prejudice and racism in their daily lives regardless of where they lived.

Yet Japanese Americans tried to hold on to certain traditions within their communities. The JACL developed new principles which became their traditions while trying to keep some of the traditions of the past.

How can we maintain the strong and important traditions that made the JACL unique and a cut above many other community-based organizations while at the same time move forward in a different kind of society and community than in the past? Can we rebuke old institutional barriers to progress and at the same time embrace new and innovative avenues to advancement and success in our programs? This is the challenge that we face within our organization.

In many respects we have begun the process of change to create a "New JACL" which will be in tune with the future. We have instituted new programs which were not part of our history. While we would like to see an increase in the number of units or chapters within the JACL, we have recognized that there is need for some consolidation and realignment of chapters and districts which may no longer be functioning satisfactorily. We have moved from the biennial national convention to an annual convention which will allow better continuity and more effective budgeting.

The JACL National Board reflects a newer generation of leaders, and we have been able to bring younger staff members on board with the addition of a fellowship program that provides us with the talents of some of the brightest college minds in the nation. Some of our newer programs are aimed specifically at the age demographic that will provide new and fresh leadership in the decades ahead. So rather than maintaining a status quo, we are looking forward to the future with new ideas and programs in which our young adults and young families can become an integral part.

With civil and human rights as our backdrop, we continue our work to bring equality and fairness to the laws of our nation. But the scope of equality and fairness reaches beyond the Japanese American community and is broader than what is defined as a right in our Constitution. Our right to good health and access to health care is a new initiative where we are seeking fairness in our institutions. We are supporting the rights of Filipino veterans and working to lessen the bigotry against American Muslims and Sikhs. We are working toward comprehensive immigration reform.

The JACL is working jointly with OCA (formerly the Organization of Chinese Americans), NAVASA (National Alliance of Vietnamese American Service Organizations), and other Asian American groups in increasing our effectiveness in working on common goals and interests. We continue to work with coalition partners in the civil rights arena and with Asian and Pacific Islander American groups. We are no longer an organization that works exclusively for and with the Japanese American community. Our reach has been broadened.

The communications function of the JACL will need a more aggressive movement toward the Internet. With new and exciting platforms that have high use among younger generations, it will be necessary to shift toward expanding and perfecting the use of our website for communicating, fundraising, and developing membership. While some seem to be wedded to the printed media, which is very expensive and not cost effective, most of our members are discovering the opportunity that lies within the reaches of the computer and Internet for both individuals and the organization. Many of our oldest senior citizens, as well as virtually all of our younger members, are using the computer regularly.

Change is inevitable and in the air. Some will always fight change, but it can be positive and beneficial. Certain traditions will remain important, but change will be necessary for our growth and sustainability as an organization.

JACL APPLAUDS THE NOMINATION OF GENERAL ERIC SHINSEKI

Article Originally Written for
the JACL Membership
December 7, 2008

Members of the Japanese American Citizens League (JACL) are very happy to learn that President-elect Barack Obama has nominated Ret. Army general, Eric K. Shinseki, to become Secretary of Veterans Affairs on the Obama Cabinet. The JACL applauds the President-elect for his selection of General Shinseki, a Japanese American native of Hawaii and former United States Army chief of staff.

Shinseki was born in Lihue, Kauai, to an American family of Japanese ancestry. His grandparents had emigrated from Hiroshima to Hawaii in 1901. He grew up in a sugar plantation community. After graduation from high school, he attended the United States Military Academy at West Point where he graduated with a Bachelor of Science degree. He earned a Master of Arts degree from Duke University.

General Shinseki served two combat tours in Vietnam, where he was awarded two Purple Hearts and three Bronze Stars. After serving as the thirty-fourth Chief of Staff of the United States Army from 1999 to 2003, General Shinseki is the nominee to become the seventh United States Secretary of Veterans Affairs. He is the first Asian American to become a four star general in the US Army and the first to lead one of the five US military services. He is an innovative leader of the Army who is dedicated to helping veterans. He is not afraid to stand up for what he believes is right. General Shinseki was retired in June 2003 after thirty-eight years in the Army.

In naming General Shinseki as the nominee, President-elect Obama noted that General Shinseki won the respect and admiration of our service people because they have always been his highest priority. He is a man of principle and integrity. He has a great sense of duty and commitment to the veterans and the nation.

General Shinseki has been a spokesman for the Go for Broke Education Foundation. He actively supports the Japanese American Veterans Association (JAVA) and other veterans' groups. Only two weeks ago he was the featured speaker at a Japanese American veterans' gathering in Los Angeles, California.

As a decorated soldier and officer in the US Army, General Shinseki is especially qualified to become Secretary of Veterans Affairs. The JACL is pleased to see such a respected American of Japanese descent be given this opportunity to continue his leadership abilities in President-elect Obama's cabinet. His commitment to all veterans and to the Asian American veterans' community is noteworthy.

It has been my privilege to become personally acquainted with General Shinseki, and I feel that he will be an outstanding addition to the cabinet. General Shinseki is an excellent choice for Secretary of Veterans Affairs. He is a great role model for Japanese American and all Asian American young people. He has served his country well and will continue to do so in the position of Secretary of Veterans Affairs. Americans everywhere can be proud of this great American general who has become an outstanding leader for the entire nation.

Floyd Mori was invited to attend the confirmation hearing for General Shinseki and heard absolutely no negative comments about General Shinseki on his proposed appointment. It was a total praise fest at which General Shinseki was given the utmost respect and honor.

YEAR IN REVIEW/2008

Article Originally Written for
the JACL Membership
January 4, 2009

This past year saw many very visible changes in our nation. The so-called *"change we can believe in"* was embodied in the election of Barack Obama as the first United States President of African American heritage. Other new faces emerged that reflect a fresh air of generational change. David Gregory became the new moderator for *"Meet the Press."* Speaker Nancy Pelosi completed her first term as the first woman to be the Speaker of the House in the United States Congress. The Phillies won the World Series. There was a revitalizing of so many facets of our society. *Diversity* and *Youth* were themes that seemed to prevail.

The JACL, an organization that has a rich tradition in its people and its mission, was not exempt from change and revitalization. The changes that we are seeing are significant and provide immense opportunity for the future work and mission of this great organization which has been in existence for eighty years. Some changes that may seem negative and pessimistic can be turned into tools to build and reconstruct. Our decline in membership numbers has given us the incentive to fill in with new members of a new generation and broader ethnic backgrounds. The same membership-based funding mechanism has forced us to look to innovative measures to finance new programs and initiatives. The narrowing of policy alternatives allowed us to develop a new drive toward programs that will benefit and involve members for generations to come.

The institutional shift from a biennial to an annual convention for the JACL will trigger a new era of better communication and awareness among members and chapters. In fast changing times in funding, membership, and programs, an annual convention will allow quicker response to a dynamic nonprofit environment. The mobility of today's membership requires a different approach to organizational problem solving. Youth and young adult professionals will have the tools and motivation to become more involved in programs that will enhance leadership and build meaningful relationships to the Asian American community and its causes.

There has been a new shift in JACL staff responsibilities among the regional directors (Bill Yoshino in the Midwest District, Karen Yoshitomi in the Pacific Northwest District, Patty Wada in the Northern California, Western Nevada, and Pacific District, and Craig Ishii of the Pacific Southwest District in California) that focus on programs that benefit membership. The two main focus areas are toward youth and health. These kinds of programs involve members and their families and help them to move toward individual excellence. They provide a renewed understanding of the cultural values that enhance their own lifestyle and that of those around them. New opportunities for JACL fellowships and internships have broadened experience and increased commitment to community and to a nation free of intolerance and inequality while at the same time giving support to an overburdened full-time staff.

We are not without challenges and difficulties. But we are better equipped and organized to solve the problems before us. With this "*New JACL*," we will use the best technology available to us along with the continued dedication of members, leaders, and staff to break ground we have heretofore felt unreachable.

We merely have to lengthen our stride just a little toward our goal of developing better Americans for a greater America for all of us as individuals and as families.

Thanks for your support of the JACL. I wish you the best in this New Year.

JAVA HONORS BRONZE STAR MEDAL AWARDEES

Some True American Heroes
Article Originally Written for
the JACL Membership
January 22, 2009

The Japanese American Veterans Association (JAVA) held its quarterly luncheon meeting on January 17, 2009, at the Harvest Moon Restaurant in Falls Church, Virginia. The emcee was Col. Mike Yaguchi, US Air Force (Ret.). Officers were installed with Robert Nakamoto retained as JAVA president for another term. Vice president is LTC Martin L. Herbert, US Army (Ret). Treasurer is LTC Earl S. Takeguchi, US Army (Ret.), and Secretary is Col. Bruce Hollywood, US Air Force (Ret.). Terry Shima is the executive director for JAVA.

Highlighting the lunch was an awards ceremony officiated by Maj. Gen. Tony Taguba, United States Army (Ret.). Six Japanese American veterans of World War II were presented with the Bronze Star. Ranger Tech. Sgt. Grant J. Hirabayashi and Tech 4 Yeiichi Kuwayama were present to receive their Bronze Star awards in person. Etsu Mineta Masaoka received the Bronze Star for her late husband, Tech 4 Mike M. Masaoka. Hanako Hankie Hirose accepted the award for S/Sgt. Goro Hirose. Bina

Kiyonaga accepted the Bronze Star for her late husband, 1Lt. Joseph K. Kiyonaga. Dr. Ray Murakami accepted the award for S/Sgt. Hideyuki Noguchi.

Ranger Tech. Sgt. Grant J. Hirabayashi was born in Kent, Washington, and incarcerated in Heart Mountain, Wyoming. He enlisted in the Army Air Corps and subsequently entered the Military Intelligence Service Language School at Camp Savage, Minnesota, where he volunteered for Merrill's Marauders. He served behind enemy lines in Burma and later in New Delhi, India, and the China Theater. After his discharge in 1945, he obtained Bachelors and Masters Degrees and served in various US government departments, including the National Security Agency.

Tech 4 Yeiichi Kuwayama was born and raised in New York City and graduated from Princeton University. He was inducted in the US Army about one year before the attack on Pearl Harbor. He volunteered for the 442nd when it was activated in 1943, and was assigned to its Medic Unit. He served as a Medic in Italy and France. He was awarded the Silver Star for gallantry, French Legion of Honor, Knight Cross of Military Valor, and Combat Medic Badge. He obtained an MBA from Harvard Business School and was the US general manager for Nomura Securities, was a specialist in the US Securities and Exchange Commission, and an official in the US Department of Commerce.

Tech 4 Mike Masaoka, who was an early leader within the Japanese American Citizens League (JACL), was born in Fresno, California, and his family later moved to Utah when he was a boy. He graduated from the University of Utah where he won All American ratings as a debater. He was appointed as executive secretary of the JACL in 1941. He advocated for Japanese Americans to be allowed to serve in the military which resulted in the formation of the 442nd Regimental Combat Team, and he was first to volunteer. Four Masaoka brothers joined the army with one being killed in the rescue of the trapped Texas battalion in the Vosges Mountains of Eastern France. Following his discharge from the Army, he served as the Washington, DC representative for the JACL, where he worked tirelessly for many years on Japanese American issues and advocating for civil rights. He then went on to start his own consulting firm. Mike passed away in 1991 of congestive heart failure at the age of seventy-five.

S/Sgt. Toro Hirose was born in Los Angeles, California, and was incarcerated at Manzanar. He was inducted in the US Army on November 5, 1941, and volunteered for the 442nd. He served in five campaigns in Italy and France. He worked for a printer for seventeen years and the federal government for twenty years.

1Lt. Joseph K. Kiyonaga was born in Hawaii and volunteered for the 442nd. He fought in Italy and France. He attended the University of Michigan Law School and Johns Hopkins University School of Advanced International Studies. He joined the Central Intelligence Agency (CIA) in 1949 and served in Asia and Latin America. He passed away at age 59 of cancer.

S/Sgt. Hideyuki Noguchi was born near Sacramento, California, and graduated from the University of California, Berkeley. His parents were incarcerated at the Tule Lake camp. He was incarcerated in 1942 the same year he volunteered for the 442nd. He served in Italy, in the liberation of Bruyeres and other towns, including the rescue of the trapped Texas Battalion. He settled in Washington, DC with a career as an engineer with the Federal Communications Commission.

These awardees were truly all American heroes who served our country and paved the way for a better life for Japanese Americans. They and all the Japanese American veterans of World War II are to be commended for their bravery and courage in the face of huge adversity. They are part of the story of Japanese Americans who served valiantly and patriotically while enduring persecution and hardship. They continued their lives honorably after their time in the service of our nation.

MERCED ASSEMBLY CENTER CEREMONY

Speech at a Day of Remembrance Event
Merced, California, February 21, 2009

On behalf of the national office of the Japanese American Citizens League (JACL), I am happy to express a welcome to all who are in attendance tonight at this Day of Remembrance Banquet where we remember the past and make plans for the future with the erection of the Merced Assembly Center Memorial Monument. I am honored to be on the program with two great gentlemen, who served together in the California State Assembly where I was also privileged to serve many years ago. These two leaders, Reps. Dennis Cardoza and Mike Honda, continue to serve with distinction now in the United States House of Representatives.

Last night I had a nice visit with my brother and his wife in Pleasanton, California. My brother Tom and I remembered back to our early years of living on a farm in Utah and the impact of World War II on our lives. Since our family lived in Utah, we were not forced to leave our home. However, we did face discrimination even in our rural area. Tom joined the United States Army while still a teenager in college and was on his way to Germany to join the ranks of the 442nd Regimental Combat Team when the war ended.

My sister in law Betty recalled her early childhood before the war in Lindsay, California, in this central valley. She talked about the shame and embarrassment that Japanese Americans felt at being uprooted as they were forcibly removed from their homes on the West Coast. She still has friends from those early days in Lindsay with whom she keeps in contact. She related that some of those friends have a hard time remembering and talking about, even today, that era in their lives. They have discussed the fact that they cannot recall the exact happenings of that time period. Some of the bad memories may have been unconsciously erased or suppressed because of the emotional stress the experience of incarceration caused.

Many Japanese Americans blocked out the painful memories for many years and seldom spoke of the experiences of the war years.

When the JACL and others earnestly worked for the Redress Movement in the 1970s and 1980s, which finally resulted in the passage of the Civil Liberties Act of 1988, which brought about a Presidential apology and reparations to Japanese Americans who were incarcerated, many of these people were forced to recall those memories. Those who testified before the Commission on Wartime Relocation and Internment of Civilians (CWRIC) told heartbreaking stories. Others who did not testify began to talk to their families about their experiences during the war. Some healing started from the remembering and talking about that devastating period of their lives.

Over 4,600 individuals were uprooted from their homes and placed here temporarily at the Merced County Fairgrounds in 1942 before being shipped off largely to Amache, Colorado, to a hastily constructed camp where they lived surrounded by barbed wire and watched over by armed guards.

The planned Merced Assembly Center Memorial Monument which will be completed and dedicated a year from now will help the community and nation to remember. This is a time for the Japanese American community to remember the past. Remembering history is important in understanding who we are and what we are made of so that we can move forward. Forgetting or suppressing the memories deprives us of that knowledge. Remembering helps us to create a better today and a brighter tomorrow.

For the Japanese American community and the community at large, this is a time to remember and think about another time when things did not go well for our nation's Constitution. World War II was a time when hysteria and racism reared their ugly heads.

This is a time for all of us to remember that we are a nation with what I believe to be a sacred Constitution. We cannot forget the rule of law that governs our nation and how we should behave toward each other. This is a time to be grateful for those who were faithful and strong, even at the peril of their own well-being.

Last week a similar Day of Remembrance event was held in Fresno at which I was also privileged to speak. I know many of you were there. We thank Judge Dale Ikeda for his leadership in that effort. That event included a dedication ceremony for the Pinedale Assembly Center Memorial which is now completed and where others of Japanese ancestry were temporarily housed. These memorials and monuments have an important purpose in telling the Japanese American story. Sharing the Japanese American experiences of incarceration during World War II helps others to understand. It is essential that we remember the past in order to not repeat the same mistake when racism and wartime hysteria caused the nation to make some huge errors in judgment.

I am happy to be here to encourage all of you to support this great endeavor at preservation and remembrance. The Merced Assembly Center Memorial will be a beautiful reminder of a painful part of history.

I would like to thank Congressman Cardoza, who represents this area, for his efforts to create a lasting legacy of remembrance. Thanks also to Congressman Honda for his support and endorsement of this project. He was just a baby when he came here with his family from their home in San Jose to be incarcerated at this site in Merced before being moved to Camp Amache.

I commend my fellow Utahan, Bob Taniguchi, and his committee for undertaking this tremendously important project. Again, I urge all of you to work with this great group of people and to be generous when they call upon you for your support.

Thank you.

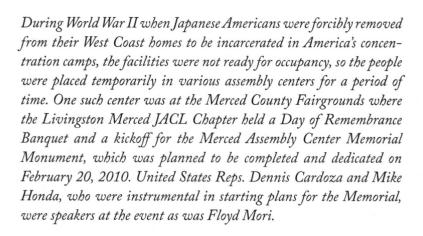

During World War II when Japanese Americans were forcibly removed from their West Coast homes to be incarcerated in America's concentration camps, the facilities were not ready for occupancy, so the people were placed temporarily in various assembly centers for a period of time. One such center was at the Merced County Fairgrounds where the Livingston Merced JACL Chapter held a Day of Remembrance Banquet and a kickoff for the Merced Assembly Center Memorial Monument, which was planned to be completed and dedicated on February 20, 2010. United States Reps. Dennis Cardoza and Mike Honda, who were instrumental in starting plans for the Memorial, were speakers at the event as was Floyd Mori.

The dedication for the memorial was held on February 20, 2010, with the unveiling of the sculpture of a young girl sitting on top of a pile of suitcases and holding a doll. Titled, "Never Again," the sculpture was inspired by the "bring only what you can carry" order that limited each person to one suitcase which would be given a tag with a family identification number. A wall behind the sculpture contains most of the names of the 4,669 Japanese Americans sent to the Assembly Center with the words, "To Remember Is To Honor." The beautiful sculpture was created by Artist Dale Smith of Berkeley, California.

ASIAN AMERICAN HERITAGE

Speech Given for Asian American
Heritage Month
To Asian American and Pacific Islander
Army and Civilian Personnel
Fort Belvoir, Virginia, May 4, 2009

Ladies and Gentlemen:

It is a great pleasure for me to speak to you today regarding heritage. This month of May is, of course, Asian American and Pacific Islander Heritage Month.

When a person thinks of heritage, one's own parents come to mind first. Tomorrow would have been my mother's 103rd birthday if she were still living, but she passed away at age 95. My father immigrated to the United States as a young man at about the time my mother was born.

My father came from the southernmost part of Japan when times were tough, particularly for his family. He lost his mother, and his father was in ill health. There were younger siblings who needed care, so his solution was to come to America as a teenager in order to earn money for the family. He had enough to get to Hawaii where he labored for about a year to earn and save money to come to the mainland of the United States. He arrived in San Francisco and worked as a cook in a restaurant.

Later he succumbed to the call of "big money" by working on the railroad, laying tracks across the Sierras and over the Nevada desert. He almost lost his life when he was run over by one of the small rail cars used in construction. But he survived and ended up in a small farming community in Utah where he was allowed to own land (unlike California where Japanese immigrants were not permitted to purchase land).

So he began farming on the Utah-Idaho border in a small town named Lewiston, raising sugar beets. After about a dozen years of hard work, he was able to return to Japan to get a wife. His bride, who became my mother, was very young and was from the same village. She was the apple of her father's eye. My father told her father that it was only going to be a matter of a few years until he saved enough money to come back and live comfortably in Japan. For many different reasons, mostly economic, they never did make it back to Japan to live. Much later in life, when they were finally able to return to visit Japan, my mother realized that America had become her home and where she preferred to live.

My father had a large farm by the standards of those days and brought other Japanese immigrant men to work on his farm. My mother had to learn to cook and feed about a dozen men while beginning a family. The first two of their eight children were born on this farm in northern Utah before they moved farther south.

My dad knew little English, but he humbled himself to attend an elementary school class occasionally during the winter months as he was allowed to do with the children in the community in order to learn some basic English. My mom never did learn to speak much English as she was busy being a wife and a mother although she was extremely well versed in current affairs as she read Japanese language newspapers and magazines regularly throughout her life.

Over time, my father gained a reputation as a hard worker. He also helped newer immigrants get their feet on the ground in this new land. He did this while also sending money to his own and his wife's family back in Japan. He was kind to the neighbors as well. I remember as a child going around to the neighbors at Thanksgiving and distributing the best celery and onions of the crop for their Thanksgiving dinners. My mom always thought he was generous to a fault, but I think he was appreciated by others.

My childhood days were largely spent in the fields with the rest of the family. When I was old enough, I had to do my share of the work. We would go to school during the day and go right to the fields when we got home in the afternoon, working into the evening hours. My father taught me by example the importance and results of hard, honest work. When he was the age that I am now, he still was hard to beat in any kind of hoeing, lifting, or shoveling on the farm. My father taught me much by example. I think that I learned to be competitive because he always challenged me to do better in all that I did.

Although I was the next to the youngest in my family with a wide spread between the oldest and the youngest, my childhood, like that of my older brothers and sisters, was not without hard times in trying to fit into the American society. I was like other minorities who were often the object of taunting and teasing because we looked different and because our parents did not speak "good" English. As I became an older teenager, I had my share of being turned down on dates in the predominantly white community where we lived because, especially in those days, mainstream American parents generally did not allow their daughters to date people like me who were of a different race. Even after the Second World War had been over for many years, we were still seen as the enemy and strangers by some people.

So during and after the war, we were encouraged to become totally American and to fit into mainstream America as much as we could. That is when I was actually given an American or English name at the time I started elementary school. The handicap that we had was the perception that we did not "look American." To this day, this is the barrier that Asian Americans often face in the United States. We are still sometimes looked at as foreigners, although our families may have been in this country for several generations. Even today, Americans of Asian descent who were born in the United States and have never been to the country of their heritage occasionally experience being considered by others as if they were recent immigrants.

Prejudice remains among people in our society even today. The newer Asian immigrants face some similar issues that the early Japanese and Chinese immigrants faced in the 1920s, the 1930s, the 1940s, and the 1950s. The anti-immigrant rhetoric and sentiment today have the same tone as when Japanese and Chinese people were particularly targeted as new immigrants generations ago. Their children who had been born in America faced discrimination as well. While Asian Americans worked on the railroad which helped to lay the infrastructure that allowed the industrial revolution to take place, they were seen as taking jobs and business away from the people who were thought of as "real Americans." This type of thing continues to happen today.

I believe as an economist, and it is my contention, that the American dream is built on the dreams of immigrants. That dream becomes a reality because of the values upon which that dream is based. This is true whether somebody came here in the 1600s to escape religious intolerance in Europe, the 1700s for political freedoms, or the 1800s and 1900s for more economic opportunity and liberty.

Asian immigrants generally came to this country, in the past and today, endowed with a strong set of values and morals. Family and respect for parents are important. Doing an honest day's work reflects upon the family. Children were admonished not to bring shame to the family name. The immigrants are basically loyal to their new country but proud of the heritage of the country of their birth. Today we call all of this *integrity* or *character*. We trusted each other because most possessed these same values. So one of the most important reasons to be concerned with heritage is because that is where we derive values and morals. Without knowing who we are or for what we stand, it could be said that anything goes.

Although the early Chinese and Japanese immigrants had been enlisted as laborers who worked on the infrastructure of our nation and the primary industries of extracting raw materials from the earth, American society did not want to have anything more to do with them after that work was completed. Politicians responded by constructing legal barriers for new Asian immigrants to come to this country and barriers for those here to complete their American dream. The ugly head of prejudice once again was reared against the immigrants.

Many laws were passed such as an anti-Asian immigration law in 1924 which prevented new Japanese immigrants from entering the country and kept families from forming. Asians were denied the ability to gain citizenship.

It was not until the 1950s when the Japanese American Citizens League or JACL, which was established in 1929, worked to change and pass laws that Japanese immigrants were actually allowed to become citizens of the United States. My father became a citizen, and my mother finally gained American citizenship in the 1970s when laws were further changed to allow people of limited English proficiency to become citizens. My parents were proud to be American citizens. They had spent most of their lives here raising a family, having two sons who served in the United States Army during World War II with one returning home in a casket, and two younger sons who subsequently served in the US Army Reserves.

Many people of Asian heritage were subjected to physical and social exclusion during those early days and that period of time. Then World War II happened, and the people of Japanese ancestry faced a denial of due process as they were rounded up from their West Coast homes and treated like cattle as they were taken to places strange and unknown to them. War hysteria and prejudice allowed the government to persecute people and take away their freedom simply because of their physical characteristics and the color of their skin. President Franklin D. Roosevelt signed Executive Order 9066 on February 19, 1942. This allowed the military commander to remove any persons from a designated area. Around one hundred twenty thousand people of Japanese ancestry were affected with most of them being United States citizens. They were incarcerated in American concentration camps hastily constructed in desolate areas of the country. Because the order was only used against the people of Japanese heritage, it clearly showed that it was carried out due to the prejudice and discrimination that existed at that time.

The camps took time to construct, and people were sent to temporary assembly centers. These were often horse stalls at racetracks and at fairgrounds such as Tanforan near San Francisco, Santa Anita, or similar places up and down the West Coast. The shame and loss of dignity from being isolated from the rest of society and given a number to identify them have been carried by many even to this day. The lack of privacy and primitive, crowded living conditions took a toll which adversely affected them. Although they tried to make the best of a bad situation by making small improvements to the often one room per family that they were allotted in the barracks, it was still an extremely emotional and physical hardship. While teenagers may have enjoyed relative freedom and lack of supervision within the camps, families were affected adversely as older children seldom ate meals with their families. Family unity suffered.

The values of their heritage became important to the Japanese immigrants and their children during this time. There were the values of loyalty, respect for authority, upholding the family name, and to stick out against any hardships which were pitted against the value of justice. Of course, the incarceration was neither just nor right, and some voiced that opinion. But in the end, the old prejudices and discrimination won out. To prove their patriotism, the entire community of Japanese Americans on the West Coast had no choice but to subject themselves to this forced incarceration (although a few protested and were arrested).

Some Japanese American young men tried to volunteer for service in the Armed Forces of the United States immediately after the war began, but they were rejected and found that they had been reclassified as enemy aliens who were ineligible to serve. The desire to prove their loyalty resulted in many immediately joining the segregated military unit of Japanese Americans when it was established in 1943. Others were drafted.

This segregated unit, the 442nd Regimental Combat Team, was combined with the 100th Battalion of Japanese Americans from Hawaii which had the slogan, "Go for Broke." Sen. Daniel Inouye tells the story about how the mainland and the Hawaii soldiers did not get along until some of the Hawaii group were invited to visit Japanese Americans in one of the camps. After they saw the families of their fellow servicemen in the 442nd locked up in the camps, the soldiers from Hawaii had compassion. The two groups started to get along.

The 442nd Regimental Combat Team/100th Battalion fought in the European theater of the war and became the most highly decorated unit for its size and length of service in the history of the United States military. They were famous for the rescue of the Texas Lost Battalion while suffering eight hundred casualties in the process of saving just over two hundred lives.

The Japanese Americans in the military intelligence service did their work in the Pacific theater. US military leaders have said that thousands of lives were saved because of the work of these men in gathering intelligence and listening in on Japanese radio transmissions. These soldiers were also instrumental in the peaceful occupation of Japan after the war, playing an important liaison role between Japanese and American entities. My oldest brother was among those who served in Japan. Perhaps the transition of Iraq could learn a lesson from the occupation experience in Japan.

The Asian American community has begun to enjoy the fruits of its cultural values of hard work, honesty, and loyalty. Any institution, private or public, would like to see these values in its employees and executives. For the Japanese American community, attitudes against them have generally shifted from disdain and even hatred during those war years to respect today. While the rise of Japan's economic power brought back some detractors who lashed out against Japanese Americans and other Asian Americans in recent times, now our community is not alone in defending our rights and who we are.

The Japanese American community's general acculturation and assimilation into the mainstream of American society have allowed us to remove many of the barriers of the past. There is a higher degree of social acceptance, and we are among the highest achieving minorities in the nation. Much of this is due to the sacrifices of the Japanese American soldiers in the 442nd/100th in proving loyalty and patriotism during those difficult times. They made the world better for all Japanese Americans who followed.

This overassimilation, in my mind, also has its negative side. If it means that there is difficulty in preserving cultural heritage, then there is a resulting loss of self-identity and self-worth. Then important cultural values may be lost.

Today, we see an emergence of placing more value on status than on traditional values. Therefore, often in order to gain status, anything goes. We see what has happened to our economy and society when we have allowed the end goal of status, personal wealth, and greed to justify any means to attain those goals. Basic human and moral values have been compromised because people have lost the values of our ancestors, that of honesty, hard work, and plain old integrity.

Asian American and Pacific Islander Heritage Month can help us to reflect and remember who we are and what values embody our souls. Our nation faces a major question today as to what our core moral values really are. Are status and financial gain the only things that govern our behavior as individuals and as a nation or are honor and integrity still important? Of course, honor and integrity are of great importance.

It is my hope that Asian American and Pacific Islander Heritage month will help Asian Americans and all Americans to understand the great values that are embodied in all cultures. I hope that it will cause you to appreciate and reflect upon the great values of your own forefathers and the cultural heritage that you bear.

Military culture was born of the values of honor and integrity. We fight wars to preserve freedom and that part of our way of life. Values are most important, more so than status and economic gain. The military helps us to remember that we should always be a nation of integrity and character.

As I mentioned earlier, my two older brothers joined the United States Army during World War II when the country of their birth was at war with the country of their heritage. They wanted to prove their loyalty to the United States—their country and their home. I have many friends and some relatives who served in the 442nd Regimental Combat Team. My younger brother and I served in the Army Reserves. I have a grand nephew who is currently a cadet at West Point.

While we look at the military as protecting us and fighting our enemies, we are all proud of the role it plays in preserving values that make the United States of America the great nation that it is. So while we reflect on our heritage, let us be reminded that we not only have a cultural heritage to which we owe our existence today, but there are many other aspects of our great heritage, of course including the military, that make this a great country.

Thank you for your commitment to serve our country and the values that you maintain in order that future generations have a legacy upon which they can build.

Thank you for allowing me to share a few thoughts with you this morning. God bless you and God bless the United States of America.

———— ∞ ————

When Floyd Mori graduated from high school, young men were routinely being drafted into the US Army unless they joined the Army Reserves, the National Guard, or the ROTC. Many from his graduating class joined the Reserves and went to Ford Ord in California for basic training, including close friends Don Campbell, Russell Larson, Harold Rawson, and others.

Floyd's grand nephew, Kyle Kiriyama, attended the US Military Academy at West Point, took time out to serve a mission for the Church of Jesus Christ of Latter-day Saints, and then returned to finish at West Point.

ASSEMBLY BILL 37— *NISEI* HONORARY DEGREES

Testimony to the California State Assembly
The California State Capitol
Sacramento, California, March 17, 2009

Mr. Chairman and Members of the Committee:

My name is Floyd Mori, and I am the national executive director of the Japanese American Citizens League (JACL), the nation's oldest and largest Asian American civil and human rights organization. Established in 1929, the JACL currently has approximately fifteen thousand members with over one hundred chapters, most of which are located in California.

Thank you for the opportunity to represent the Japanese American community and the JACL this morning in the matter of Assembly Bill 37 which would provide Honorary Degrees for Japanese Americans who were attending college when World War II began and who were forced to leave school to be incarcerated in America's concentration camps.

After Japan bombed Pearl Harbor on December 7, 1941, and President Franklin D. Roosevelt signed Executive Order 9066 on February 19, 1942, approximately one hundred twenty thousand people of Japanese ancestry who were mostly US citizens were forcibly removed from their homes on the West Coast. They lost virtually everything they owned and were detained in assembly centers which were often horse stalls at fairgrounds before being moved to the ten camps hastily set up in remote and desolate areas of the country. Life was very difficult for these incarcerated persons.

Although some Japanese immigrants arrived in the United States during the late 1800s, they had begun to come to America in larger numbers in the early 1900s. By 1942, many had married and had families. They had children who were young adults attending college. There was much discrimination and prejudice against the Japanese Americans which prevented many with college degrees from finding gainful employment in their fields of study even after graduating from college. Believing that an education was important regardless of the trials they faced, the young *Nisei* who were the second generation of Japanese in America, born in this country and American citizens, were attending college in large numbers. They wanted to make a better life for themselves, their future families, and their parents. Education was stressed by their parents, and attending college was a manifestation of an important family and cultural value.

Many of those college students who had to interrupt their studies went on to serve valiantly for their country in the armed services of the United States. The 442nd Regimental Combat Team, which was joined with the 100th Battalion from Hawaii, became the most highly decorated unit for its size and length of service in the history of the United States military and contained a good number of those college students. It was a segregated unit of Japanese Americans within the military. Yet the reality of being uprooted and denied a goal so ingrained in their culture and dreams, resulted in great heartache, shame, anger, and denial. Many were unable to share or talk about this traumatic experience of incarceration until decades later when the government acknowledged that it was a major injustice and finally apologized.

The University of California at Berkeley had the greatest number of Japanese American students of any United States institution of higher learning at the time that the war broke out. The University of Washington was second with four hundred fifty Japanese American students who had to leave the university in 1942 to relocate to the American concentration camps. Last year the University of Washington awarded honorary college degrees to those remaining students who were forced to leave the university during the war. Some other universities on the West Coast have also awarded honorary degrees to Japanese Americans who had been incarcerated.

Although some of those former students had later gone on to complete their college degrees at other universities after the war, the symbolic graduation ceremony and the honorary degrees more than sixty-seven years later were meaningful. The ceremonies brought a flood of memories and tears to the recipients of the honorary degrees.

Former secretary of transportation, Norman Y. Mineta, who gave the keynote address at the University of Washington ceremony, said, *"The message of today's event is a simple one, and one that I believe none of us should ever forget. It's never too late to do the right thing. It's never too late to rejoice that the right thing has been done. It's never too late to be grateful to people who do the right thing."*

The Japanese Americans who were forced to leave the universities to enter barbed wire camps with armed guards holding guns facing inward are now mostly in their late eighties or in their nineties. Extending honorary degrees to individuals who were incarcerated and unable to complete their post secondary education in California's public institutions of higher learning due to the forced removal of innocent Japanese Americans from their homes and schools during World War II would be an attempt at righting a wrong. It is long overdue.

In the year 2008, last year, commemoration events were held throughout the country to celebrate the twentieth Anniversary of the passage of the Civil Liberties Act of 1988 which provided that an official Presidential apology letter and reparations be given to Japanese Americans who were still alive who had been unconstitutionally removed by the US government from their homes during World War II. The nation recognized that Japanese Americans were unjustly discriminated against solely because of their ethnic origin. Racial prejudice and wartime hysteria coupled with a failure of political leadership had caused around one hundred twenty thousand people of Japanese ancestry to be wrongly persecuted with their freedoms stripped from them.

The passage of Assembly Bill 37 would not only right a wrong, but it reminds us that we should never again let war hysteria and racism override the basic civil liberties and due process promised to each one of us, regardless of the color of our skin. The Japanese American Citizens League, JACL, urges your support of this bill.

Thank you.

THE TULE LAKE PILGRIMAGE

Article Originally Written for the JACL Membership
July 2009

There were ten World War II concentration camps for Japanese Americans as has been stated many times on many occasions. I am one who placed the Tule Lake camp as one of the ten, knowing that there was something different but only knowing the academic differences. Going on the 2009 Tule Lake Pilgrimage opened my eyes a little wider and enriched my mind a little deeper. But more importantly, it engaged my heart as I began to experience the feelings that have existed among those who were there during the war.

Initially, Tule Lake was a destination for those Japanese Americans and Japanese immigrants from a specific geographical locale, which is much like the other camps. If you found out in which camp a person was detained, you had a pretty good idea of which region of the West Coast that the family resided when the war started. Tule Lake began to change when the government identified persons whom they suspected of being potential spies, and it also became home to those who had voiced some degree of dissatisfaction with the way they were being treated. These included those called Resisters of Conscience who expressed and showed dissent regarding the unfairness and the injustice of the whole episode.

The naming of the Tule Lake Camp as a *segregation center* changed the entire landscape and led to this camp being very unique and with a stigma that has lasted over the decades. Much like a quarantine, which isolates people from the "healthy society," this designation had the same effect. I remember as a child when two of my classmates who were sisters were isolated from the rest of the students because they had lice. Until the day they moved from the community, they faced teasing and taunting, which I am sure caused undue heartache and long-term mental stress that probably still lives with them until this day. Yet as children, they had little control over what a life of poverty dealt to them, including the lice (although we now know that lice can affect anyone).

We, as Japanese Americans, are of different backgrounds, but we have been fortunate in inheriting a legacy of strong values from our forefathers. Loyalty, upholding the family name, hard work, fairness, and justice are values that the first generation immigrants from Japan and the second generation born in America forbearers engrained in their posterity. At times these values may be in conflict with each other, or one places more importance on one value at a particular point in time. Family, health, and well-being may influence which value is manifest at any given time.

Like my fellow first grade students who had lice, Japanese Americans had little control on what the war had dealt to them. Yet, each confronted the situation the best they could with the values that were important to them. That is the matter with which we need to come to grips. They did what was important to them in their specific circumstance. This took a great deal of courage. In fact, others have since said that they wished they had shown such courage as did the Resisters during that difficult period.

Actions that were based on the principle of justice were not cowardice nor unpatriotic. It has been unfair for that stigma to remain after all these years. It is important to understand that all had their reasons for making the decisions that they did, and it all related to the basic values that they knew to be right. It is particularly vital for us all to respect that one individual's reason for action is of no less importance than another's. Many of the Resisters were making their decisions in the hope that it would make the situation better for their families.

In the early 2000s after some young JACL leaders learned of the Resisters [many of whom were sent to Tule Lake for stating their views] who protested the incarceration and refused to serve in the US Army unless their families were released from the American concentration camps, the issue was brought up to the JACL. A resolution was passed at the National JACL Convention in the summer of 2000 for the JACL to apologize to this group because JACL leaders had not treated them kindly in the past. The JACL held an official ceremony in San Francisco on May 11, 2002, at the Japanese Cultural and Community Center of Northern California, to apologize to the Resisters which included some of the residents of the Tule Lake Camp.

Because I was the national president of the JACL at that time, I wrote and offered the apology speech. It was a privilege to meet a number of the Resisters who attended. They had been valiant young men who stood up for the Japanese Americans' civil rights during a difficult period of time. Many subsequently served in the US military, and some were just sticking up for the principles in which they believed even though they were not in the group of young men who would have been subject to the draft. Such was the case of Frank Emi, who was married and was a father at that time, so he was exempt from the draft.

Many of those who were considered as unpatriotic and labeled as troublemakers at Tule Lake were people of great principle and conscience. Some of the residents of Tule Lake carried a stigma for years and still feel the pain. Even after the war ended, they were often ostracized by some in the Japanese American community and within the JACL.

The JACL needs to have further conversations about Tule Lake. It would do well for each of us to feel the emotion and frustration of so many who were incarcerated there. The understanding of how an era dealt with values, rejection, and conflict may heal some of the hurt and anger that have existed in the community since the war. The time to overcome these differences and the anger is long past. Those who actually experienced the pain and suffering have mostly passed on, but their descendants carry on their legacy by attending the Tule Lake Pilgrimages.

The Tule Lake Pilgrimage held every other year has been regularly attended by Japanese Americans who were incarcerated at the Tule Lake Camp and by family members and friends. The relationship between former Tuleans and the JACL has not always been amicable. In 2009, it was said to be a historic first to have a representative of the National JACL attend the pilgrimage. Floyd Mori attended as national executive director of the JACL. He was questioned during the pilgrimage about the JACL's wartime activities against the Resisters who were at Tule Lake. [See the Resisters Apology Speech of May 11, 2002, for further information.] Another first at that pilgrimage was to have the attendance of San Francisco's consul general of Japan, The Honorable Yasumasa Nagamine, with his wife, Ayako, and Yoshiro Tasaka, the consulate's liaison to the Japanese American community. Some people who attend the Tule Lake Pilgrimages are members of their local JACL chapters, but apparently no one representing the National JACL had previously attended the Pilgrimage.

INTRODUCTION OF DALE MINAMI

Speaking to Introduce Dale Minami
Utah Valley University
Provo, Utah, September 22, 2009

It is an honor to introduce to you a great American. Dale Minami is a third generation Japanese American who was born in Los Angeles. Although he grew up with an all-American background, including baseball and boy scouts, his parents, grandparents, and older brother suffered untold discrimination and hardship before Dale was born. When World War II began and the persons of Japanese ancestry were forcibly removed from their West Coast homes, Dale's family was sent to an assembly center at the Santa Anita Racetrack in California where they lived in horse stalls. They were later transferred by train with other Japanese Americans to what is considered an American concentration camp in Rohwer, Arkansas.

Because they were wrongly suspected and perceived by the United States government as being a national security risk, people of Japanese ancestry living on the West Coast were sent to hastily constructed camps where rows and rows of barracks were built in remote and desolate areas of the country. They lived in crowded conditions without the normal comforts of home. It is a dark period in our nation's history of which many people are unaware. One of the ten concentration camps was the Topaz Camp near Delta, Utah, to the south of us here not too far from the location of your campus.

Dale's grandparents had come from Japan, but his parents were born in America and were citizens in this great country where the Constitution proclaims that everyone should be treated equal. They had grown up saying the pledge of allegiance in school. They believed in its words that there should be *"...liberty and justice for all."* Yet, they were imprisoned and stripped of their freedoms, possessions, and honor without any due process as guaranteed by the Constitution. This experience would greatly affect their future lives. They taught their sons that they should treat all people with respect.

While he was a boy in Southern California living a comfortable life, Dale became aware of the civil rights struggle in the South where African Americans were treated badly and suffered daily discrimination. He was a student at the University of Southern California, from which he graduated magna cum laude, when he became extremely interested in social conscience. As a college student, he witnessed the Watts Riots in 1965, six days of civil unrest that left more than thirty people dead and more than a thousand injured. Determined to find out why these people felt such anger, he read many books about the history and challenges of African Americans.

Dale decided to pursue a career path in social justice and almost went into social psychology. His father suggested that the field of law would be more practical, and Dale entered Boalt Hall School of Law at the University of California at Berkeley. It was a place of anti-war protests, free speech demonstrations, and rebellious students in the late 1960s.

I had completed my education from Brigham Young University in the mid 1960s and had started my career teaching Economics at a community college just down the freeway from Berkeley in

Hayward, California. I witnessed busloads of protesting students being taken to the county jail in Pleasanton, a city where I lived and where I would later become mayor.

Not only did Dale learn of the injustices against his own family and other Japanese Americans during World War II, but he developed a true commitment and passion for social justice. He became an advocate for the disenfranchised. He has spent his life helping others. After completing law school and receiving his Juris Doctor degree in 1971, he was recruited to help start the Asian Law Caucus in 1972. With cultural and economic issues keeping many Asians from obtaining adequate legal services, the Asian Law Caucus sought to provide legal access and to empower Asians in America.

They took on many important cases in the various areas of civil rights. Today the Asian Law Caucus is known as the country's oldest legal and civil rights organization serving low income persons in the Asian American and Pacific Islander communities.

Dale later went into private practice and began the firm of Minami, Lew & Tamaki in San Francisco. He continued to take civil rights cases on a pro bono basis although today they specialize in personal injury law and entertainment law. Kristi Yamaguchi, the Olympic gold medal ice skater, is one of Dale's clients.

In the early 1980s, Dale was the lead attorney on a legal team of pro bono attorneys in successfully reopening the Fred Korematsu case about which he will be speaking today. Fred was an American citizen of Japanese descent, twenty-three years of age, who dared to question the practices being perpetrated against Americans of Japanese ancestry at the beginning of World War II. He had a Caucasian girlfriend, and he refused to submit himself to the government's incarceration camps. This caused him to be arrested and convicted of defying the government's order. He appealed his case all the way to the Supreme Court which ruled against him in 1944. The case resonated with Dale because of the experience of his own family being incarcerated during the war.

Aiko Herzig-Yoshinaga had discovered documents in the 1980s that government intelligence agencies had hidden from the Supreme Court in 1944. She became a researcher for the Redress Movement, and her findings were used by Professor Peter Irons, a legal historian. The documents showed that Japanese Americans had committed no acts of treason to justify mass incarceration. Dale and the legal team re-opened the forty-year-old case of Fred Korematsu on the basis of government misconduct. On November 10, 1983, Fred's conviction was overturned in a federal court in San Francisco. Fred Korematsu received the Presidential Medal of Freedom, the nation's highest civilian honor, from President Bill Clinton in 1998.

I have had the privilege of knowing Dale for a long time. I met him early in his career. I remember him when he came out of law school and began his career as a young attorney. After he started his work with the Asian Law Caucus, I watched his career with interest as he became well known as a lawyer who worked hard for the rights of others. I had some dealings with Dale and as our paths crossed from time to time over the years, we became friends. We could be related as Dale's wife, who is also an attorney, has the same last name as I do.

Besides starting the Asian Law Caucus, Dale is co-founder of the Asian American Bar Association of the Greater Bay Area, the Asian Pacific Bar of California, and the Coalition of Asian Pacific Americans.

Dale has received numerous awards including the American Bar Association's 2003 Thurgood Marshall Award, the 2003 ACLU Civil Liberties Award, the California State Bar President's Pro Bono Service Award, and an Honorary Juris Doctor Degree from the McGeorge School of Law.

Dale is an extremely popular and sought after speaker. You are fortunate to have him speak to you today about an important topic of civil rights. It is a pleasure for me to introduce to you a truly great American with a big and caring heart, who has done much good in the world—my friend, Dale Minami.

Floyd Mori was invited to introduce Dale Minami, a prominent civil rights attorney in San Francisco who was a guest speaker at Utah Valley University in Provo, Utah.

Fred Korematsu was born on January 30, 1919, in Oakland, California. The State of California commemorates the Fred Korematsu Day of Civil Liberties and the Constitution on January 30th, his birthday. The Fred T. Korematsu Institute for Civil Rights and Education is named in his honor. Fred Korematsu passed away on March 30, 2005, of respiratory failure at the age of 86.

Brent Mori, Floyd Mori's son, became friends with Fred Korematsu and his wife while Brent was attending the University of California at Berkeley and was involved with the Berkeley JACL chapter. Brent worked with Fred on an early Day of Remembrance event for the JACL. Floyd met Fred Korematsu several times.

EARLY JAPANESE IMMIGRATION TO THE UNITED STATES

The Wakamatsu Colony
Article Originally Written for
the JACL Membership
November 17, 2009

The Japanese American Citizens League (JACL) has been involved indirectly for some time with those who are trying to work on preservation of the Wakamatsu Colony.

Believed to be the first Japanese settlement in the United States, The Wakamatsu Tea and Silk Farm Colony was established in 1869 by John Henry Schnell, a Prussian who was married to a Japanese woman. Seven Japanese citizens and a European expatriate sailed across the Pacific to San Francisco. They made their way farther east and purchased some land in Gold Hill near Coloma and Placerville in El Dorado County, California. The Japanese immigrants brought with them, mulberry trees, silk cocoons, tea plants, and bamboo roots.

The group from Aizu-Wakamatsu in Fukushima Prefecture grew to twenty-two people. The Japanese settlers began producing traditional Japanese crops such as tea, silk, rice, and bamboo.

The Gold Hill Ranch was the site of the Wakamatsu Tea and Silk Colony from 1869 to 1871.

The American River Conservancy announced on August 7, 2009, that measures are expected to make the purchase of the Gold Hill Ranch possible. A grant, along with legislative action by Sen. Barbara Boxer (D-CA), will help to preserve and protect an important part of the history of Japanese immigration to the United States.

The Gold Hill Ranch is also the gravesite of Okei, a nineteen-year-old girl who died in 1871 and is believed to be the first Japanese person to be buried on American soil. She left her native Japan to be a governess for the Schnell children. In acknowledging Okei's significance, Fred Kochi, the president of the Gold Hill Wakamatsu Colony group, said that the site represents the "hardship" that immigrants from Japan endured as "agricultural settlers" in the United States.

The colony only lasted a few years with the residents leaving after the drought of 1871. The Schnell family is said to have left two years after the colony was established. Drought and financial problems forced the colony's members to disperse and settle throughout California beginning in 1871. The Veerkamp family purchased the property in 1875.

Though the colony was short-lived, many of the original structures on the site remain intact including a farmhouse, barn, artifacts, and agricultural plantings. The two hundred seventy-two acre ranch encompassing the original colony site has been passed down for generations through the Veerkamp family. The site has been preserved for visitors to come and learn about the history of the Wakamatsu colonists and Japanese culture. It also provides wildlife habitat, hiking trails, and picnic areas, as well as grazing and pastureland.

The first measure to advance the Wakamatsu Colony project is a $488,000 Farm and Ranchland Protection Program (FRPP) grant that was recently approved for funding by the Natural

Resources Conservation Service (NRCS). The grants will be matched by approximately $500,000 in private donations that have previously been received by the American River Conservancy.

On August 6, 2009, Senator Boxer introduced the Gold Hill Wakamatsu Preservation Act (Senate Bill 1596), which would authorize the State Department of Interior, through the Bureau of Land Management, to acquire the Gold Hill Ranch and work with the American River Conservancy and the Japanese American community to permanently preserve the cultural history, agricultural character, and open space of the area which is significant in Japanese American history.

"This legislation will protect this historic site in California's Gold Country, where a small band of immigrants established the first Japanese settlement in the nation more than a century ago," Boxer said in a statement.

Kochi said the Gold Hill Wakamatsu Colony preservation group plans to develop parts of the land into a Japanese garden. The organization also hopes to recreate the barn into a theater where plays and folk dances can be performed just as they had been "in those days," he added.

The Japanese names of Okei, Sakurai, and Kuninosuki Masumizu, three names known to researchers as being in the group identified as "Japanese Colony," do not appear on the 1870 census rolls which were taken in June 1870. The colony had been in existence for one full year at the time of the census. The 1870 census records show fifty-five Japanese then in the United States (excluding Hawaii and Alaska) with thirty-three in California and twenty-two of those in El Dorado County.

Newspaper accounts of the period suggest the colonists were traveling, however, infrequently between Gold Hill and Japan. Because of this, there may have been other colonists whose home was actually in Gold Hill on June 1, 1870.

There were one hundred forty-eight Japanese people living in the United States by 1880. The Japanese government did not allow laborers to leave Japan legally until after 1884 when an agreement was signed between Japan and the Hawaiian sugar plantations. Many Japanese who immigrated to Hawaii later moved to the mainland of the United States. By 1890, two thousand thirty-eight Japanese people resided in the United States.

Because of their expertise in agriculture, hard work, and willingness to travel, Japanese laborers from the Hiroshima, Kumamoto, Yamaguchi, and Fukushima areas in Japan were recruited to work in the Hawaiian sugar plantations. Japanese immigration continued, but white supremacist organizations, labor unions, and politicians caused a "Gentlemen's Agreement" to be enacted to curtail immigration from Japan. The agreement did permit wives and children of the laborers already in the country to enter the United States. From 1908 to 1924, many Japanese women had immigrated to the United States as wives or "picture brides."

The Japanese population increased, so a movement to totally exclude Japanese immigrants led to the Immigration Act of 1924. This legislation curtailed immigration from Japan until 1952 when 100 immigrants per year were allowed. A few refugees entered the United States during the 1950s along with Japanese wives of United States servicemen.

Some of this information was taken from The Wakamatsu Colony Centennial, a booklet that was published by the Japanese American Citizens League (JACL) in commemoration of the centennial celebration in January 1969.

WAT MISAKA HONORED BY THE NEW YORK KNICKS

Article Originally Written for the JACL Membership
December 21, 2009

Wat Misaka was honored by the New York Knicks basketball franchise in December 2009 during their game with Charlotte in New York City. Wat was the first non-white person to play in the National Basketball Association (NBA which was then known as the Basketball Association of America or BAA). Wat, who was drafted by the Knicks in 1947, was recognized and honored before the crowd at Madison Square Garden. He was accompanied by his wife, Katie, and several friends.

Wat is a longtime member of the JACL and belongs to the Salt Lake City JACL Chapter. The JACL is happy to congratulate him for this outstanding and well-deserved honor.

A second generation American born in this country of immigrant parents from Japan, Wat was born in Ogden, Utah, on December 21, 1923, where he grew up with a single mother and his brothers after his father had died. Except for his stint playing basketball with the Knicks and his military service, he has lived in Utah his entire life. He and his wife make their home in Bountiful, just north of Salt Lake City.

After finishing high school in Ogden where he was an outstanding player on his school's basketball team, Wat played basketball at Weber College in Ogden, which was then a junior college in his home town. He later transferred to the University of Utah in Salt Lake City, where he became a star on its basketball team. Upon his return from the 1944 NCAA tournament championship which the University of Utah won, Wat's mother told him that he had a letter waiting for him. He found that he had been drafted into the United States Army so his college studies and basketball were interrupted and put on hold. He served for two years with the army in the occupation of Japan at the end of World War II after which he returned to school at the University of Utah for his senior year.

It was 1947 when Wat, as a five-foot-seven-inch point guard at the University of Utah, was drafted by the New York Knicks after playing at Madison Square Garden when Utah won the NIT Championship that year. The Knicks drafted Wat as the first NBA player of Asian descent or any ethnic minority in the first round. It was the same year that Jackie Robinson broke into major league baseball. Although Wat's professional basketball career soon ended, he has the distinction of being the first non-white player in the NBA.

Wat played in the pre-season and in three regular games in the 1947–1948 season before he was cut from the team. Although it was not long after the end of World War II when Japan and the United States had been at war, Wat said he experienced little racial intolerance while with the Knicks.

Wat said: *"Whether real or not, I felt less prejudice against me in New York than I did anywhere. Playing for Utah at Madison Square Garden, New Yorkers are great fans of underdogs, and they really backed us up, even against St. John's. When I went back as a Knick, there were people who remembered me from playing for Utah and would say hello on the streets sometimes."*

Despite the good feelings he had in New York, he was given little explanation about why he was being let go from the Knicks team. He said he does not know if the war having recently ended with Japan had anything to do with it.

Wat was offered a chance to play for the Harlem Globetrotters when he left the Knicks, but he decided to instead return to Utah to complete his schooling in engineering. He was inducted into the Utah Sports Hall of Fame in 1999. In 2009, President Barack Obama heard of Wat's outstanding achievement in basketball and invited him to attend a ceremony at the White House at which he mentioned Wat's accomplishments in his speech. Wat and his son Henry attended the White House event.

While visiting the office of Paul Osaki in San Francisco, New York actress, singer, and playwright, Christine Toy Johnson, saw a photo of Wat Misaka in a basketball uniform. She asked about him and heard a small portion of his story. Being intrigued with it, Christine and her husband, Bruce Johnson, also an actor, singer, and filmmaker, produced a documentary about Wat called, *Transcending, The Wat Misaka Story.* This is the story of a true American hero, and the film also tells some of the Japanese American history of that era.

Christine and Bruce Johnson were instrumental in having the New York Knicks honor Wat at halftime of a recent game at which time Wat was honored and recognized. Young people in the crowd were impressed with Wat as they approached him after the game to meet him and offer congratulations.

Wat Misaka has since been honored for his accomplishments after other Asian American and civil rights groups became aware of him and his story. The Japanese American National Museum in Los Angeles had featured Wat years ago with an exhibit, but his story had not been widely known until the documentary about him was produced. His name was also mentioned in the media when Jeremy Lin became a star with the Knicks in 2012.

UTAH DAY OF REMEMBRANCE EVENT

Speech Given at a Day of Remembrance Event
Honoring Wat Misaka and Raymond Uno
Weber State University
Ogden, Utah, February 20, 2010

It is a great honor for me to be here today, and I am humbled to be on the stand with these two great leaders who are men of outstanding accomplishments, Wat Misaka and Raymond Uno, as we commemorate the Day of Remembrance and as they are presented with special honors of which they are most deserving. Wat is receiving recognition from Weber State University by having a scholarship established in his name after achieving great success years ago as an outstanding basketball player on their college team. Raymond is receiving the 2010 Human Rights and Social Justice Award which exemplifies his life and his work. He has been serving others throughout his career and in all aspects of his life.

It is fitting that these awards are presented at this Day of Remembrance event which we commemorate to remember the experiences of Japanese Americans during World War II. We note the achievements and celebrate the accomplishments of these great men since that dark time in our history.

May I begin by going back to what I can remember as a small child? I was born in Murray, Utah, close to where a Lowes Hardware Store is now located on Forty-Eighth South and I-15. We were a large family with Japanese immigrant parents and at that time, seven children of which I was the seventh, trying to get through the trials of daily life before the start of World War II. My father was farming, and my older brothers and sisters all worked hard alongside our parents, which I eventually did also. I remember the crops—sorting, washing, and packing the vegetables although I was very young while we lived there.

When I was still a small child, we moved a little farther south to a farm in Sandy. After the war started, some relatives came from California and moved in with us. They were cousins of my mother and were "voluntarily evacuated" from their homes on the West Coast. Because they had someone (our family) living inland who would sign for them, they received permission to move to Utah in the days before the camps were a reality and to avoid being imprisoned. They arrived in the spring of 1942. It was kind of fun for me to meet relatives whom I had never seen or met.

I started school during the war, and first grade wasn't much fun. We lived in a small, rural community, but there was a fair amount of taunting and name calling because I was Japanese. Being the only one who was "different," I was excluded from a lot of activities going on around me at the elementary school. As I was growing up, I liked sports, especially baseball and basketball. I did not see many role models for me to look up to at that time except for my older brothers.

The Japanese community in Utah held picnics in the summer, and I looked forward to those events. It was one of the few times I associated with other Japanese American young people. There were some guys my age at the picnics, Paul Terashima, Frankie Imai, and some of those tough Ogden kids.

I was taken to JACL basketball tournaments and baseball league games by my older brothers and sisters. Japanese American players then became my role models as a child. Here were people who looked like me who were able to do something. I thought then that I wanted to become a first baseman because that was the position where my older brother played, and he was one of my role models.

In the cold winter nights during my childhood, our family gathered around the radio to listen to the University of Utah basketball games. There were names like Arnie Ferrin, Vern Gardner, and, of course, Wat Misaka. I must have been around seven or eight years old at the time. Wat, as has become better known in recent years, was the first non-white player ever to play in what is now the National Basketball Association (NBA), having been drafted by the New York Knicks from the University of Utah. It happened in the same year that Jackie Robinson broke into major league baseball.

Although Wat's basketball career with the NBA was cut short, that was a huge accomplishment. My wife and I were honored to be at Madison Square Garden with Wat and Katie when Wat was honored by the New York Knicks last December. This was arranged by Bruce and Christine Toy Johnson, who have produced a DVD about Wat's story.

Going to school at the time for me was a challenge and still was not that fun. What did I have to look forward to?

Listening to Wat having such great success on the basketball floor as a college student gave me hope. He gave me dreams toward which I could work. Wat's example gave me an identity and confidence that I could compete. My brothers had put up a basketball hoop on a wall of the chicken coop at our farm. There was bare dirt under it, and I think they measured it wrong. It was too high for me as an eight and nine year old then, but I spent hours shooting baskets even in the snow. I got so I could shoot baskets quite well and could beat the neighborhood kids, which brought some measure of acceptance. I was able to make the Draper Junior High School Braves basketball team as a seventh grader, playing with ninth graders. I remember my dad coming in his overalls to watch me play basketball at school games.

Baseball was different from basketball. I decided that I wanted to pitch. I had to push myself on to be a pitcher because I knew that I was pretty good at the time. I became a feared pitcher by the opposing teams. I later played short stop and second base. I was nurtured by coaches and went on to become All State in baseball in high school. I say this not to boast, but to tell you that it was Wat who gave me hope to be able to try and to have some success at sports. He became my role model in many ways. He was always a gentle giant of a man. While I never made it to the Yankees or the Lakers, the attitude that I was able to develop through Wat's example helped carry me on to other venues and adventures. It was my privilege later in life, after moving back to Utah, to become close friends with Wat and to share many memorable experiences with him.

Raymond Uno, as one of the early lawyers and the first judge of Asian American ancestry in the state of Utah, has been an example within the community for decades. Although Ray was born in Ogden, Utah, his family had moved to California when Ray was about eight years old so they were removed from their home at the outbreak of the war. He was incarcerated at the Heart Mountain concentration camp as a young child. He continues to work diligently with the Heart Mountain Wyoming Foundation to build a lasting learning center which will preserve the camp and the memories. He has been a giant among civil rights advocates and served as a national president of the JACL in the 1970s. He was, along with Jimi Mitsunaga, instrumental in starting the Minority Bar Association in Utah.

I knew of Ray and was familiar with his name long before I ever met him and became friends with him. We have since worked together on the planning for numerous events and activities. We have been on committees together where I have seen his leadership and commitment firsthand. He is an outstanding leader and a person who has dedicated himself to the community and to service. He continues to help and serve others in many capacities today to make this a better world. I hope we understand what Raymond Uno has sacrificed in order that we could gather here today. We commend him for his many great accomplishments which are too many to list.

So I think it is good that we have a Day of Remembrance. While we remember Executive Order 9066 (EO 9066) signed by President Franklin D. Roosevelt on February 19, 1942, which caused the people of Japanese ancestry, mostly citizens of the United States, to be forcibly removed from their West Coast homes and incarcerated in hastily constructed camps in remote and desolate regions of the country, we also celebrate the rescinding of EO 9066 many years later by President Gerald R. Ford in 1976. We remember all that it means to our nation and community. It is *essential* that we remember what this day symbolizes.

We need to look to and remember our heritage. What are the *values* that embody that community from whence we came and grew?

Hard Work, Honesty, Hope for a Better World. These are values instilled in us by our Japanese immigrant parents and grandparents.

And, *Yes*, this "hopey, changey" stuff is important to remember. Those who don't understand that hope is important have lived with a silver spoon and do not understand who they are, nor do they remember from where they came. Many good changes have come about because of the hope that the Wat Misakas and the Raymond Unos of the Japanese American community have instilled in us.

There was *sacrifice* and a *cost* that allows us our place in life and society today. The matter of *involvement* is a critical theme of those like Wat and Raymond. They were not caught up in their own glory, but they became involved in a team or the community in order to make it better for all of us. Their involvement was in others rather than being concerned with personal ego and position in life. Because they did so and because of their accomplishments, our position in life and in the community as Americans of Japanese ancestry is better today.

Today is a *Day of Remembrance*. So I would say, let us remember what happened some sixty-eight years ago when many were called to prove to the nation that we are as red-blooded and patriotic as they, even though our skin and appearance may be a little different. Let us remember that there was a price paid for where we are today, and we are obligated to repay that debt by becoming involved just as our early leaders were involved in making a better world.

By remembering, may our involvement, sacrifice, and recognition of how we got to where we are today motivate each of us to be the Wat Misaka or the Raymond Uno in somebody else's life. Young people still need role models.

It has been my distinct privilege and honor to have become personally and closely associated with both of these outstanding individuals through the years. I have worked and played with them on a regular basis on many committees, socially, and on the golf course. I am happy to call them my friends.

I would like to say *"Thank You"* to these two great gentlemen who have done so much for all of us. They are true American heroes who have led the way.

Thank you, Wat and Raymond, for your leadership and example.

JACK TOBE JOINS THE JACL DC CHAPTER BOARD

A Young Japanese American Leader
Article Originally Written for
the JACL Membership
February 2010

While attending the Japanese American Citizens League (JACL) DC Chapter Mochitsuki event (a social where they make and serve the traditional Japanese rice cakes called *mochi*) in December 2009, my wife and I were greeted warmly by an impressive teenager. He was especially attentive, helpful, personable, and kind. We wondered who this great young man was as we were then not acquainted with him. We found that his name is Jack Tobe, a thirteen-year-old member of the chapter.

Service is nothing new to Jack, who has just become the youngest member of the Board of the JACL DC Chapter, which takes in Washington, DC, Maryland, and Virginia. He was installed at the Chapter Installation Luncheon in January 2010 at the MeiWah Restaurant in Bethesda on a very snowy day in the Washington, DC area. It is quite likely that Jack is the youngest board member serving within the entire organization of the JACL.

Jack has been attending important functions for years with his father, John Tobe, a Japanese American from Los Angeles who is an alumnus of the University of Southern California (USC). Jack is a dedicated fan of USC along with his father who works for the Japan Embassy in Washington, DC. Jack is a regular visitor to the Japan Ambassador's Residence in Washington, DC, accompanying his father to significant events.

A seventh grader at St. Patrick's Episcopal Day School in Washington, DC, Jack is on the varsity basketball team and was on the varsity cross country team. He received the "Coach's Award" for his performance and dedication on the cross country team. He earned a black belt in Karate several years ago. However, Jack's first love is baseball where he plays first base, pitcher, and outfield on his team. He has been playing Little League for seven years.

Volunteering is a way of life for Jack, who has been a four-year volunteer of "Gifts for Good" (GFG), which is an alternative gift fair at his school. He has also participated in the "grate patrol" program which helps to feed the homeless. In August 2008, Jack did volunteer work for the Democratic National Committee (DNC) Secretary's Office at the Democratic National Convention in Denver, Colorado. He was a runner and floor whip for the DNC.

Jack is a fourth generation Japanese American whose grandfather was incarcerated at the Minidoka, Idaho camp from 1942–1943. Jack's great grandfather was held in a detention camp in Santa Fe, New Mexico. His great grandfather and his grandfather were part of an exchange program where incarcerated Japanese immigrants and Japanese Americans were allowed to return to Japan. They did so and left the United States at that time because it was the only situation which allowed the family to be reunited after being imprisoned and separated. They traveled to Fort Dix in New Jersey and were put on a Swedish flagged vessel which sailed to Goa, India. There, they were transferred on to a Japanese flagged vessel and sailed to Yokohama, Japan. Jack traveled to Japan in 2006 and visited relatives who still live in the Tokyo region.

A member of the JACL for the last several years, Jack is also a member of the Japanese American National Museum (through his father's membership). He has volunteered at the JACL DC Chapter's annual *mochitsuki* and other events. He also volunteers at the *Shin-Shu Matsuri* (a New Year's festival in Washington, DC sponsored by the Japan Commerce Association of Washington/JCAW).

Jack has always had a keen interest in Japan and the Japanese culture. Among his favorite foods are *soba, musubi, and mochi.* He is on the road to true leadership within the Japanese American community, the JACL, and the nation. Hopefully, other young people will follow Jack's example and become more involved in leadership within the JACL. Young people are our future, and they are extremely important to the organization. The JACL would greatly benefit by having many more young members like Jack who are willing to put forth the effort to become leaders at a young age.

JACL RECEIVES NATIONAL PARK SERVICE GRANT

Article Originally Written for
the JACL Membership
May 14, 2010

The National Park Service (NPS) has announced the grant award recipients for the Fiscal Year 2010 Japanese American Confinement Sites Grant Program. NPS has awarded twenty-three grants totaling $2.9 million to help preserve and interpret historic locations where Japanese Americans were detained during World War II.

Jon Jarvis, director of the NPS, stated: "*The Japanese American internment experience is an important chapter in American history. The National Park Service is honored to be part of this shared effort to preserve these sites, which are a tragic reminder of a shameful episode in our past, and a compelling lesson on the fragility of our constitutional rights.*"

The NPS grants range from $17,295, to re-establish the historic honor roll at the Minidoka National Historic Site in Jerome County, ID, which commemorates Japanese American servicemen from that camp, to $832,879, to build the interior of the Heart Mountain Interpretive Learning Center in Park County, Wyoming.

The Japanese American Citizens League (JACL) has been awarded a grant of $151,790 for a program called "Passing the Legacy Down: Youth Interpretations of Confinement Sites in the Western United States," which will include the Manzanar Relocation Center, Inyo County, California; Tule Lake Relocation Center (Tule Lake Segregation Center), Modoc County, California; Colorado River Relocation Center (Poston), La Paz County, Arizona; and Minidoka Relocation Center, Jerome County, Idaho. The Japanese American Confinement Sites Grant Program was established in 2006 by Congress to preserve and interpret the places where Japanese Americans were incarcerated during World War II. The law authorizes up to $38 million in grants for the life of the program to identify, research, evaluate, interpret, protect, restore, repair, and acquire historic confinement sites. The program seeks to teach and inspire present and future generations about the injustice of the Japanese American confinement and demonstrate the nation's commitment since then to equal justice under the law.

Congress appropriated $3 million in the current fiscal year for grants which were awarded on a competitive process, matching $2 in federal money for every $1 in non-federal funds and "in-kind" contributions raised by groups working to preserve the sites and their histories. Congress appropriated $1 million for fiscal year 2009, the first year of the grants. Rep. Doris Matsui has been instrumental in getting the grant money appropriated.

Locations eligible for the grants include the ten War Relocation Authority camps that were set up in 1942 in seven states: Gila River and Poston, Arizona; Amache, Colorado; Heart Mountain, Wyoming; Jerome and Rohwer, Arkansas; Manzanar and Tule Lake, California; Minidoka, Idaho; and Topaz, Utah. There are also forty other locations in sixteen states, including civilian and military-run assembly, relocation, and isolation centers.

Gerald Yamada, national coordinator for the Japanese American National Heritage Coalition, had been working on the camp preservation issue for some time when Floyd Mori joined in the effort representing the JACL.

Rep. Bill Thomas of Bakersfield, California, chairman of the House Ways and Means Committee, after introducing the bill in the House, shepherded its approval on the House floor. With Manzanar located in his district, Congressman Thomas took a personal interest in ensuring passage of the House version of the bill. With his leadership position in the majority party of the House of Representatives, the congressman was possibly *the key factor* in the passage of the bill. As Congressman Thomas retired from the House of Representatives after his fourteenth term, this was one of his last major acts in his distinguished career as a member of Congress.

The bill was originally introduced in January 2005 and died in committee. It was introduced on April 6, 2005, by Rep. Bill Thomas with Rep. Doris Matsui and Rep. Mike Honda as cosponsors along with 112 others. HR 1492 passed the House of Representatives overwhelmingly in November 2005. The sponsors of the bill on the Senate side were Sen. Daniel Inouye. (D-HI), Sen. Bob Bennett (R-UT), and Sen. Daniel Akaka (D-HI).

The result was Public Law 109–441: Preservation of Japanese American Confinement Sites including provision of grants to organizations "to preserve and interpret the confinement sites where Japanese Americans were detained during World War II." It was signed into law by President George W. Bush. The bill established the Japanese American Confinement Sites Grant Program.

Mori stated, *"The JACL is grateful to the NPS and to Congress for this grant which will help us continue to tell the Japanese American story in order to ensure that no other people will have to endure the horrific experiences which Japanese Americans did during World War II. We appreciate the efforts of Craig Ishii, the JACL Pacific Southwest regional director, for his considerable and outstanding work in the grant application process necessary for the JACL to secure this funding."*

Larry Oda, National JACL president, added, *"These grants will allow the JACL and other organizations to tell the important story of the Japanese American experience of incarceration. We thank those involved in awarding this grant to the JACL."*

JACL CELEBRATES UNVEILING OF SECRETARY MINETA'S PORTRAIT

Article Originally Written for
the JACL Membership
July 28, 2010

The Japanese American Citizens League (JACL) congratulates former congressman, Secretary of Commerce, and Secretary of Transportation, Norman Y. Mineta, whose portrait is now part of the permanent collection at the National Portrait Gallery (NPG) in the nation's capital. With a growing number of Asian American Pacific Islander (AAPI) leaders in government today, it is with the greatest pleasure that the JACL joins in honoring Secretary Norman Mineta, who was one of the first wave of great AAPI leaders in government and who has opened many doors for the AAPI community.

Secretary Mineta's portrait, painted by artist Everett Raymond Kinstler, was unveiled on July 26, 2010, with a reception following the ceremony honoring the former cabinet member at the NPG as part of the *New Arrivals* Collection. It was a gift from the Smithsonian Asian Pacific American Program to the NPG with donors from within the community. Remarks were made by the deputy director of the NPG, Carolyn K. Carr; the Smithsonian Institute's undersecretary for History, Art, and Culture, Richard Kurin; and acting director of the Smithsonian Institute's Asian Pacific American Program, Konrad Ng.

When addressing those in attendance to celebrate the unveiling of his portrait, Secretary Mineta reminisced about his past which has made him the person he is today and has resulted in a permanent place at the Gallery for his portrait. He shared stories of his experience in service to the nation and of his family and their struggles as Japanese Americans living in an American concentration camp during a time of animosity against them.

"It is with great pride that we see Secretary Mineta's remarkable story of leadership and service honored in the Portrait Gallery," said Asian Pacific American Program Acting Director Ng. *"He represents the key roles that Asian Pacific Americans have played in US culture, history and politics."*

A pioneer in AAPI politics, Secretary Mineta was born in San Jose, California, where he later became mayor. He served for many years as a member of Congress, co-founding the Congressional Asian Pacific American Caucus (CAPAC) and leading the passage of H.R. 442, the Civil Liberties Act of 1988, an official government apology for the incarceration of those of Japanese ancestry during World War II. Appointed Secretary of Commerce by President Bill Clinton and later Secretary of Transportation by President George W. Bush, Mineta served until his retirement in 2006. He was awarded the Presidential Medal of Freedom, the highest civilian award. For many decades, Secretary Mineta has been an active part of the JACL, and today serves as a great presence in the AAPI community.

Inclusion in the NPG is an attestation to an individual's contribution to American culture and history. Each portrait is recognition of the importance of an individual in US history. The Portrait Gallery includes Presidents, visionaries, and activists among those whose lives tell the American story. The Secretary's portrait is also part of an effort in having more sittings of people still living as part of the collection of portraits at the gallery.

The JACL supported the project from its inception. JACL national executive director, Floyd Mori, who attended the unveiling ceremony, stated, *"Norman Mineta has been a great member and supporter of the JACL as well as an outstanding leader for all Asian Americans and the country as a whole. We are proud of him and congratulate him for his accomplishments and example of true leadership. The JACL joins with others in expressing thanks for his many years of service to the nation. This latest honor is well deserved."*

VETERANS' EXHIBIT DEDICATION

Speech Given for Opening of the Exhibit at Ellis Island New York, August 8, 2010

It is an honor for me to represent the Japanese American Citizens League/JACL at this dedication. I have been asked to tell you a little of the history of the JACL and of Mike Masaoka, to whom this exhibit, *"Go for Broke: Japanese American Soldiers Fighting on Two Fronts,"* is dedicated.

As a small boy in Utah during World War II, I remember two of my older brothers joining the Army. My oldest brother was in the Military Intelligence Service (MIS). He was serving with the United States Army in the occupation of Japan at the end of the war when he lost his life in the crash of a military plane. Another brother was on his way to Germany with the US troops as a replacement for the 442nd when the war ended. So this exhibit has special significance to me personally and to many others who are in attendance here today.

We would like to thank Eric Saul, the curator of the exhibit, and the Japanese American Wartime History Project for putting together this exhibit and for their efforts to tell the story of the Japanese American veterans of World War II. Thanks also for dedicating this exhibit to Mike Masaoka. It is largely believed, and has been stated by Mike, that the initial concept of the formation of a military unit to be comprised of American citizens of Japanese descent which became the 442nd, was Mike's idea at a time when Japanese Americans were regarded as noncitizens who could not serve in the United States military.

Although there were some Japanese people who came to America before the turn of the century, the Japanese immigrants started to come to the United States in larger numbers in the early 1900s. They were hard working and enterprising. They found some limited success in this new country where they did not speak the language and the customs were unfamiliar. They were often looked upon with distrust and disdain. They endured hardship and faced prejudice on a daily basis.

As the American-born children of these Japanese immigrants became young adults and attended college, they still faced discrimination. They were told that no one would hire them even after they completed their university studies and earned degrees. There were many laws aimed at keeping their immigrant parents in a subservient state. As immigrants from Japan, the parents were not allowed to become United States citizens and could not own land in California and other areas. The Japanese immigrants and their children faced difficulties and bigotry at every turn. In fact, by 1925 further immigration from Japan had been banned.

The Japanese American Citizens League/JACL was formed in 1929 by the second generation American children of Japanese immigrants to combat the prejudice, intolerance, bias, and racism that they and their families experienced. Just as in its beginnings, the mission of the JACL remains to secure and uphold the civil and human rights of Americans of Japanese ancestry and others, to preserve the cultural heritage and values of Japanese Americans, and to combat social injustice against all people regardless of color or circumstances.

Mike Masaoka was not one of the originators of the JACL, but he became an early leader of the organization. Mike was born in Fresno, California, on October 15, 1915. He was the fourth of eight children born to Japanese immigrant parents. When he was a child, his father moved the family to Salt Lake City, Utah, where he was able and allowed to buy some land, which Asians immigrants were not permitted to do in California. Mike attended West High School and the University of Utah. He was a champion debater and graduated from the University of Utah in 1937.

It was my privilege to meet Mike when he lived in Utah, and I was a young boy there. I remember him coming to our home to encourage my older brothers to prepare for college. I would much later become better acquainted with him through our involvement with the National JACL.

Mike became a leader in the JACL after organizing the Intermountain District Council (IDC) of the JACL in Utah and Idaho. His first major involvement happened in 1938 when he attended an annual gathering of the JACL. At the age of 25, Mike was named the JACL national secretary and field executive, which began a long history with the JACL. Mike has stated that during World War II he was the only executive of the JACL with two girls as secretaries. Saburo Kido, an attorney, was serving as the national president. These two young men sought the advice of many others in guiding the JACL. They have received a lot of criticism over the years for actions taken by the JACL during the war years. They did what they thought was best for the Japanese American people at that time given the circumstances with which they were faced. They had huge responsibilities for their age.

With the bombing of Pearl Harbor by Japan on December 7, 1941, Japanese immigrants and Japanese Americans faced increased discrimination in the United States. They were immediately looked upon as the enemy. In fact, as a leader in a Japanese

American organization, Mike was arrested by the FBI on that day and taken from a meeting where he was trying to organize a chapter of the JACL in Nebraska. He was escorted from the meeting and placed in jail.

On February 19, 1942, seventy-three days after the United States entered World War II, President Franklin D. Roosevelt issued Executive Order 9066 which gave the military commander the authority to remove people from a designated area. The long held prejudices endured by those of Japanese ancestry came to the forefront as nearly one hundred twenty thousand men, women, and children were uprooted from their homes on the West Coast with most being incarcerated in hastily constructed camps in desolate areas of the United States where they were surrounded by barbed wire and armed guards facing inward with guns pointed toward those who were being held there. Although there were young Japanese American men who wanted to serve in the United States military and tried to enlist right after Pearl Harbor was bombed, they found that all Japanese Americans had been reclassified as enemy aliens and were deemed ineligible to join the armed forces of the United States.

Mike Masaoka went to Washington, DC to represent the JACL to work for the abolition of the detention camps and mitigate the effects of the forced removal of Japanese Americans from the West Coast. After meeting with government officials and hearing the alternatives, he suggested that the Japanese American community should cooperate with the government. He worked for the reinstatement of Japanese Americans into the military, and the result was the creation of a segregated unit of Japanese Americans which became the 442nd Regimental Combat Team. Mike and government leaders had expected ten thousand young men from the camps to volunteer for the 442nd, but only three thousand did, so others were later drafted. The unit was joined with the 100th Battalion of Japanese Americans from Hawaii. The motto of *"Go for Broke"* which was used by the 100th Battalion became the motto for the entire 442nd.

Even before Mike was married to his wife Etsu, he had signed up to join the Army. He became a soldier in the 442nd which served with distinction in Italy and France during World War II. He was awarded the Bronze Star, the Legion of Merit, and the Italian Cross for Military Valor. Three of his brothers also served in the Army with one losing his life in the war. Mike received some military awards after his passing.

After returning from military service, Mike resumed his work with the JACL and was the JACL Washington DC representative for many years. He worked tirelessly to gain, protect, and preserve the civil rights of Japanese Americans and others. He tried to reform immigration and naturalization laws, resulting in the repeal of the so-called Oriental Exclusion Act and the abolishment of the National Origins Quota Immigration System. He was instrumental in making it possible for Japanese immigrants to finally become naturalized citizens of the United States. He lobbied for reparations for losses suffered by Japanese Americans who had been imprisoned in the American concentration camps during the war. This assisted in the passage of the Evacuation Claims Act of 1948 which provided small repayments for some of the financial losses suffered.

Mike later played a role in the proceedings of the Commission on Wartime Relocation and Internment of Civilians from which The Civil Liberties Act of 1988 (the Redress Bill) became law. This Act allowed for redress and a Presidential apology for the Japanese American people who had been forcibly evacuated from their homes on the West Coast to be incarcerated in the camps during World War II and who were still living on August 10, 1988. A main purpose of the Redress Bill was to ensure that no other Americans would ever have to suffer the discrimination and indignities inflicted upon Japanese Americans by the incarceration which they experienced during World War II.

The National Japanese American Memorial to Patriotism in Washington, DC, which is a remembrance of the camp experience and which honors the Japanese American veterans, came about largely due to the vision of Mike Masaoka, who said, *"... the placing of an appropriate monument to our heroic dead in the nation's capital where, among the nation's heroes, it would be in proper company as a constant reminder to all Americans that the slant of one's eyes does not reflect the slant of one's heart, that the cost of racial intolerance runs high, that all Americans are of a common patriotism..."*

Also placed at that memorial are these words written by Mike: *"I am proud that I am an American of Japanese ancestry. I believe in this nation's traditions. I glory in her heritage. I boast of her history. I trust in her future."*

The honorable Norman Y. Mineta, former congressman from California, former secretary of the Department of Commerce, former secretary of the Department of Transportation, and Mike's brother-in-law, has this quote in stone at the Memorial: *"May this memorial be a tribute to the indomitable spirit of a citizenry in World War II who remained steadfast in their faith in our democratic system."*

The National Japanese American Memorial to Patriotism honors the Japanese Americans who served in the United States military which this exhibit is also honoring here today. They exemplified true patriotism.

Mike Masaoka has received many awards and was the JACL *Nisei* of the Biennium in 1950. In 1968, he was awarded the Third Order of the Rising Sun by the Emperor of Japan, and in 1983, he was honored with the Second Class Order of the Sacred Treasure by the Emperor of Japan. The JACL has an ongoing Congressional Fellowship established by Mike's friends and named in his honor, in which a young college graduate is able to work in the Washington, DC office of a member of Congress. Mike Masaoka was a true leader and a valuable part of the Japanese American history and legacy.

Mike met his wife, Etsu Mineta Masaoka, at a JACL Northern California District Meeting in Monterey, California. He was working in San Francisco, and she and her family were living in San Jose. They rode the same bus to Monterey after she boarded in San Jose although they did not meet until later at a social event during the district meetings after which their courtship began.

After the war broke out, Etsu's family was incarcerated at Heart Mountain, Wyoming. She left the camp alone in 1943 on a bus to Salt Lake City where Mike was living and where they were to be married. He thought it better that he not go to Heart Mountain to pick her up because of some sentiments against him and the JACL at the time. He had already enlisted in the US Army, which Etsu found out after arriving in Salt Lake City. They went ahead and got married on Valentine's Day. Mike had work to do in Washington, DC after which Mike went off to serve in the 442nd, the segregated unit of Japanese Americans in the Army. Etsu stayed in Chicago where her sister lived while Mike was at war. After the war ended, Mike and Etsu made their home in Maryland. Mike worked for the JACL as the Washington, DC Representative for many years after which he started his own consulting firm. Mike passed away in June of 1991 at the age of seventy-five of congestive heart failure after suffering with heart problems for a decade. His wife Etsu supported him in all he did. Etsu and their granddaughter Michelle Amano continue to live in Maryland.

This exhibit at Ellis Island is a tribute to the patriotism and heroism of the Japanese Americans who served their country during extremely difficult times. It honors Japanese American soldiers of the 100th Infantry Battalion, the 442nd Regimental Combat Team, the 522nd Field Artillery Battalion, the Military Intelligence and Language Services (MIS), and the Japanese American women in the Women's Army Corps who served valiantly during World War II at a time when they were looked upon as the enemy.

We commend Eric Saul for the excellent work on this exhibit and thank him for honoring Mike Masaoka and Chet Tanaka, who worked with Mike in the PR department of the 442nd and was responsible for writing many of the medal recommendations and reports on the 442nd. We thank Eric for recognizing the JACL and its role.

Thank you to all the veterans of that era and especially to those who are in attendance today. You sacrificed much to make a better world for all of us.

It is important that the Japanese American story, including that of our Japanese American veterans of World War II, be told and retold in order to guarantee that the liberties which we enjoy today will be available for all people. We owe a lot to the brave men and women who served and continue to serve our country in the military. This exhibit helps to keep history alive for future generations.

Thank you.

This dedication ceremony was held at Ellis Island for an exhibit done by Eric Saul about the Japanese American men and women who served valiantly for the United States Army in World War II. This included Japanese American soldiers of the 442nd Regimental Combat Team/100th Infantry Battalion, the 522nd Field Artillery Battalion, the Military Intelligence and Language Services (MIS), and the Japanese American women in the Women's Army Corps. The exhibit was dedicated to Mike Masaoka, an early leader of the Japanese American Citizens League/JACL, and to Chet Tanaka. Floyd Mori was national executive director of the JACL and was asked to represent the JACL to speak about Mike Masaoka. An article about the event follows.

DEDICATION HELD FOR THE GO FOR BROKE EXHIBIT AT ELLIS ISLAND

Article Originally Written for
the JACL Membership
August 10, 2010

The dedication ceremony for the exhibit, *"Go for Broke: Japanese American Soldiers Fighting on Two Fronts,"* was held at the Ellis Island Immigration Museum on August 8, 2010. The exhibit was created by the Japanese American Wartime History Project with Eric Saul as curator. Saul, former director of the Presidio Army Museum, created the original *"Go for Broke"* exhibit in 1980. Saul said, *"This is a wonderful tribute to the veterans on the sixty-fifth anniversary of the end of World War II. Their history is one of the great stories in American history."* Tribute was paid to the veterans of World War II, several of whom were in attendance.

George Takei served as master of ceremonies with the United States Park Police posting the colors. The national anthem was sung by Abbi Bingham Endicott. Chaplain Lt. Commander US Navy John M. Miyahara gave the invocation and benediction. Remarks were made by Ambassador Shinichi Nishimiya, consul general of Japan in New York, and Robert Nakamoto, president of the Japanese American Veterans Association (JAVA). Floyd Mori, national executive director of the Japanese American Citizens League (JACL), spoke about Mike Masaoka, to whom Saul has dedicated the exhibit, along with Chet Tanaka, who worked with Masaoka in the 442nd Regimental Combat Team. Mr. David Luchsinger, Superintendent of the Statue of Liberty and Ellis Island, also spoke at the dedication as did Joanne Oppenheim, author of *Dear Ms. Breed.*

The keynote address was given by Major General Kelly McKeague, USAF, Office of Joint Chiefs of Staff, Department of Defense. He spoke of the Hawaii National Guard which had been in existence since 1893. They were discharged in 1898 and reorganized in 1899 under the Territory of Hawaii. Japanese Americans were a large part of the National Guard. Members of the 100th Infantry Battalion from Hawaii were sent to Camp Shelby in Mississippi and were joined by the Japanese Americans from the mainland who made up the 442nd Regimental Combat Team. They did not get along at first until the Hawaii soldiers were taken on a visit to the American concentration camp in Rohwer, Arkansas. When they saw the conditions from which many of the 442nd enlisted with their families incarcerated, their attitudes changed. They began to understand each other and get along. [This story has often been related by Sen. Daniel Inouye, who was from Hawaii and a member of the 100th/442nd.] Major General McKeague mentioned President Harry Truman's remarks to the Japanese American soldiers after the end of the war that they had not only fought the enemy but fought prejudice and had won.

Some of Mike Masaoka's friends who attended the exhibit and ceremony from the Washington, DC area were Dr. Ray and Mary Murakami and Frank and Barbara Nekoba. Also shown for those who attended the dedication at the Museum was the film, *"442: Live with Honor, Die with Dignity."* Viewing the film is highly recommended for anyone who would like to know more about the history of the 100th/442nd and the Japanese American soldiers of World War II.

Comprising the exhibit are 150 rare photographs collected from a number of prominent government agency archives and private collections from Hawaii and the mainland United States. The exhibit opened to the public on Monday, July 5, 2010, and will be open throughout the summer at Ellis Island.

LET'S NOT PERSECUTE THE INNOCENT

Op Ed Article Written for
Various Media Outlets
September 2, 2010

It was the day after Pearl Harbor when fathers were taken from their homes under FBI escort to places unknown to them and their families. These were law abiding citizens who happened to be Buddhist priests and Japanese language teachers or business owners and community leaders who were obviously of Japanese ancestry. Some families were not aware of the disposition of their fathers for months. There was no appearance before a magistrate of any kind. There was no ability to retain legal counsel. They were just carted away to federal detention centers and held as prisoners, and yet their only crime was that they were of a particular religion and a specific ethnicity. It was years, in some instances, until they were reunited with their families. Many families were torn apart, and much suffering was experienced.

The good part of this story is that the federal government recognized the egregious error that was made, and many years later apologized with a letter from the President of the United States and through Congressional legislation with the passage of the Civil Liberties Act of 1988. The Congress found, through congressionally sanctioned hearings, that this injustice happened because of war hysteria, poor political leadership, and racism. This recognition of error and Presidential apology were done in order that future generations would learn from this mistake and never repeat it again.

As we fast forward to 2010, another non-Christian religion is being singled out and the character and integrity of their teachings, much of which mirrors the teachings of Jesus Christ, are being questioned. Their basic right to construct a community center which houses a place of prayer is being opposed by those who declare that dying for a democracy, such as we have in this country, is a noble thing. The American Muslim community in essence is being told that it does not belong among the rest of us doing the things, even worship, which we do each day, because the Constitution allows us that privilege. They are being denied the rights and privileges of the Constitution because of the very reasons found to be in error when Japanese Americans were denied their basic rights after the attack on Pearl Harbor.

Why is there any debate regarding the location of a community center that is within a few blocks of "Ground Zero," but not even within view? Have we forgotten that two decades ago we apologized for such bigotry in order to stop it from happening again? So where is the lesson that was to be learned from the World War II experience of the Japanese Americans? Is this the same wartime hysteria that prevails and causes innocent citizens of this country to suffer and experience humiliation? Is this the same kind of poor political leadership that allows the demagogues to use this issue to propel their warped political agenda? Is this the same kind of bigotry that looks down upon that which they do not understand and holds guilty those whose culture is not the same as theirs?

Then lastly, aren't we, after all is said and done, citizens of the nation that has sent its sons to harm's way to protect and preserve the precious principles written into our Constitution? High on the list of our freedoms that many have died to protect is the freedom of religion.

———◆◆◆———

Op Ed dated September 2, 2010, by S. Floyd Mori, national executive director of the JACL.

JACL APPLAUDS PASSAGE OF THE CONGRESSIONAL GOLD MEDAL BILL

Article Originally Written for
the JACL Membership
November 2011

The Japanese American Citizens League (JACL) applauds the passage of the Congressional Gold Medal Bill, which passed the House of Representatives unanimously with 411 votes. On May 13, 2009, US Rep. Adam Schiff from California introduced the Congressional Gold Medal Bill, HR 347, to award the Congressional Gold Medal collectively to the 100th Infantry Battalion and the 442nd Regimental Combat Team.

US senator Barbara Boxer also of California introduced S 1055 in the Senate. I was able to serve on the National Veterans Network (NVN) steering committee, representing the JACL, to assist with the grassroots push to lobby support from senators who had not signed on to the bill. The JACL supported this effort with JACL Fellows in the Washington, DC office, Phillip Ozaki and Jean Shiraki, making appointments and visiting many Senate offices along with Terry Shima and Grant Ichikawa,

World War II veterans and leaders in the Japanese American Veterans Association (JAVA).

The Senate passed S 1055 on August 1, 2010, which included an amendment to include the Military Intelligence Service (MIS). The House passed an amendment to include the MIS on September 23, 2010. President Obama signed the bill into law on October 4, 2010, awarding the Congressional Gold Medal collectively to the Japanese American veterans who were members of the 100th Infantry Battalion, 442nd Regimental Combat Team, and the Military Intelligence Service during World War II.

The Congressional Gold Medal events which took place in Washington, DC were held to honor the Japanese American veterans of World War II and were attended by over 2,500 people. There were more than three hundred Japanese American World War II veterans in attendance. The festivities were planned and executed by the NVN, led by Christine Sato-Yamazaki, and others. Subsequent Congressional Gold Medal events are being planned around the country to honor the Japanese American veterans in local areas.

Representing my family as a next of kin for my brother, Shigeru Mori, whose name is inscribed on the wall of the National Japanese American Memorial to Patriotism in Washington, DC as a soldier who was killed during military service in World War II, I was honored to receive the replica Congressional Gold Medal in memory of my oldest brother who was in the MIS serving in Japan during the occupation. Although I was a small child when he left for the war, I have fond memories of Shig as a kind and generous individual who was a good brother. He paid the ultimate price for the country he loved as did all the eight hundred twelve Japanese Americans whose names are on the wall. Our hearts are filled with gratitude for them and for all the Japanese American veterans who gave so much to make a better world for all of us.

The JACL has honored Japanese American veterans many times over the years at conventions and other events. At its 2009 JACL Gala held in Washington, DC, the JACL paid tribute to all veterans. Awards were presented to some of the organizations which have served the Japanese American veterans and which are keeping alive this important part of United States history. The groups honored were the Go for Broke National Education Center, the Japanese American Korean War Veterans (JAKWV), the Japanese American Veterans Association (JAVA), and the National Japanese American Historical Society (NJAHS). World War II veterans who were present were honored with a certificate of appreciation and a small gift. Everyone in attendance who had ever served in the military was asked to stand and be recognized. We were extremely honored to have Vice Admiral Harry B. Harris, who is one of the highest ranking officers of the United States Navy, serve as master of ceremonies for the Gala. Vice Admiral Harris, whose father was also in the Navy and whose mother is Japanese, attended the Congressional Gold Medal Ceremony at the Capitol.

The Japanese American veterans of World War II helped provide a better life for those who came after them. Their efforts are often extolled as being an important part of ushering in the civil rights movement. President Harry S. Truman desegregated the US military after World War II. The Japanese American veterans definitely made life better in this country for all Japanese Americans. They are deserving of every honor, and we owe them a great deal. We salute all Japanese American veterans and indeed all American veterans.

Japanese American veterans of that era are now in their eighties and nineties. They were extremely grateful that their efforts were recognized at long last after seventy years. It was very emotional to listen to many members of Congress extol the valor of the Japanese American soldiers who served their country during World War II in spite of the fact that many of their families were incarcerated behind barbed wires in America's concentration camps.

The ceremony held in the Capitol at which House Speaker John Boehner conducted was considered a rare moment of unity for the Democratic and Republican members of the Congress as they praised the Japanese American veterans of World War II for their contributions and sacrifices. It was a great lesson that patriotism is beyond color and ethnicity.

Rep. Adam Schiff, who introduced the House version of the bill stated: *"Man for man they were the most highly decorated combat units of the war. I can't imagine a group more deserving of Congress's highest honor."*

Admiral Harry B. Harris is now a Four Star Admiral, one of six who hold this rank which is currently the highest in the United States Navy. In October 2011, he served as the direct representative to the Secretary of State for the Chairman of the Joint Chiefs of Staff. Admiral Harris assumed command of the US Pacific Fleet in Honolulu, Hawaii, in October 2013. A graduate of the United States Naval Academy at Annapolis, Admiral Harris has logged 4,400 flight hours and has received many awards.

The Nisei Soldier Congressional Gold Medal returned to the Smithsonian National Museum of American History on February 19, 2014, after a year-long, seven-city tour. It is on special display at the Smithsonian and will be added to the World War II section of the Price of Freedom exhibit in July 2014. President Barack Obama greeted seven Nisei veterans at the White House Oval Office on February 18, 2014, and thanked them for their extraordinary service. The veterans who represented all Japanese American veterans are: Nelson Akagi, Grant Ichikawa, Susumu Ito, Joseph Kurata, Tommie Okabayashi, Terry Shima, and James Takemori. Christine Sato-Yamazaki and Floyd Mori accompanied them.

YOUNG PEOPLE ARE VITAL TO THE JACL

National Executive Director's Report
Article Originally Written for
the JACL Membership
September 29, 2010

As the National JACL scholarship recipients for this school year have been announced, we would like to congratulate these exemplary young people who received scholarships to assist them in furthering their education. Because we believe that education is so important, the scholarship program has been a significant part of the JACL for many years. The JACL is privileged to make this financial investment in young people, thanks to the many generous donors. Thanks to David and Carol Kawamoto and all others who helped administer the scholarship program as volunteers. The scholarship program will now be under the direction of Patty Wada, regional director of the Northern California Western Nevada Pacific (NCWNP) district of the JACL, and vice president of Planning and Development, Jason Chang.

About ten years ago, the JACL began to require scholarship applicants to be members of the JACL. It is anticipated that by having a JACL membership, these students will learn about the organization and will become involved with the JACL in their local areas, hopefully before they are of the age to apply for the JACL scholarships. Past participation in the JACL is a consideration in selecting the scholarship recipients, which makes it a good idea to get involved in the JACL at an early age.

The cost of a student/youth membership in the JACL at its current level of $25 a year is a good investment for the chance to receive a scholarship award of $1,000 to $5,000. Students may be awarded more than one National JACL scholarship during their college years. Most chapters also have scholarships available to their members.

Of course, this is not the only reason to join the JACL, and we hope that all youth and students will want to become members to participate in a great civil and human rights organization which provides social and leadership opportunities as well. The young people who serve on the JACL National Youth/Student Council and youth members of the various chapters are to be commended for their service to the JACL. They are gaining valuable experience which will help them to become our future leaders.

It is a fact that a large percentage of the JACL membership is now older in age with a substantial number of senior citizens. It is absolutely essential to the future of the JACL that we do a better job of bringing in more young people and retaining our student/youth members after they leave college. We would like to encourage all National JACL and chapter scholarship winners and applicants to remain active members of the JACL throughout their lives. The organization can benefit you as you serve and grow within the JACL. Giving should be a part of our lives, and remaining active in the JACL after receiving a scholarship is a good way to help the organization and others.

The JACL has found it difficult in the past to entice our younger generation in great numbers to become members of the JACL or to keep their memberships active. Having more youth members and members with young families will help to build the organization. The National JACL Convention held in

Chicago last July saw several families with small children and babies in attendance, which was a refreshing change reminiscent of the past when the conventions had more boosters and children attend. We appreciate the participation of young professionals and those who are involving their families in the JACL.

JACL fellowships and internship programs have been sponsored by State Farm, Eli Lilly, Ford Motor, Southern California Edison, UPS, AARP, AMGEN, and AT&T among others over the years. Some of the past fellows who have worked in the JACL offices are the following: Brandon Mita, Elaine Low, Jacki Mac, Naomi Lim, Meilee Wong, Crystal Xu, Shirley Tang, Jean Shiraki, Leslie Toy, Hillary Nakano, Stephanie Otani-Sunomoto, Jason Hata, and Amy Watanabe. In addition, Christine Munteanu and Phillip Ozaki worked as JACL Fellows before being hired as full-time staff for the JACL. Craig Ishii became the Pacific Southwest District regional director after serving as an intern for the JACL. Tim Koide was hired as JACL membership coordinator after being a JACL intern in the Washington, DC, office. These young people served the JACL well in assisting the full-time JACL staff. An outstanding opportunity to serve as a fellow in the Washington, DC office of a member of Congress has been afforded for over the past twenty years by friends of the late Mike M. Masaoka, an early leader of the JACL. Fellowships and internships are also offered in some of the JACL offices. Southwest Airlines has become a partner of the JACL and is providing airline tickets for youth events and fellowship recipients. Student/youth members are invited to avail themselves of the JACL fellowships and programs.

Chapter and district leaders need to strengthen their outreach to Asian American young people and other interested youth in their neighborhoods to encourage them to become members of the JACL. The scholarship program is an excellent selling point.

Although keeping track of students may be difficult when they move away from their home chapters, it is important to maintain contact with the scholarship applicants and recipients to keep them involved in chapters either at their home or where they attend college. Chapters in areas where colleges and universities are located should welcome the participation of students. College students are encouraged to stay involved with the JACL wherever they are attending school if a chapter is available in the area. The advanced technology of today makes it easier to stay in touch.

The older generation which has been the backbone of the JACL for decades is appreciated for their dedication to the JACL, but the young people are vital as they are our future leaders.

———— ✺ ————

Some of the people listed served the JACL after 2010, and names were added after the original printing of this article.

JACL Fellows, Phillip Ozaki and Jean Shiraki, are shown with Floyd and Irene Mori in the photo on page 40.

The Mike M. Masaoka Fellowship was funded by Mike's friends and established in his honor in 1988. The Fellowship was administered for twenty years from its inception by Dr. H. Tom Tamaki of Philadelphia with the help of a committee. Dr. Tamaki turned the handling of the fellowship over to the JACL DC office in 2008. Some of the recent Masaoka fellows have been: Mackenzie Walker, Michael Misha Tsukerman, Scott Sakakihara, Leslie Tamura, Nina Fallenbaum, Dana Nakano, and April Tsuki.

Some of the interns who served in the JACL DC office were: Kaitlin Inamasu, Greg Stillman, Emily Mitarai, Ide Viriya, Mai Suzuki, Kan Tagami, Bruce Kang, Bonny Tsang, and Rebecca Tien.

DAY OF REMEMBRANCE EVENTS ARE GOOD REMINDERS

Article Originally Written for
the JACL Membership
February 24, 2011

Many of our JACL chapters recently held Day of Remembrance (DOR) events to remember the signing of Executive Order 9066 (EO 9066) which happened on February 19, 1942, and the rescinding of EO 9066 which occurred in 1976. We encourage these events and think they are a good reminder so that the horror of the unjust incarceration of Japanese Americans during World War II will never be repeated against anyone. The past should be remembered and recalled in order to make the future better. We want to ensure that there is justice for all Americans and that the mistakes of the past are not repeated.

It was a dark day in history when President Franklin D. Roosevelt signed EO 9066 on February 19 in 1942. The order gave the military commander the authority to remove any person from certain geographic areas. The order was used only on those of Japanese ancestry and affected around one hundred twenty thousand innocent people who were living on the West Coast of the mainland United States. They were not protected by the Constitution, and there was no justice as men, women, and children who had done no wrong were forced to leave their homes. Before the camps were ready, they were held in assembly centers at fairgrounds and racetracks in horse stalls which had been white washed but still smelled of horses. Then they were taken to barbed wire enclosed camps in desolate regions of the country where they were imprisoned. Allowed only to take what they could carry, families were required to abandon homes, friends, pets, farms, businesses, and most of their earthly possessions. Some remained in those camps until 1945 after the war ended. Except for a fortunate few who left their belongings with trusted friends who took care of them, the people generally returned to find that items they had stored had been stolen or ruined while they were gone.

During the late 1970s, I was able to introduce a resolution in the California State Assembly which paved the way for the first official Day of Remembrance events held in California. It was a privilege for me to be with the group that was in the Oval Office at the White House when President Gerald R. Ford rescinded EO 9066 in 1976.

DOR events were being held in California regularly, but in the mid-1980s a Mount Olympus JACL Chapter event occurred which I believe was the first DOR event held in Utah where I was then living. This was a small gathering in our home to commemorate the event. It was soon after my family had moved from California to reside in the state of my birth. A JACL chapter member was asked to speak. Years before, he had been incarcerated in the camp at Minidoka, Idaho, having been born and raised in Seattle. He had been a member of the 442nd, the segregated unit of Japanese Americans in the US Army during World War II. He was a young adult man when he was forced from his home and imprisoned at Minidoka. Although he attended the event, he declined to speak at that time because it was too painful and emotional for him. He was unable to talk about the experience. He choked up with tears coming to his eyes when he even thought about speaking about those years of his life and his experiences of incarceration.

Since that first small DOR gathering, the DOR events are now a major annual JACL happening in Utah. The three JACL chapters in the state now jointly collaborate to hold a yearly event at which they remember EO 9066 and celebrate the events which followed such as the passage of the Civil Liberties Act of 1988 (The Redress Bill) which provided for a Presidential apology and token monetary reparations for the incarceration and wrongs committed against Japanese Americans during World War II. DOR events are held throughout the country to remember that fateful day of February 19, 1942, the rescinding of EO 9066, the Redress Bill, and the triumphs achieved by Japanese Americans since those days.

Last year I was asked to speak at the DOR event held by the three Utah JACL chapters which honored two old friends, Wat Misaka and Judge Raymond Uno. Both are outstanding long-time members of the Salt Lake Chapter of the JACL. Wat Misaka, who was born and raised in Ogden, Utah, was having a scholarship established in his honor. Raymond Uno, who was incarcerated at the Heart Mountain Camp was receiving an important award. DOR events often recognize people who have made a difference as they remember the errors of the past in order to prevent them from happening again.

It was a happy occasion when President Ronald Reagan signed into law the Civil Liberties Act of 1988, which is also called The Redress Bill. President Reagan had opposed the monetary reparations part of seeking redress. However, he became convinced to sign it when he was reminded of when he was an Army officer in 1945 and was present when Gen. Joseph W. Stilwell presented the Distinguished Service Cross to Mary Masuda for her brother, Kazuo Masuda, who had lost his life in the war. Kazuo was a staff sergeant in the 442nd Regimental Combat Team. A newspaper article about the event was produced which stated that a young actor by the name of Ronald Reagan had said: *"Blood that has soaked into the sands of a beach is all of one color. America stands unique in the world: the only country not founded on race but on a way, an ideal. Not in spite of but because of our polyglot background, we have had all the strength in the world. That is the American way."*

Redress was the culmination of over a decade and a half of hard work by many people to bring about redress and reparations, coupled with a Presidential apology, to those innocent Japanese Americans and Japanese immigrants who were incarcerated in illegal detention camps during World War II. The JACL and other groups, and many individuals, spent countless hours on redress to ensure that this experience would never be inflicted on any other people in the United States of America.

Over the years those who were incarcerated in the camps and could speak about the experience in public forums such as school classrooms have generally been those who had been young children or teenagers during World War II. The Japanese Americans at that time suffered great shame because their own government did not trust them and considered them as not even citizens. Most of those incarcerated did not speak of the experience even to their own families. It was and still is an emotional issue which caused great pain.

After the JACL and others began the Redress Movement and a commission was formed to hear the stories, those who had been incarcerated began to open up and speak about the experience. Some talked to their families about it for the first time. However, it is still difficult for many to talk about those horrible years of being denied their freedom and being locked up in America's concentration camps.

In spite of their humble beginnings, the DOR events held by JACL chapters everywhere have become major JACL events which are open to the public. They are held around the time of

February 19 each year. These various activities throughout the nation are good reminders to all Japanese Americans and the general public that this travesty of justice occurred to citizens of this country and should never be allowed to happen again. We must not forget our history, and others need to hear it or be reminded of it.

Since my schedule was to be in California during February of this year, I was able to accept invitations to attend the DOR events at Merced on February 19 and in Fresno on February 20. The event in Merced was the one-year anniversary of the monument erected at the Merced Fairgrounds to commemorate the assembly center in which Japanese Americans were temporarily housed in 1942 before the camps were ready for occupancy. JACL National Board members from the area and present at those events were Jason Chang, vice president of planning and development, and Marcia Chung, district governor of the Central California District Council.

Consul General of Japan in San Francisco Hiroshi Inomata and Rep. Jim Costa, who represents the area and has been very supportive, were also present. Bob Taniguchi and Judge Dale Ikeda, along with many others, were instrumental in having impressive monuments erected and presenting great programs in Merced and Fresno.

Special DOR events are held throughout the nation. The Washington, DC JACL Chapter and the Japanese American community regularly celebrate DOR in conjunction with the Smithsonian. This year they held a screening of the film, *442: Live with Honor, Die with Dignity*, which is a depiction of the experiences of the 442nd Regimental Combat Team/100th Battalion which served honorably during World War II. We owe much to these brave Japanese American veterans who showed the world the patriotism and loyalty of the Japanese Americans. They are in large part the reason for the success and acceptance which Japanese Americans generally now experience.

All those who have helped to organize and present the JACL DOR events around the nation are to be commended. Thanks to all who attend these events. We hope that more of the DOR events will reach out to the surrounding communities to invite others to learn of the Japanese American history.

SIKH FUNERAL AFTER A TRAGIC SHOOTING

Remarks Given at the Funeral of Surinder Singh
Sacramento, California, March 12, 2011

Today is a day of mourning for many. The family of Surinder Singh has lost a loved one. The community has lost a friend. The world has lost a worthy human being who had no reason to be shot and killed. We are all dismayed that this type of thing still happens in today's society.

The Japanese American Citizens League (JACL), the organization which I represent, is the nation's oldest and largest Asian American civil and human rights organization. We join with the many, who are saddened by such a senseless tragedy as the drive-by shooting which caused the death of an innocent Sikh gentleman, Surinder Singh, and injury to his friend.

We are all here because of our *hope* for our families and a better future. We pay tribute to a person who did not deserve to die at this time and in this manner. When something like this tragedy happens, we are reminded of the hate which exists in the world around us. It may question our resolve to work for more tolerance and understanding. It is difficult to make any sense of such an occurrence.

Hate and violence are nothing new in this country, but unfortunately, they still exist as evidenced by the reason we are here today.

Some 165 years ago, a small religious group was persecuted to the point that the governor ordered them exterminated. Members of the Church of Jesus Christ of Latter-day Saints (Mormons) had settled in Missouri where they were becoming a considerable political and economic influence because they tended to vote as a bloc. This caused hostilities and the issuing of an executive order by Missouri Gov. Lilburn Boggs, which has since been called the Extermination Order: *"The Mormons must be treated as enemies and must be exterminated or driven from the State."* Because of persecution and hatred, the Mormons left the state and migrated to Utah. The Extermination Order was not formally rescinded until 1976.

Almost seventy years ago, a whole community was rounded up and imprisoned simply because of their ancestry. President Franklin D. Roosevelt signed Executive Order 9066 on February 19, 1942, which caused the entire Japanese American and Japanese immigrant population on the West Coast of the United States to be forcibly removed from their homes and placed in America's concentration camps. Most of them were citizens of the United States, incarcerated by their own nation, the country of their birth. The Japanese Americans and their immigrant parents were discriminated against and were seen as a threat as they were finding some success in America. Pearl Harbor became the excuse to persecute an entire group of people and to lock them in camps in remote and desolate areas of the United States. Many stayed there for the duration of the war and then had to start over at the war's end. Executive Order 9066 was rescinded by President Gerald R. Ford in 1976.

Japanese Americans and our organization of the JACL worked for over ten years to get the government to apologize and to gain redress for those who were incarcerated during World

War II. The Constitution did not protect or defend its own citizens. A commission later determined that the evacuation and incarceration of Japanese Americans was due to racial bigotry, war hysteria, and a lack of competent political leadership at that time. These people were being discriminated against and treated unfairly simply for how they looked. One of the main purposes of the Redress Movement which finally provided an apology and reparations to Japanese Americans was to ensure that this type of thing should never happen again to any other people.

However, since the terrorists' actions of 9-11, we see innocent persons who may have appearances similar to the terrorists being routinely faced with racism and hate. They are persecuted simply because of their ethnicity or how they look instead of because of anything they did.

The senseless, tragic act which caused the death of Surinder Singh and the injuries to his friend, Gurmej Atwal, shows us that our work is not done. There are some around us who are full of hate for anyone who is not like them. There are those who will blame innocent persons based only on appearances. It is an excuse to show the hate they feel. There was no logical reason for Surinder Singh to pass from the world at this time. He was healthy and able to go for an afternoon walk with his friend on a regular basis. He was taken from this life through no fault of his own. He did not deserve this fate.

Today we continue to work for justice for all people. We, who remain and are saddened by this tragedy, must continue the efforts in which we are engaged. We need to be vigilant in order to try to ensure that this type of thing does not happen again. People should be able to feel safe enough in their own neighborhoods that they can take a walk without fear of harm.

May this unfortunate tragedy cause us to remain more steadfast in our quest for tolerance, understanding, and justice. The JACL extends its deepest sympathy to the family of Surinder Singh, to his friends, and to the entire community.

Thank you for allowing me to be here to share these thoughts at this sad and difficult time.

This tragic shooting occurred on March 4, 2011, when two Sikh gentlemen were mercilessly gunned down as they took an afternoon stroll in their neighborhood in Elk Grove, California, near Sacramento. Surindir Singh, 65, was fatally shot and died at the scene. His friend, Gurmej Atwal, 78, lived but died from his injuries on April 15, 2011. The two friends, who were immigrants from India, were merely taking a walk when they were shot at 4:25 p.m. by individuals in a passing vehicle.

The victims had beards and wore turbans. The incident was being investigated as a possible hate crime. Floyd Mori was asked to represent the JACL and give some remarks at the funeral of Surindir Singh on March 12, 2011. A candlelight vigil was held the night before the funeral at the scene of the shooting, and over five hundred people attended.

A Los Angeles Times Article about the incident and the funeral mentioned Floyd Mori, national executive director of the Japanese American Citizens League, speaking at Singh's funeral and said the JACL has noted similarities in the reactions to 9-11 and Pearl Harbor when groups of people were accused of being disloyal and unpatriotic simply because of their religion or their heritage.

THE DEVASTATING EARTHQUAKE AND TSUNAMI IN JAPAN

Speaking at a Press Conference
California State Capitol
Sacramento, California, Spring, 2011

Our hearts go out to the victims of the terrible disaster of a devastating earthquake and tsunami which struck Japan just last week. Many have lost family and friends in these tragic events. I have two sons who live in Tokyo. They and their families are safe, but we and they all feel for those affected most in the hard-hit areas.

We marvel at the resolve of the Japanese people to get through this, to help each other, and to plan to rebuild. Although Japan is possibly the best prepared nation for such a disaster, no one can be completely prepared for a calamity of this magnitude.

The Japanese American Citizens League (JACL), the organization which I represent here today, is the largest and oldest Asian American civil and human rights organization in the nation. We have over one hundred chapters in twenty-five states and actually have a Japan Chapter. Some of our members have friends and family members affected by this huge disaster which has struck.

The JACL has joined forces with Direct Relief International or DRI, a well established humanitarian organization, to form the Japan Relief and Recovery Fund. One hundred percent of the donations collected will go directly to the relief effort in Japan. DRI is a top rated relief organization with high efficiency. They have donated medical supplies when disasters have hit in various areas of the world.

The effort and involvement of the JACL will include helping to identify effective relief organizations in Japan where funds can be targeted and given. We know that these kinds of organizations which are locally based will have great pressures for resources, so we want to help those who are actually doing the work on the ground with the victims.

We are aware of many fundraising efforts within the Japanese American and broader Asian American communities across the nation as well as here locally and the concern of people around the world. We appreciate and commend all for their concern and their willingness to open their pocketbooks to help our friends and family in Japan.

Thank you.

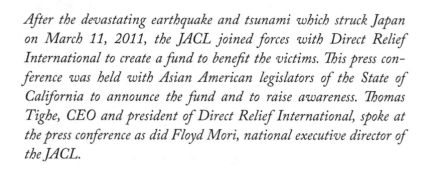

After the devastating earthquake and tsunami which struck Japan on March 11, 2011, the JACL joined forces with Direct Relief International to create a fund to benefit the victims. This press conference was held with Asian American legislators of the State of California to announce the fund and to raise awareness. Thomas Tighe, CEO and president of Direct Relief International, spoke at the press conference as did Floyd Mori, national executive director of the JACL.

JACL AND DIRECT RELIEF INTERNATIONAL PROVIDE FUNDS TO JAPANESE

Article Originally Written for
the JACL Membership
March 22, 2011

The Japanese American Citizens League (JACL) and Direct Relief International announced an initial cash transfer of $400,000 from its jointly established Japan Relief and Recovery Fund to Association for Aid and Relief Japan (AAR Japan), a thirty-one-year-old leading Japanese nonprofit, nongovernmental organization (NGO).

This support will replenish funds that AAR Japan has expended on extensive emergency relief operations and enable the organization to continue and expand its urgently needed emergency activities, which are focused on persons with disabilities and elderly persons affected by the earthquake, the resulting tsunami, and damage to a nuclear power plant.

AAR Japan responded immediately after the March 11 earthquake and tsunami by dispatching emergency teams and providing essential supplies. AAR Japan's relief efforts are being conducted with the approval from all local governments in the affected areas of Miyagi Prefecture. It includes support to twenty institutions, evacuation camps, and schools that have become temporary shelters for displaced residents.

This initial infusion of cash from the JACL-Direct Relief fund was made possible by thousands of individual donations and a $500,000 grant from Amgen. The amount is twenty-five percent of the $1.6 million in Japan-designated funds the organization has received since the March 11 earthquake.

In addition to the emergency cash grants, Direct Relief also has offered medical and personal care inventories available for immediate transport upon approval from the government of Japan, which has thus far requested private international aid groups to defer transporting material aid until needs can be identified and distribution channels cleared.

JACL's Japan Chapter members, including President John Ino, and Brent Mori, in cooperation with Professor Keiko Tanaka from Meiji Gakuin University, have been helpful in serving to advise and identify Japanese NGOs conducting response activities.

JACL National Executive Director Floyd Mori and Direct Relief's Chief Program Officer Brett Williams will be traveling to Japan to conduct additional assessments and meet with Japanese counterpart organizations.

"The intent with this initial donation is to provide immediate, direct assistance to people who suffered an enormous tragedy and are experiencing severe hardship in Japan," said Floyd Mori. *"Through the JACL network and close coordination with Direct Relief, we are very pleased that these resources will enable AAR Japan to continue its essential work in the affected areas. One of the critical issues to donors is that money donated will directly assist the stricken which this will do. We are grateful to all who have donated."*

Direct Relief CEO and President Thomas Tighe stated: *"We recognize that this emergency caused AAR Japan to tap whatever resources it had to respond fast, and this initial transfer of funds is intended to ensure that they are able to replenish funds and maintain urgently needed activities."*

In an article written by George Hadley-Garcia and special to the Japan Times in August 2011, Brad Pitt speaks about the earthquake and tsunami in Japan. He mentions Direct Relief International as a responsible and worthwhile organization which has been around since 1948. He said it is an outfit he feels comfortable about supporting. He also stated that Direct Relief works with the Japanese American Citizens League toward Japan's relief effort.

REMEMBERING OUR HERITAGE

Speech Given at a Veterans Administration (VA) Hospital
Veterans Administration Hospital Group
Washington, DC, May 23, 2011

Thank you for inviting me to speak to you today regarding heritage during this month of May, which is Asian American and Pacific Islander Heritage Month. Heritage means many things to different people, but we generally cannot consider heritage without thinking of our own parents and their influence on our lives. I will speak today primarily about the Japanese American experience in the United States and about my family. Remembering our heritage helps us to better understand and appreciate who we are.

The early immigrants from Japan were not the high upper class members of society. They were mainly men from poorer families who were looking for an opportunity to earn money and get to a better state in life. Japanese immigrants came to the United States in the late 1880s when federal legislation had excluded the further immigration from Chinese laborers who had come earlier. There was a demand for new immigrant workers, and railroads in particular recruited the immigrants for manual labor. Thousands of Japanese workers helped construct the railroads in the West as did Chinese immigrants. These people were also sought out as laborers for the sugar beet industry.

My parents both immigrated to the United States many, many years ago. My father came first as a young man in the early 1900s and years later went back to Japan to marry my mother. He brought her back to this country with the intent of returning to live in Japan one day. Although they had planned to save enough money and go back to Japan, that never happened. America became their home where they raised their family and where they were eventually buried. They became naturalized citizens of the United States later in life. My mother always thought she wanted to return to Japan to live. When they finally did visit Japan after their children were grown, she realized that America was home to her and her family. Her desire to live in Japan was gone.

My father was born and raised in the southernmost part of Japan in a place called Kagoshima. His family was suffering hard times with a father who was in ill health and his mother already having passed away. My father left his homeland in search of a way to earn money to help his family. He was still a teenager, and there were younger siblings. Like so many other Japanese immigrants, he came to America because this was the land of opportunity where riches were thought to be possible. He had enough money to get to Hawaii where he stayed and worked until he had saved money to come the rest of the way to the mainland of the United States. He arrived in San Francisco and was able to find work in a small restaurant as a cook. He worked hard and tried to save his money as much as possible on what would have been meager wages.

When an opportunity came to work on the railroad which meant earning more money, he jumped at the chance. It was hard work with other immigrant laborers, laying track across the desert of Nevada. They probably did not realize at the time that they were helping to build the transcontinental railroad which would bring the country together. His life was threatened when he was run over by a small rail car which was used by the workers. He suffered some physical damage, but he survived. He ended up going to Utah where he was allowed to buy a piece of property. He went to a small farm in Northern Utah and began raising sugar beets. There were some few other Japanese immigrants in that area at the time. They did not speak the English language and the customs were strange to them, but they worked hard.

After a number of years had passed, he had earned enough money to be able to return to Japan for a wife. He married my mother and brought her back to America. She planned to only come for a few years to this land strange to her before her husband would take her back to her homeland and her family. She must have been brave to leave her home at such a young age with a man she barely knew. It was a hard life, but eventually things got better.

They worked hard on the farm. They had single immigrant young men from Japan who came to work for them to help with the crops. It was not an easy life in unfamiliar and generally unfriendly surroundings. Although my mother had a good life in Japan, she now found herself working long and difficult hours. She had to cook meals to feed the help. It was under these conditions that they started their family.

My dad could not speak English, but he tried to learn. He studied the language and even attended some elementary school classes with children during the winter months when the farm work was reduced and he had more time. He was able to get by over the years with a small command of the English language.

As a hard worker who cared for others, my father gained a reputation as a kind and generous person. He tried to help newer immigrants after they arrived in America from Japan. He was good to his white American neighbors and shared his produce with them. It was not uncommon for him to give the best crops to the neighbors. He also sent money back to his own family and my mother's family in Japan. It is difficult to imagine how he could have managed as well as he did as he likely was never earning a lot of money throughout his lifetime.

All the family worked on the farm. I had my chores and did my share of the work in the fields over the years. The children learned from the example of our father and mother who were hard workers until their final days upon the earth. My father taught us by example to give our all. He challenged us to do better.

I was the next to youngest of eight children. There was a wide range in our ages so the oldest siblings were in high school when I was very young. Life must have been harder for them, but I can remember the challenges as well of living as a distinct minority in a white farming community. We tried to fit into the American society, but we regularly experienced prejudice and discrimination because we looked different and were from a family where our parents spoke little English and had strange customs.

By the time I was a young boy in elementary school in my rural area, World War II had ended. However, we as Japanese Americans were still seen by some people as the enemy. We were encouraged to become as much like mainstream America as we could. When I started school is when I was actually given an American name. My first name is Shiro, which means fourth son. My oldest sister, Meg, recently told me that my mother was the one who picked the name of Floyd for me although she always called me Shiro throughout her entire lifetime. The handicap that we had was the perception that we did not look American. To this day, Americans of Asian descent still regularly face that situation in the United States. We are sometimes looked at as perpetual foreigners even though our families may have been in this country for several generations.

Prejudice against Asian Americans remains a factor among some in our society even now. Today's recent Asian immigrants may face similar issues that the Chinese and Japanese faced in the 1920s and 1930s. The anti-immigrant sentiment today sounds remarkably similar to what the earliest Asian immigrants experienced when they were new to this country decades ago. While my father and people like him helped lay the infrastructure that allowed the industrial revolution of this country to take place, they were often seen after doing this work as taking jobs and business away from the people who were thought of as "real Americans." We see this same situation occurring today to the newer immigrants coming to the United States.

By profession I am an economist, and it is my belief that the American dream is born of immigrant dreams which are based upon the values one has from past generations. This is true no matter when the immigrants arrived on these shores. They came for different reasons, but this was a land of opportunity where their dreams had the possibility of fulfillment.

Family is foremost and of utmost importance for existence to most immigrants. This is generally true of those who came from Asian countries. Respect for parents is paramount. People are expected to give an honest day's work for an honest day's pay. They are loyal to their new country but proud of the heritage from which they came. Values are more important than status.

After my father's generation of immigrants had completed the main job of labor on the rails and the primary industries of extracting raw materials from the earth, American society did not have much use for them. Politicians responded by constructing legal barriers for new immigrants to come to this country and for those here to complete their American dream with their families. The government tried to curtail the growth and progress of the immigrants.

Many laws were passed against the immigrants. Asians were prevented from gaining citizenship. It was not until the 1950s when the Japanese American Citizens League or JACL, the organization which I represent today, worked to pass laws that allowed Asians such as my father to actually become citizens of the United States.

My mother was still barred from gaining citizenship until the 1970s because of her limited English ability. Yet she had spent most of her adult life here raising a family, two sons of whom served in the United States Army during World War II with one returning home in a casket.

Many people of Asian heritage were subjected to physical and social exclusion during the 1930s. World War II precipitated a new reason to discriminate. After Japan bombed Pearl Harbor, war hysteria allowed the government to do the unspeakable by denying people due process simply because of the color of their skin. Executive Order 9066 was signed by President Franklin D. Roosevelt. This allowed the forced evacuation of one hundred twenty thousand people of Japanese ancestry from the West Coast. The majority of them were United States citizens, the children and grandchildren of the immigrants. They were sent to American concentration camps located in remote and desolate areas of the country. They were given just a couple of weeks or less to settle their personal matters and were allowed to take with them only what they could carry to places unknown.

The Japanese immigrants were understandably nervous about what would happen to them, but they believed that their children were safe because they were citizens of this country. They thought that the government surely would protect its own citizens. Yet the rumors were rampant about the impending doom for Japanese Americans.

The shame and loss of dignity from being isolated from the rest of society and given a number to identify them have been carried by many until this day. The lack of privacy and terrible living conditions took a toll on individuals and on family life. Their health suffered. Their loss of freedom for several years had horrible effects on self-esteem and well-being.

The Japanese Americans and their immigrant parents felt they had no choice in the matter. Although there were some who protested the inhumanity and injustice of the acts against them, the entire community in the end had to go along with the wishes of the government. The Japanese Americans wanted to prove their loyalty so they did as they were ordered. The few who dared to test the orders or who disobeyed were arrested.

There were Japanese American young men who tried to enlist in the United States Army as soon as the war broke out. They were rejected because all Japanese Americans had been reclassified as enemy aliens or noncitizens, who were ineligible to serve. Eventually, through the efforts of the JACL and the government, a segregated military unit of Japanese Americans was formed. It was the 442nd Regimental Combat Team which was joined by Japanese American soldiers from Hawaii, the 100th Battalion. Those brave men desired to prove their loyalty to a country which had rejected them. They adopted the slogan of "Go for Broke," which had been used by the Hawaii group, and they became the most highly decorated unit of its size and length of service in the history of the US Army. They served in the European theater, and their casualties were immense.

Other Japanese Americans served in the military intelligence service and did their work in the Pacific theater. Former secretary of state, Colin Powell, has stated that thousands of lives were saved because of the work of these men in gathering intelligence and listening in on Japanese radio transmissions. These soldiers were also instrumental in the peaceful occupation of Japan after the war, playing an important liaison role between Japanese and American entities. There were some scattered individuals of Japanese ancestry who served in various non-segregated units of the military.

The Asian American community has come a long way. There has been much progress made. Japanese Americans credit much of their acceptance in society today to the work of the 442nd, the Japanese American soldiers who heroically served their country during times of extreme hatred, hostility, and discrimination against them, their families, and their friends.

There will always be a need for vigilance in defending the civil and human rights of all people. Although Asian Americans have much more acceptance in society today, there is still discrimination and prejudice which need to be faced and addressed. Our work will continue in trying to make this a better world for all.

As Asian Americans and Pacific Islander Americans, this month helps us to think about who we are and how important our heritage is. It is my hope that remembering our heritage will help us to better serve our fellowmen. We need to appreciate those who have gone before us and continue the fight they fought so valiantly.

The United States military is of great importance in our nation's history, and it remains valuable today. Thank you for your service to this great country. Thank you to all those of you who extend help to those in the armed forces who need medical assistance here at this facility. You are to be commended for your willingness to give of yourselves in order to benefit others. It has been an honor to spend this time with you today.

Thank you.

SEABROOK JACL CONTINUES ITS RICH HERITAGE

Article Originally Written for the JACL Membership
May 23, 2011

While my wife and I were attending a JACL Eastern District Council (EDC) meeting at Medford Leas, New Jersey, John Fuyuume, who is a former JACL Seabrook Chapter president, mentioned that the Seabrook Chapter would hold its *Keiro Kai* (an annual event to honor the senior citizens of the community) later that day. John was representing the chapter at the meeting since the chapter co-presidents, Sharon Yoshida and Lenore Wurtzel, were busy preparing for the event of which Linda Ono was chair. We had some free time after the EDC meeting finished in the afternoon, so we decided to drive to Seabrook, a few hours away to visit the JACL chapter there.

John made arrangements by phone for us to attend the Seabrook *Keiro Kai* event and gave us instructions for driving to Seabrook. It was an honor to be present and to meet the attendees. We were able to talk with former residents of the Poston, Gila River, and Topaz camps who had made their homes in Seabrook during and after the war.

The Seabrook Chapter of the JACL continues its rich heritage by holding the *Keiro Kai* each year, which it has been doing
for over sixty years. The dinner is held to honor the Japanese
Americans in the area who are sixty-five years and older. The
oldest male at this year's event was Hank Furushima, and the oldest female was Mitsuko Omura. They take a group photo of the
attendees each year and have photos going back to the late 1940s.

During World War II when the Japanese Americans were
removed from their West Coast homes, they were incarcerated
in ten camps built in remote and desolate areas of the country.
Some people were given the opportunity to leave the camps
before the war ended if they were accepted into colleges or found
work in areas away from the West Coast. This involved mostly
young adults and some families.

Seabrook is a small town in a farming district of Upper
Deerfield Township in southern New Jersey. Charles F. Seabrook
and his sons ran a frozen food business with 20,000 acres under
cultivation. Near the end of World War II when they were faced
with a labor shortage because of the war, they recruited Japanese
American people from the camps along with other displaced persons to become crop pickers and workers for their food process-
ing plants. In 1944 and 1945, about 2,500 people of Japanese
descent received permission to leave the camps and migrate to
Seabrook to work. Many stayed after the war ended as most people found it difficult financially to relocate back to California,
Oregon, and Washington.

The Japanese Americans in Seabrook adapted well to the
surrounding culture and area while maintaining their traditions
and heritage. A museum begun by Japanese American residents
in 1994, the Seabrook Educational and Cultural Center, helps
preserve their identity and provides a platform for telling the
Japanese American story. The museum is staffed by volunteers
and was directed for many years by John Fuyuume, who grew
up in Pasadena, California, where his parents grew vegetables

and had a family grocery store. Forced from their Pasadena home in the evacuation of Japanese Americans from the West Coast after the start of World War II, his family was incarcerated in 1942 at Gila River, Arizona, where they stayed until relocating to Seabrook in 1944.

John with his wife Setsuko, whose family also lived in Seabrook, moved to Philadelphia from Seabrook a few years ago to a retirement area where they joined Setsuko's sisters and brother-in-law, Eiko and Bunji Ikeda, Chizujo Sakata, and Miyoko Wong. They all drove to Seabrook to attend the *Keiro Kai* event.

The *Keiro Kai* is held at the Seabrook Buddhist Temple, which was founded in 1945 by the Japanese people who came out of the camps. Entertainment was provided by the *Minyo* (folk) Dancers and the *Hoh Daiko* Drummers *taiko* group. The Minyo dance group began in 1975 under the direction of Sunkie Oye. They were formed as part of a cultural presentation by members of the Seabrook Japanese American community at the 1975 Smithsonian Festival of American Folklife. The *taiko* group in Seabrook began in 1991.

Most of these residents of Japanese descent or their parents were incarcerated in the American concentration camps before relocating to Seabrook for work during World War II. Most who stayed liked the community and continued to make it their home after the war ended in 1945. Although they may not have had other options at the time, Seabrook has become their home.

COLUMBIA UNIVERSITY CANDLELIGHT VIGIL

Speech Given After Japan Disaster
For Victims of the Earthquake
and Tsunami in Japan
Columbia University
New York, New York, April 6, 2011

It is a pleasure for me to be here tonight to share this time with you in a candlelight vigil for the victims of the devastating earthquake and tsunami in Japan. I am representing the Japanese American Citizens League (JACL), the oldest and largest Asian American civil and human rights organization in the nation. The JACL was established in 1929 by young Americans of Japanese ancestry to fight the bigotry, prejudice, and discrimination faced by them and their immigrant parents. It was an era when Asian Americans faced extreme racism that was aimed specifically toward them only because of their ethnicity. The West Coast treated Asians probably not much better than African Americans were treated in the South at that period of time. They were rebuffed or ignored.

The JACL is an American organization that was formed under the laws of the United States. During World War II, we went out of our way to make sure that the nation understood that we were really American. But even with that said, we continue to have close ties to Japan through family and friends. Heritage is an important part of who we are. So when something terrible happens in Japan, it is happening to friends and family of the JACL and regardless of our citizenship, our hearts are there for the people of Japan at this difficult time. The entire world has shown support for Japan in this recent disaster.

While preparing to leave for the airport for a trip from Washington, DC to California early in the morning on March 11, almost a month ago, I heard the horrible news of the terrible earthquake and tsunami in Japan. Earthquakes occur in Japan fairly frequently, but they generally do little or no real damage because the country is basically prepared for them. This was different. It was an earthquake of great magnitude followed by a tsunami which caused massive destruction. Most of their preparations for a disaster were in vain.

As I have two sons who reside in Tokyo along with their families, and I have many other relatives, friends, and business associates living in Japan, it was immediate cause for concern. We did not hear from one of our sons until a day later because of his travel away from home, but all my family members were safe. The JACL has a chapter in Japan, and those members appeared to be safe as well. We do have close personal friends who were doing church missionary work in the area hardest hit by the tsunami. It took a while for them to get word out that they were okay although they experienced hardship and trials from the tsunami. They were greatly involved in some of the relief efforts. There was great devastation and much suffering in some parts of Japan.

After I arrived in California on that fateful Friday, I was busy on the phone with the JACL staff, the Japan Embassy in Washington, DC, and staff from the White House. We worked with the White House to prepare for a conference call to Japanese American community leaders as they knew that there were many close relationships in Japan. The conference call took place that afternoon. There were many offers to help. People throughout the world were anxious to do what they could to help Japan with the disastrous results of the earthquake and tsunami. We were overwhelmed with the immediate outpouring of care and support. Members and friends of the JACL were asking what they could do to help.

A close personal friend of mine in Virginia, John Tagami, who is also a friend of the president, Thomas Tighe, of Direct Relief International which is based in Santa Barbara, California, contacted me with a proposal that the JACL partner with that organization. Direct Relief is a privately funded humanitarian organization which was established in 1948 and which has decades of experience in emergency response and humanitarian assistance worldwide. After doing some due diligence, we found Direct Relief to be one of the premier disaster relief organizations in the world.

It was not a difficult decision for the JACL to join into a partnership with Direct Relief International to support relief and recovery efforts for this huge crisis in Japan. We set up The Direct Relief/JACL Japan Relief and Recovery Fund. This fund will use one hundred percent of donations received directly toward assistance for the victims in Japan.

This partnership of the JACL with Direct Relief came about because of the large number of inquiries to the JACL from concerned members, coalition partners, associates, and friends who were anxious to help in a meaningful way and who wanted to join with the JACL in doing so. Although we had initially suggested on the morning of the disaster that our members donate through another organization, the JACL felt a partnership with Direct Relief was a better way for us to become more directly involved and to help.

The donations which come in to The Japan Relief and Recovery Fund will support the immediate health and human needs of people by working with local emergency relief groups who are culturally sensitive and who are friends and neighbors to those who have lost family, friends, and homes in this disaster. These local groups are the ones which respond first because they are part of the community. However, being small and not used to this kind of catastrophe, they may quickly burn through any inventory of goods and cash that they have on hand. These are the ones that we feel do the most good, but on the other hand they need financial assistance the quickest. These are the kind of local NGO (non-governmental organization) groups that our effort intends to help.

The response has been gratifying and impressive. Direct Relief is a good partner for the JACL as it has been doing this kind of work for a very long time, and it has built relationships with businesses and groups which immediately came forward with meaningful donations and some very large contributions. Their experience with disaster relief has been invaluable.

Members and corporate partners of the JACL also quickly made contributions. The JACL has over one hundred chapters throughout the United States with a chapter in Japan, which is positioned to maintain a closer relationship to the work that is progressing on the ground in Japan. Our relationship with corporations and foundations plus the basic grassroots nature of the JACL gives the partnership a broader width and community thrust in doing the right thing. One of our corporate partners, UPS, phoned on the first day and offered a $50,000 grant to use as we see fit towards the relief effort. Just yesterday, a prominent foundation offered an anonymous $50,000 grant to the fund. Today I received notification that a middle school in Maryland will be having a carwash to raise funds to contribute to the cause. The spirit of giving and wanting to lend a helping hand has been overwhelming. As of today, the fund has received over $3.5 million, which does include some of Direct Relief's large donors who regularly give when a disaster strikes.

There are a number of NBA players who have joined in this effort at raising relief funds. Some of these professional basketball players paid $1,000 per point which they scored over a particular weekend. Others pledged a set amount.

Last week I was able to travel to Japan along with Brett Williams, Direct Relief's director of international programs and emergency response, to see the affected area firsthand. We did not travel to the very hardest-hit areas, but we witnessed large evidence of the devastation. Here we were able to speak to some of the victims and heard many stories of heartbreak and uprooted lives.

One young, newly married woman with whom I was able to speak told of how they had just moved into their first new home. Now the house was unlivable and would have to be completely destroyed. She was distraught and worried about how her mental state would be in the long term.

A young man told the story of how he and his mother were on their way up the stairs to the second floor of their home to escape the tsunami when his mother heard the cries of her sister outside. She had come to their house to escape the tsunami, but the earthquake had jammed the front door and she was feverishly trying to open the door. The mother rushed downstairs to help open the door, but it continued to stay stuck. The son yelled from the second floor for his mother to hurry and come upstairs because he could see the oncoming wave of water. The mother did not heed his pleas and continued to struggle with the door. The wave hit, and both women lost their lives.

These stories can be told over and over hundreds or thousands of times. It is heart wrenching, but people were helpless at the time. The force was too great to withstand.

I try to think of the most severe natural disaster I have had to face. Although I have experienced some rather mild earthquakes, I think the worst natural disaster problem was the winter of 1948. We lived in what was farmland near Salt Lake City, Utah, and the severe winter weather caused drifts of snow to reach over ten feet high. We could not get out of the yard and had to stay home. School was cancelled. To a nine-year-old boy these drifts became a winter wonderland without having to go to school, but for others it was a difficult time. It was many days before the plows could make it through all of the country roads to free the people to get back to school and work. We were fortunate that we had warm homes and enough fuel and food. This small problem of nature can in no way compare to the devastation that has taken place in Japan with this recent earthquake and tsunami disaster.

The main purpose of our going to Japan was to evaluate the effectiveness of our community NGO groups who were helping with the relief effort. We met with several and have decided that at least four with whom we met deserve to have additional funding which we are able to provide to carry on their good works. These nonprofit groups are much like the JACL. They rely on donations to keep up their work. In stressful times, their resources are often taxed to the limit. We were able to distribute $400,000 to an NGO that has done heroic work in providing emergency goods such as fuel, tons of food, blankets, sleeping bags, and other supplies directly to victims. They will begin to provide a mobile medical unit with the grant which was given to them from our fund.

In times of stress it is interesting to see how communities react. At the start of World War II Japanese Americans were sent to illegal, detention centers and camps without any due process. They faced physical and mental stress that many humans could not endure. Yet they weathered that storm of injustice and came back to their communities to play important roles in the social movements of the 1950s and 1960s. They have become stalwart leaders in their communities and have even risen to become elected officials in Congress and advisors to Presidents and a cabinet member in two Administrations.

During the relief efforts after Katrina, the Asian American community along the Gulf Coast became virtually invisible to relief agencies, both private and governmental. Weeks after the disaster when many others did not want to return to the Gulf Coast, the Vietnamese came back and rebuilt their communities largely without any help from government or relief agencies. Within a few short months, eighty percent of the community had returned to rebuild and to restore while more than half of the other communities stayed away.

There is something in the basic values of the Asian culture that puts self-dignity and self-reliance high on the list. We have been through much hardship, and we know how to handle hardship. Thus, I trust that the Japanese people affected by this recent disaster will continue that tradition. They began that self-help immediately. I spoke to many people in Tokyo who are planning to take time off work to go to the disaster area to do their part in helping. Children are raising money for the cause. Yet with all of this, much help will be needed from outside of Japan. This is our role.

Many have suffered. Many have perished or have loved ones that have died. They need to feel the spirit of giving and the knowledge that somebody will be there to help. The healing and rebuilding will take years to be completed. There are scars that will remain for a very long time. They not only need our prayers, but they are in need of our substance.

This is the time of cherry blossoms in many parts of the world. In Washington, DC this past weekend, the blossoms were at their height. Trees that have struggled through a hard winter and many hard seasons of cold always bounce back and show a beautiful bloom each spring. Even the magnificent blooms of two days ago have partially fallen because of a heavy rain yesterday. But we know that next year the blooms will be back in all their glory.

It is not coincidence that the cherry blossoms are so symbolic to Japan. Like the cherry blossoms on the trees in Washington, DC, which were a gift from Japan to the United States, I fully expect that the Japanese people will be back in full bloom and productivity in the next spring of their lives. While they have been beaten down by the powers of nature, their spirit is strong and their will to bloom is as a cherry tree. Yet in order to bloom, the cherry tree needs the warmth of the sun. For the people of Japan to bloom again, they will need the warmth and the spirit of caring and support from good people like you.

Thank you for your generosity and concern for the people of Japan. Thank you for being here tonight to show that you care.

May God continue to bless the people of Japan with renewed life and hope and may God bless America.

LESSONS FROM HISTORY: 9066 TO 9-11

Speaking to Participants of the
JACL Collegiate Leadership Conference
Washington, DC, June 11, 2011

The Japanese American experiences of World War II are worthy of being told over and over again in order to assure that the travesty and injustice which occurred against the Japanese Americans will not happen again to any other person in this land of the free. As remote as that possibility may seem to most people, there have recently been suggestions made by certain individuals to round up innocent people and take away their freedoms as was done to those of Japanese heritage who were living on the West Coast after the start of the Second World War. Educating the general public is important to ensure that such treatment is never inflicted upon citizens of this country again.

The Japanese American story is not well known. In fact, we were made aware not long ago of an experience by a high school student in the Midwest when the class was given an assignment to write a paper about an event which happened in history. The girl who is part Japanese by heritage chose to write about the evacuation and incarceration of Japanese Americans (including her grandparents) during World War II. The teacher gave her a poor grade, stating that this could not have happened in the United States and that the girl had made it up.

It seems that little about this period and experience is written in the history books although the Japanese American Citizens League (JACL) and others have tried for years to get the story included and taught in high school US history classes. The JACL has a curriculum guide and conducts teacher workshops, so that educators will have the proper information to teach this part of history. Still, many people have never heard of the Japanese American mass incarceration of one hundred twenty thousand persons which occurred after President Franklin D. Roosevelt signed Executive Order 9066.

After the Imperial Navy of Japan bombed Pearl Harbor in Hawaii on December 7, 1941, life immediately changed for Japanese Americans. It was a Sunday, and people were attending church or social activities with family and friends. Some women who were at that time young girls spoke of having been at the movies when the announcement was made that Japan had bombed Pearl Harbor. They had never heard of Pearl Harbor, but they had a foreboding feeling as they immediately started for home. They were full of fear and apprehension. In the days that followed, the children generally kept attending school. There was some harassment, but it seems that most people did not suffer physical harm. Some teachers admonished their students to be kind to their Japanese American classmates because they were not at fault in this matter. Fathers went to work as long as they could. Rumors began to fly, and people were scared of what might happen.

Lt. Gen. John L. DeWitt of the Western Defense Command is said to have at first opposed a wholesale evacuation of the people of Japanese heritage and had suggested that only individuals that were considered to be disloyal be taken. He later recommended to President Franklin D. Roosevelt that all the Japanese people from the coastal regions of California, Oregon, and

Washington should be forcibly removed from their homes and incarcerated. Against the advice of some few leaders, President Roosevelt agreed and issued Executive Order 9066 on February 19, 1942. This order gave authority to the military commander to remove any people from a designated area. Although Executive Order 9066 could have been used against Germans and Italians as well, it was only executed by the Western Defense Command against the people of Japanese descent and was clearly discriminatory and racist.

Gen. Walter Short, commander of the United States Army's Hawaii Department, had declared martial law. He was ordered back to Washington, DC after the surprise attack on Pearl Harbor by Japan. He was reduced in rank from Lieutenant General, which was a temporary rank, to Major General. General Short was replaced in Hawaii by Lt. Gen. Delos Emmons on December 17, 1941.

Contract laborers had arrived in Hawaii from Japan starting in 1868. By 1940 three fourths of the ethnic Japanese in Hawaii had been born there and were citizens. There were nearly 158,000 persons of Japanese ancestry living in Hawaii, and they were more than thirty-five percent of the population of the territory. Less than two thousand were taken into custody, which represented one percent of those people. General Emmons resisted the order to relocate the Japanese American population. He stated that those who were deemed to be suspected of fifth column activities were already gathered up, and he felt that the rest of the Japanese Americans posed no threat.

Executive Order 9066 was put into effect to force persons of Japanese ancestry living on the West Coast of the mainland United States to be removed from their homes and incarcerated in camps which were hastily constructed in remote areas of the United States where the living conditions were brutal in harsh weather and far from comfortable. The majority of these people were American citizens, the children and grandchildren of immigrants from Japan with whom they were imprisoned behind barbed wire compounds with armed guards facing inward.

Because Asians have similar facial features and to avoid receiving the same treatment being showered upon the Japanese Americans, some Chinese people wore badges which said, "I am Chinese."

Immediately on that fateful day and soon after December 7, 1941, leaders and business owners within the Japanese community, which included Japanese Americans, were sought out by the FBI and arrested. They were taken from their homes and placed in jails or prison. Sometimes the families did not know where they were for weeks or months. Apparently, the government had been researching the leaders in the community for some time, which resulted in its quick action. These included people who were officers in Japanese organizations or Japanese American groups, prominent businessmen, store owners, teachers, and church ministers or Buddhist priests. Men in suits banged on their doors and took them from their homes.

The reasons for the incarceration, as stated by a commission many years later, were: wartime hysteria, racial prejudice, and the lack of competent political leadership. It was stated at the time of the war that it was being done for their protection and due to military necessity because all people of Japanese descent were suspected of being spies for Japan. The government went to great expense to build all the barracks, mess halls, and other buildings for the ten camps and further expense to staff the camps which imprisoned the people of Japanese descent.

The Japanese immigrants had begun to see some financial success and progress in the United States by the time the war broke out. Many had farms, small businesses, or other jobs at which they worked very hard. Although they were not allowed to own land in California, some had purchased property in the names of their adult children who were American citizens by birth. They had established successful business enterprises. They had married, were having children, and appeared to be making a home in this country. A good number of the children of the immigrants were college students or even college graduates when the war started. They were trying to make their way in the American society. Prejudice and discrimination against these and other Asian Americans and immigrants had been rampant. It was escalated against Japanese Americans at the beginning of World War II.

The people of Japanese ancestry who were directly affected by Executive Order 9066 lost almost everything they owned. Those who went to the camps were required to prepare themselves with very little notice and could take only what they were able to carry. Most were required to start over with next to nothing when they were released after the war ended. Many found that their furniture and personal possessions which had been stored had been stolen or were ruined during their incarceration.

At the JACL biennial convention held in Chicago in 1970, the JACL passed a resolution calling for recognition of, and reparations for, the injustices suffered by Japanese Americans by the incarceration which occurred during World War II. It seems to have been the original idea of Edison Uno, an activist leader in the Japanese American community for whom a JACL civil rights award is named. He wrote: *"Time has healed some of the old wounds, but the scars are not visible, they are there in the deep recesses of that psychological corner of our minds."* There was some success such as having Executive Order 9066 rescinded in 1976 by President Gerald R. Ford. I had the privilege of attending that signing at the White House. I was honored to know Edison Uno personally and thought him to be a great man who was taken from this life much too early. He passed away in 1976.

At the 1978 National Convention of the JACL which was held in Salt Lake City, Utah, the national council which is made up of delegates from the various JACL chapters approved a resolution to earnestly seek redress and monetary reparations for the wrongs committed against Japanese Americans during World War II. Some leaders within the JACL had been working for years on the issue, but they had been largely unsuccessful up to that time in making much progress in the efforts to seek redress.

The issue was not without controversy. There was contention in the ranks as some people wanted to leave well enough alone. The Japanese Americans had seen a degree of acceptance and success after the war, largely as a result of the bravery and patriotism of the 442nd Regimental Combat Team/100th Battalion, which was a segregated unit of the United States Army. They became the most highly decorated unit in the history of the US military for its size and length of service. They sustained many casualties and death which resulted in numerous Purple Heart awards being earned and presented.

Some delegates at the convention did not want to rock the boat and bring up the painful past. However, the resolution passed, and the campaign for redress was continued with increased effort. A federal investigative commission was approved by Congress. President Jimmy Carter signed the bill to form the Commission on Wartime Relocation and Internment of Civilians (CWRIC) to investigate the circumstances surrounding the incarceration of Japanese Americans and to provide a report to Congress and the President.

Japanese Americans and others testified before the CWRIC. I had the privilege of testifying for redress at the hearing held in San Francisco, not as one formerly incarcerated but as a public official supporting the issue since I was a California State Assemblyman. People who had been incarcerated started to talk of those experiences which they had kept suppressed for so many years. Some very vocal people inside and outside of the Japanese American community opposed redress and were also given the opportunity to speak at the hearings. One of the strongest opponents was a white woman. A Japanese American United States Senator by the name of S. I. Hayakawa, who had been born in

Canada, strongly opposed redress seemingly mainly because of asking for monetary reparations.

The CWRIC issued a report in 1982 which stated that the government's actions against the Japanese Americans had been unjustified and unconstitutional. The CWRIC determined that the forced evacuation and incarceration were *"...the result of 'race prejudice, war hysteria, and a failure of political leadership.'"*

It took more than a decade of hard work and dedication which finally resulted in the passage by Congress of the Civil Liberties Act of 1988 (The Redress Bill). This called for an apology including a letter from the President of the United States and a payment of $20,000 to be made to all the people of Japanese descent who had been removed from their homes on the West Coast who were still living by a specified date. It was a token payment compared to what people lost, but it was felt that the monetary sum would help to prevent a recurrence of the injustice against anyone else. The Civil Liberties Act of 1988 was signed by President Ronald Reagan forty-six years after the 1942 evacuation and incarceration.

Many of the JACL chapters throughout the country hold Day of Remembrance events on or near the anniversary of Executive Order 9066, February 19 of each year. This is a time to remember the past and educate others about the painful experiences of Japanese Americans during World War II. These occasions are used to teach the JACL members and others in the various communities throughout the United States about the Constitution and civil rights. It is important that young people learn of these events in order to ensure that they do not happen again. The Day of Remembrance events are open to the public.

Asian Americans have long felt the sting of prejudice and racism. The early Chinese and Japanese immigrants faced many difficulties and much discrimination because they were seen as being different. Vietnamese refugees were relocated to the United States in large numbers in the 1970s and 1980s. I was serving in the California State Assembly at that time when refugee camps were set up at Camp Pendleton. I was able, in an official capacity, to visit and welcome these new residents to the United States. They endured hardship, but they were enterprising and ambitious. They worked hard, and many have found success in their new home just as the earlier Japanese and Chinese immigrants eventually did. Other immigrants to the United States, such as those from South Asian and the Middle East, have faced similar experiences.

My wife and I made a trip to Japan in September of 2001 during which time I was attending and participating on a program with Prime Minister Junichiro Koizumi and former vice president of the United States Dan Quayle to celebrate the fiftieth anniversary of The Treaty of Peace with Japan which was signed on September 8, 1951, in San Francisco. I had been invited to represent Japanese Americans in my capacity of national president of the JACL. We returned home to Utah on September 10, 2001. The next morning I awoke early and was driving to a golf tournament with the radio on in the car. I heard reports about something terrible happening in New York City. The totally unbelievable acts of terrorism horrified the nation and the world. I immediately called my wife and told her that she should turn on the television. Our son, who was living in Japan, called about reports he heard of America being at war. That was 9–11.

There are parallels between the happenings in the aftermath of Executive Order 9066 and 9–11.

Unfortunately, after 9–11 the mistakes of the past which adversely affected Japanese Americans were in danger of being repeated against innocent American Muslims, Sikhs, people from India, and other citizens and immigrants who might have physical resemblances to the suspected terrorists. The Patriot Act was used, and racial profiling became apparent immediately. Innocent American men who wore turbans or had facial hair were suspected or accused of being terrorists. The government rounded up and arrested a number of these men for minor problems. Some were imprisoned or deported. Sometimes their families did not even know where they had been taken. It was surprisingly similar to what happened to the people of Japanese ancestry during World War II although it was not such a whole-sale roundup as was done to Japanese Americans.

The secretary of transportation under President George W. Bush at that time was the Honorable Norman Y. Mineta, a Japanese American who had been incarcerated with his family at the Heart Mountain Camp in Wyoming during World War II when he was a young boy. His family had been forcibly removed from their home in San Jose, California. Secretary Mineta was immediately seen on television admonishing people not to react adversely against the innocent Americans who were falsely being associated with the terrorists. He mentioned the Japanese American experience when innocent people were rounded up for no fault of their own and stripped of their freedoms simply for how they looked.

As stated, I was the national president of the JACL at the time of 9–11. We made sure that the JACL put out a press release immediately after the attacks to caution against reacting adversely to innocent Americans such as was done to Japanese Americans during World War II. Our community faced that discrimination and prejudice firsthand. We knew what could happen when the country panics at the thought of war. We did not want to see a repeat of the injustice which was done against innocent Japanese Americans. Our community had experienced the worst and did not want that to happen to any other loyal Americans who had done no wrong.

Yet fear and hysteria took over in the minds of many Americans immediately after 9–11. Innocent people were targeted with acts of racism being perpetrated against them. We must be ever watchful to assure that the horrible wrongs committed during World War II against Japanese Americans, through no fault of their own and only because of their ethnic heritage, are not repeated against any other people. Unfortunately, the danger of that happening still exists.

It takes like-minded people to fight against bigotry. We must be willing to take a stand against the discrimination and racism which can result when emotions run high against certain groups of people because of the acts of others. People should not be mistreated simply because of their physical appearance or heritage.

Our constitutional rights must be maintained, and we need to do our part to ensure that the Constitution is upheld for all citizens. Executive Order 9066 was a terrible mistake, and we must not allow it to happen again.

This presentation was made by Floyd Mori to participants of the Collegiate Leadership Conference held in Washington, DC by the JACL in 2011. It was the Japanese American portion of the panel to present the experiences of the Japanese American incarceration and the 9–11 experience. The 9–11 portion of the panel was presented by Jasjit Singh, CEO of the Sikh American Legal Defense and Education Fund (SALDEF).

The four Japanese American Democratic members of Congress who worked hard for Redress were Robert Matsui and Norman Mineta who were serving in the US House of Representatives from California and Daniel Inouye and Spark Matsunaga who were US Senators from Hawaii.

S. I. Hayakawa was a Japanese American born in Canada who was a Republican US Senator from California who served from 1977-1983. He was not in favor of the Redress Movement.

ETSU MASAOKA MEMORIAL SERVICES

Speaking at Funeral Services
Chevy Chase, Maryland, June 14, 2011

It is an honor for me to represent the Japanese American Citizens League (JACL) in paying tribute to a grand lady who is going to be greatly missed. I might mention that David Kawamoto, National JACL president, and his wife Carol are here as well as is David Ushio, who was personally acquainted with Etsu and her husband Mike when David and his family were living in the Washington, DC area. David Ushio now lives in Hawaii and is also a past National executive director of the JACL.

There are certain names that are immediately associated with something significant to our memories. The Mineta name, Etsu's maiden name, means a lot to me as Etsu's brother Norman Mineta was a role model and an inspiration for me to do something for a community that gave so much to me. The name Inouye, that of our Honorable Sen. Dan Inouye, who is speaking here today, means a lot to any of us who ever thought of having a chance of serving in public office.

For the JACL, the name Masaoka congers up a feeling of respect and gratitude for a lifetime of service in building the foundation of the organization of the JACL today. Like many institutions, the JACL has been left with a legacy of great men and women who embodied the values of greatness, who used the power of words effectively, and who also maintained a lifetime of perseverance on a focus in behalf of civil and human rights. Mike Masaoka, Etsu's husband, is a legend in the JACL.

But the reason so many of us are here today is that we recognize that all of these attributes were lifted higher by the work and support of a loving and loyal spouse. It is hard to say that Etsu stood in the background and quietly supported Mike. She was part and parcel of all the good that Mike did. Her personal support was evident from the time she became Mike's bride in 1943 until her passing from this life just this past week.

Etsu looked forward to attending the National JACL Conventions. I have attended most of the conventions since the 1970s and remember seeing Etsu always there with Mike until his passing, and then with her granddaughter Michelle and her son-in-law Richard. She had her early bird registration purchased for our upcoming JACL convention which is being held in California this July. According to her granddaughter, Michelle, Etsu was looking forward to being in Hollywood. She will be missed at the National JACL functions which she attended regularly, even after Mike's passing. Her presence was expected and appreciated.

But it wasn't only large and visible national events which Etsu attended. She was always there at the local JACL DC Chapter picnics, luncheons, installations, and other events. The night she passed, Etsu was planning her wardrobe for the chapter summer picnic that Saturday. She was always proper and exemplified the values of good grooming and proper upbringing. At the same time, she had a sparkle in her eye and was always ready for a good joke or comment that brought a smile to your face. She often supported other Asian American events and organizations as well as the JACL and the Japanese American Veterans Association.

Etsu showed great support for the National JACL Gala dinner which has been held for the past four years in Washington,

DC. We were very happy that we were able to honor Etsu at last year's Gala as we saluted champions among women. She has been a true champion and one of the best supporters of the JACL. She gave a wonderful talk at the Gala and seemed pleased with the recognition. She was an outstanding woman. The other women honored at that Gala were the Honorable Sen. Dianne Feinstein (D-CA) for her efforts to help the Japanese American community, Christine Toy Johnson (actress, singer, author, and playwright who produced the DVD on Wat Misaka), and Roxana Saberi (an American journalist and author of Iranian and Japanese descent who was held captive in Iran). Etsu stood tall and fit right in with these other exemplary women.

Young and old alike, we can all learn something from the life of Etsu Mineta Masaoka. Live life to the fullest each day. Life is much more meaningful when we include service to others. Help others to smile and feel good about themselves. Support good causes. These are all things which Etsu did. She always looked like the picture of perfection, and she was a loving person.

I strongly believe that relationships last beyond the grave, so Etsu has joined Mike in whatever work he is presently engaged. She is helping and encouraging him in all he is doing, and she is doing her part to help others. They must be so happy to be reunited.

We express our deep condolences to Michelle, Richard, Norm, Deni, and the rest of the family for the loss of Etsu in their day to day lives. At the same time, we celebrate the life that gave us all good memories and experiences that will live with us forever. Thank you to the family for allowing me to share these thoughts and to represent her many friends in the JACL.

It was a privilege to know Etsu. She was a wonderful example to all of us, a good friend, and someone who will be dearly missed.

Etsu Mineta Masaoka, wife of Mike Masaoka and older sister of Norman Y. Mineta, passed away at the age of ninety-five at her home in Maryland. The funeral service was held at the Chevy Chase United Methodist Church on June 14, 2011. Speakers included Sen. Daniel Inouye, Former secretary of transportation Norman Mineta, JACL National Executive Director Floyd Mori, and JAVA Executive Director Terry Shima.

JAPANESE AMERICANS TODAY

Speech Given to an NEA Group
National Education Association
(NEA) Conference
Chicago, Illinois, July 2011

Thank you for inviting me to participate with you at this important NEA event. It is a pleasure for me to be here in Chicago to tell you a little about the Japanese American history, about Japanese Americans today, and the Japanese American Citizens League (JACL), the organization which I represent.

The JACL was formed in 1929 by young leaders within the Japanese American community. These were the second generation. They were the children born in the United States of Japanese immigrant parents. Some were college graduates by this time, but they and their parents faced great hardship because of the prejudice against them. They felt that they needed a national organization to combat the laws which were clearly aimed at keeping them and other Asian Americans in a subservient state and curtailing their success.

As the oldest and largest Asian American civil and human rights organization in the nation, the JACL was established with the mission to secure and uphold the civil rights of Americans of Japanese ancestry, to preserve the cultural heritage and values of Japanese Americans, and to combat social injustice against all people. Today the JACL continues to operate with the same mission and an emphasis on civil rights.

There is a long history of discrimination against Japanese and other Asian immigrants. When the Japanese and Chinese immigrants arrived in the United States in search of opportunity and financial gain, they were not entirely welcomed even though America was seeking laborers. It was a strange culture and a different way of life than that to which they were accustomed. They had a different religion, they ate different food, and they did not speak the English language. There were anti-Asian and anti-immigrant sentiments, and they were made fun of for their looks, language, food, and dress. It could not have been easy, but they were determined. They felt that America was the land of opportunity, so they were willing to work hard to find the things they desired from life in this new land.

Asians came to the United States as cheap labor. They worked on the railroad laying track across the desert of Nevada, which helped to bring the country together. They worked in mining, in the fields, and in other manual labor. When it was felt that they had done their job, they were rejected. Further immigration from Japan was curtailed in 1924. It was wholesale racism.

We know of the legendary feud between the Hatfields and the McCoys in "hillbilly" lore. It was probably similar to the differences and the feelings that the Asians experienced when they came to this country. It was not easy to get along well. The Asians pretty much kept to themselves and their own people. They were seldom included or invited to participate in mainstream American culture. Life was not ideal, and it could be extremely difficult. Yet these early Asian immigrants endured the trials and persevered. They kept their dream alive.

When we think of certain people having to withstand prejudice, discrimination, and racism, the Japanese American community can say that they have "been there and done that." They have experienced these things firsthand along with a clear denial of their constitutional rights which should have been guaranteed to them by the Constitution.

During World War II right after Japan bombed Pearl Harbor, all people of Japanese ancestry were immediately looked upon as the enemy, which was shameful and hurtful to them. They were shunned and despised. Then the unthinkable happened. President Franklin D. Roosevelt signed Executive Order 9066 on February 19, 1942, which gave authorization to the military commander to remove people from a designated area. It was unquestionably aimed at only those of Japanese heritage although it could have been used against others.

The government forced the people of Japanese descent who were living on the West Coast of the mainland United States to leave their homes with little notice and be incarcerated in barbed wire compounds with armed guards. The majority were citizens of this country. Their freedoms were taken away, and most lost virtually everything they had for which they had worked hard for years. This action was later determined by a commission of distinguished Americans to have been the result of the racism and war hysteria which were prevalent at the time along with incompetent political leadership.

World War II was an excuse to show more discrimination and increased hatred toward people of Japanese heritage. They were taken away under armed guard. They were isolated from the outside world. They were subjected to terrible living conditions. Their race became shameful. Even those Japanese Americans who did not go to the camps suffered.

Although some people were able to leave the camps during the war if they found work in other inland areas or went to college, most lived in the camps for the duration of the war. When they were released at the war's end, some tried to return to their old life. A few had friends who had cared for their property and belongings, so they were able to return to them. Others found that their stored items were stolen or completely destroyed. The former internees had little money and few options. Yet they did what they needed to do to start life anew in whatever way they could.

Japanese Americans, many from the younger generation, later worked on redress for this wrongful act during World War II. The Japanese Americans had proven their loyalty even though they were locked up in the camps. They had served with distinction in a segregated unit of the United States Army and other branches of the service. It was a long, hard battle to achieve redress, but the government finally apologized to those who were forcibly evacuated from their homes on the West Coast. They received a letter of apology from the President of the United States and some monetary reparations.

Japanese Americans are better off today largely due to the service of the brave soldiers of the 442nd Regimental Combat Team/100th Battalion, the segregated unit of Japanese Americans, which gained fame during World War II. Many of these young men came out of the American concentration camps to serve their nation. It has been said by some that their patriotism and dedication actually helped usher in the civil rights movement. They proved their loyalty and served a nation which had greatly persecuted them and their families. President Harry S. Truman desegregated the army after the end of World War II.

The Japanese American population generally has done quite well since World War II. They have assimilated into the white society to a large degree, and some have achieved outstanding financial success. They have embraced the mainstream values, and many have attained their fair share of material goods. Some have risen to a very high stature in public and private arenas. There have been and are now United States senators and members of the House of Representatives who are Japanese American as well as some in the Cabinets of Presidents of the United States.

The civil rights struggle brought to the forefront many of the rights which had been denied to Asian Americans. Some remedies occurred, but there was sometimes a denial of heritage and shame of being who we were. Being looked upon as the model minority meant assimilation and acceptance into the white society. Yet everyone is not in that mold. We may have become over assimilated with acculturation causing us to become disinterested in the traditions and culture of our forebears. Many have forgotten their roots in the struggle.

There is a broader identification today as Asian Americans and Pacific Islanders instead of simply as Japanese American or Chinese American or another separate ethnicity. There are many issues which are affecting our communities today. The glass ceilings in the corporate world still exist. Medical care often does not consider the differences which Asians may face, which can cause health disparities. Environmental justice does not consider them. There are hate crimes being committed against them, which include violence and bullying.

Asian Americans always seem to be the *invisible* minority. The model minority myth is held in many circles. Japanese Americans have been considered the model minority. People think Asians are doing so well that they need no help. Many people are blind to the disparity issues.

Many newer Asian immigrants are going through similar experiences today as the early Japanese and Chinese immigrants did decades ago. Undocumented immigrants are told that they are not welcome and to go back home. Indeed, some Asian Americans whose families have been in this country for generations are sometimes told to go back where they came from as well. I have had that experience as have many others, young and old, who are ethnic Asian even though we were born and raised in America. Our race causes some to look at us as perpetual foreigners. There are still anti-immigrant attitudes by many in our society. We see anti-Chinese, anti-Korean, and anti-Muslim attitudes manifested almost daily in the media or public arenas.

Japanese Americans today are in a relatively good place with high achievements having been attained in some areas. They do not face the same kind of prejudice and racism which they did in the past, but those types of behavior sometimes rear their ugly heads even now. There will always be work to do to make this a better world for all people.

The JACL and Japanese Americans feel that telling our story is important in order to avoid a repeat of the injustice experienced by those of Japanese ancestry during World War II. We hope that educators in the schools of this nation will teach about this period in history when the Constitution did not protect innocent citizens.

Education is a high priority among Asian Americans, and education has always been stressed by the Japanese immigrant parents. Education is the key to improving our society. Educators have always been an important part of my life. I was the seventh of eight children of Japanese immigrant parents who spoke little English. Most of my older siblings moved away after the end of the war. Teachers were the ones who reinforced my value structure. They helped me gain enlightenment and self identity. Teachers can give children the encouragement and hope that they need to succeed in this world.

My first job out of college was teaching Economics at a community college in the Bay Area of California. I taught there for ten years, and I had fully intended to be a teacher for the rest of my life. My life has taken many turns since that time, but I always loved teaching.

I am grateful for the work of the NEA and for all of you. Teaching is a noble profession where you have great influence on bright, young minds. Education will continue to be extremely important in the lives of all people.

Thank you for allowing me to be here with you today, and thank you for the good work that you do in the field of education.

NATIONAL EXECUTIVE DIRECTOR'S REPORT

Speaking at Convention Opening Session
National JACL Convention
Hollywood, California, July 8, 2011

In recent weeks, people have congratulated me for retiring and have wondered what I'm going to do with all my time. Be assured that it's really not the real word, retiring. I'll still be very much involved. I expect to be at the next JACL convention in Seattle in July 2012, in one capacity or another. I made the announcement in February of this year that I will be stepping down, but I will stay around until a replacement has been found.

One of the things I want to do that I haven't been doing is spend a little bit more time with my grandkids, which I did this past weekend. We went to see the movie *Rio*. How many have seen *Rio*? It was a great story. It's about two little cockatoos. One of the cockatoos was raised in a home in North Dakota and never got outside and really never spread its wings or learned how to fly.

Somehow, the story goes, this blue cockatoo made its way down to Rio where cockatoos are native. Through certain experiences he had and certain pressures and crises that happened in this cockatoo's life and also with a great deal of passion that he found in the love of a female blue cockatoo, this cockatoo learned how to fly. He soared, and he was able to live a very happy and productive life as cartoons go.

I think one way to tell the story is that it's a little bit like the JACL. We are somewhat like the blue cockatoo. In our past environment, we thrived and we did very well like the cockatoo did in his home in North Dakota. But there are things that we were not required to do and didn't have to do. As a result, some of our talents or our muscles have atrophied a little bit, and we are not flying as we were meant to fly.

As we all know, going from North Dakota to Rio is a very major change in environment. Going from 1929 to 1940 to the 1950s and through the 1990s and into this new millennium is a very major change in environment for the JACL. We are not the same bird that we used to be. We are not in the same environment in which we used to thrive. There are things that we did not have to do in the past that we are going to be required to do in the future if we are going to be that true blue cockatoo that we are meant to be, and to soar, and to fly, and be successful and productive in the future.

We have looked at, probably, the major change within the Japanese American community as the demographics change. We are going to hear about this tomorrow in our convention, but there are many, many changes in our demographics, in our organization. I recall ten years ago when I was national president of this organization, we spoke of the average age of a JACLer or how many JACLers were above the age of sixty-five or seventy. Today, those who were seventy-five years old and older back then are either eighty-five or ninety-five or they are not with us any longer. Now we are bearing the problem of declining membership because of this attrition of our faithful *Nisei* (second generation American) members who have been loyal and committed to the JACL. Just for my curiosity, I would like all those here who are under fifty to stand. Under fifty. Now, remain standing.

Those that are under forty, remain standing. I think you get the picture. Thank you.

If we had done that ten or fifteen or twenty years ago, it would have probably been just the opposite. We have changed in terms of who we are, and there is a change in our age and in our interests. Priorities change. We look at the family structure of today compared to what it was forty or fifty years ago, and it is different. Where we live is very different. In California, there used to be over forty Japantowns once upon a time. Three remain in the major cities although some remnants of former Japantowns are still seen in some areas.

So what does that mean in a lot of the areas where our parents and your grandparents grew up and were raised? They were driving up JACL chapters. They are no longer there within the urban cities. Where have our *Sansei* and *Yonsei* (third and fourth generations) found places to live? They are in the suburbs, farther and farther away from the centers of our cities.

So in order to survive an outbreak, you have to understand some of these changes that have occurred. It is not that they are going to occur. They have occurred. I think that we may be like the blue cockatoo who still thinks he is at home in North Dakota and is not willing to really spread his wings. We need to explore the new things that need to be done to make our organization successful.

So we, I think, are at the stage where we have the minds and the will to move the JACL forward. I hope we have the passion to make some improvements upon our organization and begin to exercise some wings that we have not exercised for decades.

Technology is upon us, as we all know. Unfortunately, I think we operate in old technology as an organization in many ways. I think we need to take advantage of this technology from chapters within the JACL and adopt and use this technology to broaden who we are.

And who are we? We are the JACL. *We are the JACL.* Most people know us as the JACL, not as the Japanese American Citizens League. As we have announced, we have a new chapter in the Gulf Coast that will be primarily of non-Japanese heritage members. They are going to be people who do not have the same ancestry that traditionally has been in the JACL. As you look around you and we look around ourselves, in our communities, we are involved as Asian Americans much more that we are involved as Americans of Japanese ancestry. I think we need to understand that reality.

We are Asian Americans in Asian American communities and a country where the general population looks at us as one body and cannot distinguish between those whose heritage is Cambodian, Vietnamese, Chinese, Korean, or Japanese.

So that is one entity. I think if we look at our new, young demographic of college students within the JACL, this is how they behave and this is how they operate. They operate as Asian Americans. So I think in our chapters, as we look at our communities, our membership needs to broaden because, as the census tells us, our Japanese American community is getting smaller and smaller. That being the case, the JACL will continue to get smaller unless we reach out to others and include them.

The reality is that the JACL is a major national civil rights organization. I don't think we understand sometimes the significance that the JACL holds in the civil rights community of this country. We get tied up in some of our chapter issues, some of our local matters and our summer picnics and so on, but our talent and our abilities to impact the national civil rights community are very huge. We have that capacity, and there is really no other Asian American organization in this nation with as much influence.

You know, I have dealt now in Washington, DC on many matters for the JACL and the Asian American and civil rights community. I know some of you did not want me to remain back there five or six years ago when I became the national executive director after having been director of public policy for the JACL for a short period. However, I have found that it has been of great value to this country—to this organization—to have the JACL's presence there strongly with the national executive director based mainly in the nation's capital. People, including leaders of other civil rights and Asian American organizations, look to the JACL for many things as an example of what the Asian American community ought to be.

So as we look to the future, I think we need to awaken those muscles within us and to show that we are a major civil rights organization, that we can have an impact not only on the nation, but within our communities as we work with other organizations, and we bring in others to broaden our membership to many more different people.

As you know, one of our most successful programs in recent years has been *bridging communities* where we have brought American Muslim young people together with our JACL youth members and created a program that has been the envy of a lot of people. What it has done has helped us as an organization to develop a lot of credibility, a lot of trust not only in the American Muslim community, but in other communities that see the good work that we are doing. These young people learn about each other and about the challenges that each faces. They learn how to work together for a common good.

I could go on about the things that the JACL is doing. I hope you will stop and ask me or ask the other staff members or ask those who have been involved in the programs to find out what we are doing. Sometimes I feel that we don't know, as JACL members, all the things that we are involved in as a national organization.

But as we deliberate here in this convention, it is important that we go through the process that we do. We are a great democratic, fair organization, and we should make decisions in a very democratic way. At the same time, let's not get caught up in some of the minutia of process. Let's look at the content and the substance of the things that we discuss and rise to the level of those issues that are important to us as a community without placing so much importance as a structural organization, but on issues that affect us as human beings.

Let us be the organization that our founders expected us to be. I know that we can do that. We have the talents, and if we don't have those talents, we need to bring in some of those talents from elsewhere.

One of the things that I think we need to look at in the future is this whole governance process, and I think our president has alluded to that. We have good people that govern us in chapters and on our national board. We need to expand that goodness into skills and abilities that are needed to upgrade in this new atmosphere, this new environment that we find our organization in today. We are out there with the big boys, and we have to do as they do if we are going to compete.

So let's spread our wings. Let us show our passion. Let us express our talents and, if we are short on talents, let us reach out and find those and bring those in who have the type of talents that we need to have a very successful organization.

I look forward to many more years of involvement with the JACL. I'm not going to be there 24/7 any more after I retire, but I am going to be there. I am going to do what I can to make sure that we have a future and that your grandkids have an organization in the year 2020 and 2030 and 2050 of which we, as great grandparents, are going to be very proud.

Thank you very much.

Floyd Mori announced to the JACL staff in February of 2011 with an official announcement press release in April of 2011 that he would be retiring from the position of national executive director of the JACL when a replacement could be hired. This was his last Report in that position which he presented to the National Council of the JACL at their annual convention. He left the post on June 1, 2012, and became national executive director emeritus of the JACL.

LANA CONFERENCE KEYNOTE

Speech Given for LANA
Laotian American National Alliance
Alexandria, Virginia, August 5, 2011

It is a pleasure for me to be here with you today at your annual conference. I am grateful to have been able to work closely with Sirch Chanthyasack, your CEO, on issues of importance to the Asian American community. We commend you for the progress you have made since the launching in 1999 of the Laotian American National Alliance (LANA) to support Laotian peoples. It is also my pleasure to work closely with Doua Thor, the current executive director of the Southeast Asia Resource Action Center (SEARAC), which we are aware was instrumental in offering assistance to your organization as you were starting out.

There is an ongoing need to train youth within the Asian American community, and you are doing that. It is gratifying to see so many young people in attendance here today. This second annual conference of LANA is dedicated to you, and you are being encouraged to go out there and make a difference. Ordinary people with extraordinary hearts can make changes occur. I applaud your theme, *"Today's Youth, Tomorrow's Leaders: Unite, Educate, Advocate!"*

Although the immigrants from Laos are relatively newcomers to this land as compared to the early immigrants from Japan, the experiences and history are not that different. Life may be easier in many respects without quite the racism and prejudice which existed in the early 1900s when many Japanese young men were arriving in America, but some of the same challenges remain.

About 105 years ago, my father immigrated from the southern part of Japan to the United States to escape the poverty which was facing his family. He felt that he needed to try his hand in America which was thought to be the land of opportunity just as it is for many newer immigrants today. Life was not promising for my father's family in Japan so he sailed across the Pacific Ocean to seek his riches. When he arrived on the mainland of the United States, he did basic labor work such as washing dishes in a restaurant. Then he was able to secure work laying track for the railroad across the desert of Nevada. The money was much better, and it seemed that his dreams might find fulfillment. Although he was injured while working for the railroad, he had been able to save up some money so he moved to Utah where he was able to begin a life as a farmer. My father had no English language skills and little formal education. He tried to learn some basic English by attending an elementary school class during the winter months.

The earliest Asian immigrants to the United States faced all forms of discrimination. There were a lot of anti-Asian laws. There were legislative, administrative, and institutional barriers holding them back from full rights. Even their American-born children who were citizens of this land found that they experienced various forms of prejudice everyday. In 1929, a number of local Japanese organizations banded together to address the problems their people were facing. Thus, the Japanese American Citizens League (JACL) was born, and today it is the oldest and largest Asian American civil and human rights organization in this nation.

There were citizenship issues. Immigrants from Asia were not allowed to become naturalized citizens of this country. Marriage was unlawful between an Asian and a white person. Asians were not allowed to purchase and own land in many areas. There were many forms of segregation against the Asians similar to those against African American people. Further immigration from Japan had been halted in the mid-1920s.

World War II brought increased hysteria and hatred which amplified racism against those of Japanese ancestry living in America, who were immediately looked upon as the enemy after Japan bombed Pearl Harbor in the US territory of Hawaii. Almost three months after the bombing on December 7, 1941, President Franklin D. Roosevelt signed Executive Order 9066, which allowed the military to exclude any people from a certain area. Although the order could have been used against Germans and Italians as well, it was clearly a racist measure as it forced all the Japanese immigrants and Japanese Americans who were living on the West Coast to be removed from their homes to be incarcerated in camps surrounded by barbed wire with armed guards to watch the prisoners.

My family lived in Utah at the time of the war so we were not removed from our home. The government had tried to get people to leave the West Coast voluntarily, so those who had relatives and friends inland who would sign for them and help them could leave to avoid the camps. We had relatives who came and lived by and with us after the war began. They talked about camp, and to me as a small child, it sounded like it might be fun to go to camp. I did not learn until many years later what those camps really were and the pain and suffering they caused. When the war ended, our relatives moved back to California to resume their lives there.

The JACL worked hard to try and get Japanese Americans to be looked upon as patriotic Americans, which they actually were. With the help of JACL leaders, a segregated unit of Japanese Americans was created within the United States Army. The 442nd Regimental Combat Team/100th Battalion was made up largely of Japanese Americans from the camps and from Hawaii.

They served in the European theater and became the most highly decorated unit for its size and length of service in the United States military history. There were at the time also segregated units of African Americans and Native Americans. After the war ended, President Harry S. Truman recognized and praised the Japanese Americans who served in the military. He also desegregated the military.

Japanese Americans found some time after the end of World War II that their lives were improving somewhat. Although many of those in the camps lost everything and had to start anew with almost nothing, their lives began to change. Leaders within the JACL continued to work to reverse the discriminatory laws against Asian Americans. The Japanese immigrants were able to become naturalized citizens in the 1950s. Other laws were slowly being repealed to allow the Japanese Americans and the immigrants to experience a better life. The attitude against Asian Americans improved measurably in many areas. The Japanese American veterans were credited with much of this changed reaction to and acceptance of the people of Japanese ancestry.

During the 1960s, there was a real awakening of civil rights. People were starting to figure out that the manner in which some people were treated was not right. There were movements to get equal rights for all.

It became understood that the incarceration of Japanese Americans during World War II was one of the worst injustices in the history of this country. There were no constitutional protections or rights given to the Japanese Americans during that difficult period. In the 1970s the JACL, although it was a small organization, began a campaign to ask the government for redress. There were discussions with the four Japanese American members of Congress. One of the first organizations to support the JACL was the American Jewish Committee which began a coalition of civil rights organizations which expressed support of the effort. The Redress Movement was begun by the JACL in

1970, but it did not make much progress until it was decided at a National JACL Convention in 1978 to earnestly seek redress with some monetary reparations.

In 1976, President Gerald R. Ford rescinded Executive Order 9066 which had caused one hundred twenty thousand people to be uprooted from their homes on the West Coast. The JACL and other Japanese American groups and individuals worked very hard for over ten years on the Redress Movement. This resulted in the passage of the Civil Liberties Act of 1988 (The Redress Bill), which allowed Congress to provide reparations and a Presidential apology for those who were incarcerated who were still living. The purpose of redress was to ensure that such a travesty of justice would never happen to any other people. The innocent Japanese Americans were not protected by the Constitution of the United States, and the government finally apologized.

The cycle has come around. Unfortunately, today we see a lot of anti-immigrant hysteria. Access and equality are questioned. Families are being kept apart. Acts of aggression and discrimination still exist.

We need to tell the Japanese American story of World War II. The story is being repeated in some cases as other people are being treated poorly. Forgotten exploits need refreshing. Your stories need to be told. As Asian American organizations, we need to collaborate. We need to speak up. We need cooperation and communication among our groups.

Japanese Americans are now in their fifth and sixth generation in the United States of America. We have come a long way, but there is still much work to do. The basic general society puts all Asians together as one group. We are often looked at as perpetual foreigners even though we may have a long history in the United States. We need to work together and help each other.

There is strength in youth who have a commitment to help the community and who have values which have been instilled within them to make this a better world. As we look to the future of LANA, we can expect big things from this organization. The challenge is certainly here, but we can strengthen commitment and right the wrongs of the past. There is still a lot to learn and a lot of work to do.

We hope you will each play a significant role in helping LANA to grow and continue the good work you are doing. We congratulate LANA for your efforts and pledge the help of the JACL if we can be of assistance to you. We look forward to continuing our relationship with you.

Thank you for allowing me to be here with you today and to share my thoughts.

TIME FOR CHANGES

Article Originally Written for
the JACL Membership
September 11, 2010

When I became heavily involved in the workings of nonprofit organizations and government by beginning work on the staff of the JACL in Washington, DC five years ago as the director of public policy, I saw that there were reasons to make some changes in the JACL. This is an important organization which was formed in 1929 by young leaders within the Japanese American community. The JACL has a long history, but we needed to grow with the times. After I became National Executive Director of the JACL a little over a year later, I proposed modifications whereby we would become "The New JACL." We have since added several programs, and some changes have been made. Change is often difficult and unwelcome. It is resisted by many. Hence, some of the proposals were rejected.

Several programs have been added which primarily involve youth within our community. The Project Community Program teaches students about their heritage and culture by focusing on the Japantowns which were an important part of our history with some few still in existence today. The Bridging Communities Program has brought young people within the Japanese American and the American Muslim communities together to learn of their respective history and similarities. These programs help students to get along well together. Leadership Conferences are being held on college campuses and in Washington, DC for college age young adults in addition to the JACL/OCA DC Leadership Conference which has been in existence for many years. Youth are vital to our future, and we are trying to nurture them to become leaders.

One of the suggestions I proposed which met with opposition was to keep our name as the JACL but to change the official name from the Japanese American Citizens League to something which would be more all inclusive. It was felt that this could help us better reach out to other communities and make more people feel welcome in our ranks. There are people who will not join the JACL because they think the name implies that one must of Japanese heritage to belong although our national board regularly consists of people who are not ethnically Japanese.

Membership should be encouraged to anyone who shares our views and interests. The JACL membership numbers have been dwindling or even rapidly decreasing for years. Something needs to be done to build up membership. Stronger recruiting among the Japanese American and the non-Japanese American populations may be essential in order to sustain the JACL into the future.

Although there are a great many potential JACL members among Japanese Americans, many have never heard of the JACL or are not interested in joining. It has not been easy to convince large numbers of the children and grandchildren of former JACL leaders to become members. By the same token, our new younger members have difficulty trying to interest their parents in becoming members. If just a small fraction of the great number of Japanese Americans who are not JACL members would join, we could easily quadruple our membership rolls. Some signs of progress are evident, but we have a long way to go to fulfill the dreams of our early JACL leaders and to help this organization grow.

Since the JACL has had little luck in significantly increasing membership through trying to appeal mainly to Japanese Americans, it could be beneficial to reach out more aggressively to those who are not of our same ethnic background. We could help them as they help the organization. Our programs could be useful to them. The friendships which could be developed would be valuable. A number of our strong JACL leaders are not Japanese Americans, and they make substantial contributions to the JACL. We should be reaching out to others and inviting more people to join our organization.

Leaders within the Asian American community have been attempting to be of assistance to the Vietnamese and other Asian Americans who were adversely affected by Katrina and now by the BP oil spill. We find that these newer immigrants are facing many of the same trials and challenges which the early Japanese immigrants faced eighty or ninety years ago. The main reason that the JACL was organized in 1929 was to fight the discrimination and racism that the Japanese Americans and their parents had to endure on a daily basis. These groups of newer immigrants could benefit by joining a national organization. They may be in need of advocacy, support, friends, and even a way to obtain health insurance, things which the JACL should be able to provide.

The tragic events of 9-11 which happened nine years ago have resulted in various attacks, both physical and verbal, against American Muslims, Arabs, Sikhs, and others. This treatment continues and shows that racism and prejudice still exist toward people who look different from what most consider the mainstream. Our physical characteristics, as Japanese Americans and Asian Americans, cause many people to look at us as perpetual foreigners. Recent European immigrants who do not have a command of the English language are regularly looked upon as being American more so than Japanese Americans whose families have been in the United States for several generations.

This was brought home to the JACL recently as we were asking for a member of a United States senator's staff to represent the senator at a function because the senator could not attend. The staff member who contacted the JACL office seemed pleased that they were willing to send the legislative assistant in charge of *foreign affairs* to attend in the senator's place, as if they thought that was most appropriate even though the JACL is an American organization which should have been known to that senator's office staff.

The JACL has been around for over eighty years. Many of our parents and grandparents came to this country more than a hundred years ago. The JACL has had its own headquarters building in San Francisco since the 1970s. Our greatest membership base is in California, and we have chapters scattered throughout the country. Yet because of our name, Japanese American Citizens League, and perhaps the way we look, people still assume that we are more foreign than American.

There has been some strong opposition to changing the JACL's name, and we suggested always keeping the acronym of JACL. We would continue to be known as the JACL. There are options which would need to be discussed and reviewed before a change would ever be implemented. If it happened, it then might be necessary to explain that the JACL *was* the Japanese American Citizens League just as OCA National (formerly the Organization of Chinese Americans) does. It may be time to consider a name change although it might never happen because of resistance from some members. More important than a change in our name, however, may be a change in our attitude.

Although we are and will remain interested in preserving our Japanese heritage, we are, after all, Americans first and foremost. We have an affinity for things Japanese, but our allegiance is to America. Japanese Americans proved their loyalty to the United States of America during World War II when they faced extreme trials as citizens of this country. Even when the Constitution did not protect them, they proved their loyalty by serving our country with distinction. There were never any cases of espionage by Japanese Americans. That patriotism continues today.

Civil rights will continue to be a major force of the JACL. That is unlikely to change because discrimination still exists even with all the progress that has been achieved. It has been my privilege and honor to work closely with leaders within the civil rights and Asian American community, such as Rosie Abriam, Jeff Caballero, Sirch Chanthyasack, Christine Chen, Matt Finucane, Richard Foltin, Lisa Hasegawa, Tom Hayashi, Wade Henderson, Neil Horikoshi, Paul Igasaki, Stuart Ishimaru, Deepa Iyer, Deeana Jang, Charles Kamasaki, Kathy Ko, Daphne Kwok, Michael Lieberman, Michael Lin, Kristine Minami, Mee Moua, Karen Narasaki, Bob Sakaniwa, Hilary Shelton, Jasjit Singh, John Tateishi, Doua Thor, Dr. Ho Tran, Craig Uchida, Amado Uno, George Wu, and many others.

Japanese Americans have a long history in the United States. We have been through a lot of hardship along with some great success. The future looks bright for the JACL, but we must be willing to do what it takes to continue to succeed as a vibrant and useful organization. There is still a lot of work to be done. Change may be necessary.

Change is often resisted and unwelcome. Another change suggested by Floyd Mori along with Jason Chang, who was the Vice President of Planning and Development on the National Board of the JACL, which met with opposition was to provide a monthly payment option for collecting membership dues and donations. It was considered to be an effective way to bring in additional funds to the organization. Certain factions argued against the proposal so it did not win approval of the National Council at a JACL convention. Now it seems that most similar organizations use this method of receiving dues and donations.

INCARCERATION SPECTER RAISES UGLY HEAD IN A FORGETFUL US SENATE

Article Special to the San Jose Mercury News
November 27, 2011

The oldest generation of Japanese Americans, those who have memories of their lives and families being upended by incarceration without charge or trial in American concentration camps during World War II, at least take comfort in the hope that America is now committed to never inflicting that experience on any other group of Americans or immigrants. But our trust in that commitment is being shaken by a bill poised to go to the Senate floor that could once again authorize indefinite detention without charge of American citizens and others now living peacefully in our country.

We have reason to believe in the commitment of Americans to say *never again* to indefinite detention. In 1988, the Civil Liberties Act officially declared that the Japanese American incarceration had been a *"grave injustice"* that had been *"carried out without adequate security reasons."* In other words, the indefinite detention of Japanese Americans during World War II was not only wrong, but unnecessary.

A bill on the Senate floor raises the question of whether the Senate has forgotten our history. S. 1253, the National Defense Authorization Act (NDAA), unfortunately, has a provision in it drafted by Sens. Carl Levin (D-MI) and John McCain, (R-AZ), that would let any United States President use the military to arrest and imprison without charge or trial anyone suspected of having any relationship with a terrorist organization. Although Sen. Dianne Feinstein (D-CA) and more than a dozen of her colleagues are bravely calling for a halt to a damaging bill, they face significant opposition.

The troubling provision, Section 1031, would let the military lock up both Americans and noncitizens in the fifty states. There would be no charges, no trial, no proof beyond a reasonable doubt. All that would be required would be suspicion.

Although the details of the indefinite detentions of Japanese Americans during World War II and the proposed indefinite detentions of terrorism suspects may differ, the principle remains the same: Indefinite detentions based on fear driven and unlawfully substantiated national security grounds, where individuals are neither duly charged nor fairly tried, violate the essence of US law and the most fundamental values upon which this country was built.

As the measures to indefinitely detain Japanese Americans during World War II have been deemed a colossal wrong, the same should be true of modern indefinite detention of terrorism suspects without justification. Our criminal justice system is more than equipped to ensure justice and security in terrorism cases. We certainly should not design new systems to resurrect and codify tragic and illegitimate policies of the past.

As our history shows, acting on fear in these situations can lead to unnecessary and unfruitful sacrifices of the most basic of American values. In the ten years since the 9-11 attacks, Congress has shown admirable restraint in not enacting indefinite detention without charge or trial legislation. Now with the President seeking to end the current wars, the Senate must avoid repeating the mistakes of the past and protect American values before they are compromised. We cannot let fear overshadow our commitment to our most basic American values.

The Senate can show that it has not forgotten the lessons of the Japanese American incarceration. It should pass an amendment that has been offered by Sen. Mark Udall (D-CO) that would remove Section 1031 from the act. This Senate should not stain that great body by bringing to the floor any detention provision that would surely be looked upon with shame and regret by future generations.

PEARL HARBOR AND FALSE ACCUSATIONS OF HOMEGROWN TERRORISM

Article printed in The Hill, Washington, DC
December 7, 2011

Today, the House and Senate Homeland Security Committees are holding a joint hearing on homegrown terrorism on quite an auspicious date. The hearing, titled "Homegrown Terrorism: The Threat to Military Communities inside the United States," falls on the anniversary of the Pearl Harbor attacks.

Some seventy years ago today, nearly 2,500 Americans were killed in a surprise attack by the Japanese Imperial Navy on the US naval base at Pearl Harbor. The next day, Japanese American husbands and fathers were taken from their homes, under FBI escort, to federal detention centers. A few short months later, all Japanese Americans on the West Coast were sent to camps, most for the duration of the entirety of World War II.

They were citizens held as prisoners and charged with no crime. Driving their detention was the US government's fear of homegrown terrorism and its doubt of the loyalties and beliefs of the community—of Japanese American citizens—based on nothing more than race and religion.

The ramifications of this incarceration were enormous. Many in the community lost their homes and businesses and the ability to provide for their families. It took years, in some instances, for families to be reunited. The end result was immeasurable heartache and problems within our families that lingered for decades.

The forced evacuation and incarceration of Japanese Americans is one of the most shameful chapters in our country's history. Two decades ago, the nation apologized for the grave injustice that was based on war hysteria, racism, and poor political leadership and not justified by concerns about security.

At the National Japanese American Memorial to Patriotism, these words are carved in stone: *"The lessons learned must remain as a grave reminder of what we must not allow to happen again to any group."*

I fear we have forgotten the lessons of that time.

Today's hearing purports to look at homegrown terrorism. But in reality, it will call the loyalties and beliefs of one community of Americans into question—based on nothing more than race and religion. It is just like what occurred seventy years ago.

This very hearing is causing the harm it is intended to stop. By focusing exclusively on one group—Muslims—as the source for homegrown terrorism, we are threatening American communities. We perpetuate the discrimination and alienation experienced by American Muslims. We invite more and more harassment and hate crimes. We provide excuses for biased law enforcement practices. And above all, we harm the American values of equality, diversity, and religious freedom.

The effects of this harm are already visible all around us. Unfounded animosity and threats toward American Muslims are on the rise. A Brookings Institute poll found that 47 percent of Americans view Islam as at odds with American values. Workplace discrimination against Muslim individuals has increased 150 percent, doubling over the past ten years, and there has been an increase in bullying against American Muslim children. The FBI has used its outreach to the Muslim community as a way to gather intelligence. This discomfort toward Muslims is being fueled by anti-Muslim rhetoric spread by military, religious, and political leaders, which creates a fertile climate for discrimination.

Today is the seventieth anniversary of the *"date which will live in infamy,"* a date infamous not only for the lives that were lost, but also for the grave injustices that followed for the Japanese American community. To see that, today, our government is unfairly targeting yet another community based only on race and religion is troubling and thoroughly disheartening.

We cannot and should not let hysteria, racism, and poor political leadership take us down the same path we went down seventy years ago. We must not act in ways that sacrifice our most basic American values. We must not single out one community based on race or religion and deny them their civil rights. And we must not endanger the foundations of these communities—their families and houses of worship.

Floyd Mori was the national executive director of the Japanese American Citizens League (JACL), the oldest and largest Asian American civil rights organization in the United States. This article was prepared in conjunction with the American Muslim community.

SENATE STAFF BRIEFING ON NDAA

Speaking at a Briefing
National Defense Authorization Act (NDAA)
Washington, DC, February 2012

Good morning. My name is Floyd Mori, and I am the national executive director of the Japanese American Citizens League (JACL). As individuals and as an organization, we have had a great deal of experience with *Indefinite Detention.*

The JACL is the oldest and largest Asian American Pacific Islander (AAPI) social justice organization in the nation, having been formed in 1929. This was a time of extreme bigotry against Asian Americans. Further immigration from their homeland was not allowed. Ownership of land was prohibited in many states. Bi-racial marriage was outlawed. Naturalization was not an option for my parents, who had immigrated here in the early 1900s to raise a family of eight children, two of whom were called into military service during World War II. Anti-immigrant sentiment was strong as well as negative attitudes towards those so called *"Non-Christian heathens from the Orient."*

The bombing of Pearl Harbor by Japan only aggravated those anti-Asian sentiments. The happenings of 1942 are well documented where some one hundred twenty thousand people of Japanese descent, most of whom were United States citizens, were made to experience mass *Indefinite Detention*. They were uprooted from their West Coast homes, work, businesses, and farms. They were literally herded into temporary detention centers, one of which will be dedicated at the Fresno Fairgrounds this coming weekend as a memorial to what should not happen again. From there, they were shipped by rail to concentration camps located in extreme desolate places throughout the country. *Out of sight, out of mind*. Most Americans today are not aware that this actually happened in this country, a nation where the rule of law is paramount.

This action divided families, literally and philosophically. Communities were divided on how to respond. Some said, "We have to cooperate in order to show our loyalty."

Others went in protest, many of whom spent years behind prison bars for questioning this breach of constitutional rights. The *shame* of it all lasted for decades to where, even today, there are survivors who will not or cannot talk about the experience because it is too painful. This is seventy years later.

Many lost their sense of self-esteem and never fully recovered. A great example is my own father-in-law, who in 1941 had a thriving fruit and vegetable market in Hollywood only to lose everything. He was never again able to regain the economic status his family enjoyed before the war. While he was a good man who farmed and raised five children after that, he was never the same because of the evacuation. Life was difficult.

Then there were the years after the war when that generation was told to "Be American." We forgot our ethnic heritage but still faced lingering racial issues. This generation has had a hard time trying to determine who they really are.

The JACL grew during this time and established a Washington, DC office where we fought to undo many of the discriminatory laws that had been passed before the war. We were strong supporters of the Non-Detention Act of 1971, which was championed by Sen. Daniel Inouye (D-HI).

It states, *"No citizen shall be imprisoned or otherwise detained by the United States except pursuant to an Act of Congress."* Congress and the President said at that time that they would never repeat what happened during World War II to the Japanese Americans and *would not* subject any other American to indefinite detention without charge or trial.

To date, Congress had made no exception. It would be a major step backward if this Act were to be rendered meaningless by the provisions imbedded in the NDAA which is now before Congress.

In 1978, the JACL decided that it was time to seriously advocate for redress and an apology for the wrongdoings of the government during World War II against Japanese Americans, who were forcibly removed from their West Coast homes. The first step was to create a commission of distinguished Americans to hold hearings to study the matter. The findings of the commission were clear. The indefinite detention of Japanese Americans during World War II was unjustified and happened because of three reasons: war hysteria, racism, and failed government leadership. This then led to the passage of the Civil Liberties Act of 1988, which provided a Presidential letter of apology to those who survived the evacuation and gave a token payment to those still living by a specified date. This was signed into law by President Ronald Reagan, who had firsthand experience in seeing how Japanese Americans were faced with the bigotry that existed during and after the war when he was an Army officer many years earlier.

This blemish on our treatment of people during times of stress happened basically because we forgot the guarantees of the Constitution. Some of the details may differ, *but* the principle remains the same today. It is at the *core* of our constitutional rights. It is *basic* to our sense of values and fairness.

Indefinite detention results from fear and the hysteria of war. The rationale has never been found to be valid. For this reason, the Congress and the President apologized for government actions during World War II for the reason to *not let it happen again*.

The question today is: Are we going to learn from these past injustices?

Milton Eisenhower, who headed the World War II Relocation Agency, which was a US government agency established to handle the incarceration of Japanese, German, and Italian Americans during World War II which was only used against those of Japanese ancestry, warned that we would live to regret the actions of that time.

History shows us that the process is not only unjust but *unnecessary*. Never was any case of treason or unlawful wartime acts brought against anyone in the Japanese American community during World War II.

The same is true today. Can we allow fear and hysteria to guide us into policies that are not only contrary to our Constitution, but unfruitful in punishing the bad? Must we live to regret putting aside the basic values that make our country great?

Congress has thus far adhered to the wisdom learned by past mistakes in justice. We need to continue this path and maintain a justice system based on law and moral courage. Let us not repeat the mistakes of the past. It is a time to hold fast to proven values and maintain our constitutional rights.

Thank you.

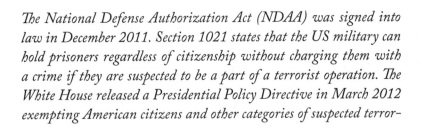

The National Defense Authorization Act (NDAA) was signed into law in December 2011. Section 1021 states that the US military can hold prisoners regardless of citizenship without charging them with a crime if they are suspected to be a part of a terrorist operation. The White House released a Presidential Policy Directive in March 2012 exempting American citizens and other categories of suspected terror-

ists from the controversial indefinite detention clause. It also imposed stricter rules on transferring detainees into military custody and coordinating with civilian law enforcement agencies. The move was made to soothe growing outrage on imprisoning American citizens and legal residents without charge. President Obama's directive corrects this unlawful action, making it difficult to transfer prisoners into military custody and exempting US citizens and legal residents arrested in the United States. The White House procedures state that the military imprisonment of a suspected "covered person" under NDAA must be approved by the Attorney General, Secretary of State, Secretary of Defense, and other top civilian officials. Even then, the FBI will retain primary responsibility for a suspect's case. This should ensure proper oversight over the prisoner program and keep the military from holding suspected terrorists indefinitely. The JACL feels this directive will help to ensure that the mistakes of the unlawful acts against Japanese Americans during World War II are not repeated. However, US citizens and residents are only protected under the directive as long as President Obama is in office. The JACL would like to have the law amended to remove Sections 1021 and 1022 permanently.

LET'S NOT REPEAT THE MISTAKES OF HISTORY

Article printed in The Huffington Post
Issued jointly by Abraham H.
Foxman and S. Floyd Mori
February 24, 2012

This week we commemorate the seventieth anniversary of a shameful and dark chapter in American history. On February 19, 1942, President Franklin D. Roosevelt issued Executive Order 9066, which provided the legal authority for the forced relocation and incarceration of one hundred and twenty thousand Americans of Japanese descent—the vast majority of whom were citizens of the United States.

The anniversary of this tragic national mistake provides a teachable moment for our nation on the dangers of stereotyping, prejudice, and racial profiling—even as we face the very real, continuing threat of terrorism.

Coming just ten weeks after the surprise attack on Pearl Harbor, President Roosevelt's executive order was issued against the backdrop of widespread, baseless fears that Americans of Japanese ancestry might pose a threat to the US—anxiety that was certainly fed by a long history of prejudice and xenophobia directed against Japanese Americans.

Executive Order 9066 authorized the creation of military zones for Japanese citizens and resident aliens, which paved the way for the forced expulsion of American citizens and immigrants of Japanese descent from their homes on the West Coast to camps throughout the United States—where they were held behind barbed wire during the war without evidence of a single individual's disloyalty toward America.

Those incarcerated in the camps were uprooted from their communities, often separated from their families, their homes, and their possessions. They lost their personal liberties and freedoms until the end of the war.

Tragically, the President's executive order was bolstered by additional congressional enactments. When the constitutionality of these actions was challenged in two main cases before the US Supreme Court—*Hirabayashi v. US* and *Korematsu v. US*—the court held that these clearly discriminatory actions by the government were, in fact, justified and constitutional.

Even Japanese Americans serving in the armed forces were segregated from their units, and a predominantly Japanese American unit was formed which became the 442nd Regimental Combat Team/100th Battalion.

In 1976, President Gerald R. Ford finally rescinded Executive Order 9066. Four years later, President Jimmy Carter signed legislation creating the Commission on Wartime Relocation and Internment of Civilians to investigate the impact of the executive order and the incarceration camps.

That commission issued its nearly five hundred page report, *Personal Justice Denied*, in 1983. The report concluded that, *"The promulgation of Executive Order 9066 was not justified by military necessity, and the decisions which followed from it—detention, ending detention and ending exclusion—were not driven by analysis of military conditions. The broad historical causes which shaped these decisions were race prejudice, war hysteria, and a failure of political leadership."*

The commission also called for Congress to apologize for these injustices. That recommendation was fulfilled in 1988, when Congress approved the Civil Liberties Act of 1988, which provided a formal apology and limited reparations to the Japanese citizens and resident aliens who had been sent to the camps or illegal detention centers.

Now, in 2012, a divisive and polarizing debate over immigration reform, as well as efforts to stereotype American Muslims as potential terrorists after 9-11, threaten the progress we have made in promoting respect and understanding among all Americans and the lessons we have learned from the forced incarceration of Japanese Americans.

Though America is, as then senator John F. Kennedy wrote in his famous 1958 essay, *"A Nation of Immigrants,"* the current white-hot, political debate over the contours of immigration reform has resulted in hateful rhetoric, profiling, stereotyping, and dehumanizing language about Hispanics, Muslims, and new immigrants to America.

Make no mistake—there is a direct connection between the tenor of this political debate and the daily lives of immigrants in our communities. Harsh enforcement-only restrictions have fostered fear, mistrust, and discrimination against immigrants and those perceived to be immigrants.

The proliferation of anti-Sharia laws directed against Muslims is an unnecessary response to a non-existent problem in America. The xenophobic references to immigrants as criminals, as a threat to our safety, and damaging to American culture have too frequently derailed meaningful policy debate—and stand in the way of the kind of reforms Americans desperately seek to fix the nation's broken immigration system.

In many communities, February 19 is annually recognized as the Day of Remembrance for the Japanese American community. Jewish Americans annually commemorate the horrors of the Holocaust during the spring, on Holocaust Remembrance Day, or Yom Hashoah. Clearly, both our communities can celebrate together the distance we have come from February 1942.

But, especially at this time, all Americans have a stake in remembering and learning lessons from the past.

———∞———

Abraham H. Foxman is national director of the Anti-Defamation League (ADL), and Floyd Mori is national executive director of the Japanese American Citizens League (JACL).

ECAASU CONFERENCE: DUKE UNIVERSITY

Rediscovery. Renaissance. Revolution.
Speech Given to University
Students of ECAASU
(East Coast Asian American Student Union)
Duke University
Durham, North Carolina, February 25, 2012

Thank you for inviting me to be here with you today. Colleges and universities have been an important part of my life. I met my wife in college, and my first real job was teaching Economics at a community college in California. It was a new school at that time, and I thoroughly enjoyed the association with college students although I was barely out of college myself at the time. What a great moment for me to be here at ECAASU! It is a wonderful sight to see so many young Asian American faces. From experience, I *can* say that we have come a long way as Asian American students.

I have lived in the West most of my life, but I think that I may have a lot in common with those of you who are from the East who grew up in communities where you were a distinct minority. Growing up in a farming community in Utah, there were not a lot of other Asian Americans around, almost none besides my family in those days.

Possibly no one else here today was around during the period of World War II, but I am one who can say that I remember that period of time as a small child. One of the real negatives was that being taunted and called the J word was hard. I just couldn't see myself as one of those "inscrutable" and "diabolical" people depicted in the comics and in the news as the enemy during the war. It was very belittling to be called the J word. (The J word is the first three letters of Japanese. It is a very racist and degrading term which was used frequently during World War II but which should never be used.)

When I started school as the child of immigrants, I spoke more Japanese than I did English so reading was not my best subject. My mom and dad did not attend parent teacher conferences because they did not speak much English. My sister or sister-in-law had to attend in their place. We ate different food than my classmates' families. These are the facts of my life that led me to dread being Japanese in the white American community in which I lived. I became ashamed of who I was. Like many Japanese Americans after the war, I was encouraged to "*Be American.*" So I tried hard to be *a regular American* and to be like everyone else.

There was a huge amount of shame among many in the Japanese American community who were uprooted from their homes and sent to American concentration camps. Although my family was not removed from our home because we did not live on the West Coast, I had similar feelings. We had something to prove. Today I cringe at war movies of that period that show the enemy to be Japanese and especially when they use the J word to describe people of Japanese heritage. It is a word that was used a lot back then, but it still brings back a flood of bad and painful memories.

I compensated for this shame by trying to be a good student, and I had older brothers and sisters who showed me the way by doing well in school. Some teachers who knew my older siblings expected me to be a good student as well. While I had to work on the farm, I was allowed to participate in sports. In grade school I began to excel in sports, and I played baseball, football, and basketball. Back in those days we played marbles, and I was the marble champion of my elementary school. In baseball I played in what was called the American Legion League for junior high school aged players. In high school I made the Utah State All Star team as a second baseman. So sports allowed me to be "one of the boys" and to be somewhat accepted in the white society.

This did little to lessen the negative feeling of being "different" because I went home to the Japanese culture of my immigrant parents. I think that some of you may have felt the same kinds of regrets in your younger life of perhaps wishing you were someone else. I did the things that the white society expected of me rather than understanding, who I really was. I had some slight occasional associations with other Japanese Americans, but my daily life in school and in the neighborhood was in an almost totally white community.

I did have some Jeremy Lins in my younger life. Some of you may have heard of Wat Misaka. He is a very close personal friend who is now making the news with Jeremy Lin because Wat was a basketball player almost seventy years ago. Although his professional basketball career was cut short, he was actually the first person of color to play in what is now the NBA. Wat was born and raised in Utah where he became a star basketball player for the University of Utah during World War II. After being drafted into the US Army and then returning from his duty in the occupation of Japan after the war's end, Wat returned to school at the University of Utah. He played on teams that won the NIT and the NCAA Championships. He was drafted by the New York Knicks back in 1947. Yes, Wat was the first non-white person to play in the NBA which occurred in the same year that Jackie Robinson broke the color barrier in major league baseball.

Although I did not know Wat personally at that time, our family used to crowd around the radio to listen to the University of Utah basketball games during the winter months. Wat brought much interest to our family, and I wanted to grow up to be like him. I was privileged to be in attendance with Wat when he was recognized at the White House by President Obama and at Madison Square Garden when Wat was honored at a New York Knicks game a couple of years ago.

Another Asian American athlete was Wally Yonemine, who played for the San Francisco 49ers and ended up being an early and longtime baseball star in the Japan Major Leagues. I can understand the impact that role models can have on the dreams and aspirations of the young. The current *"Linsanity"* because of Jeremy Lin's success is great for our Asian American youth in many respects.

Like many of you, after high school I wanted to get away from home. After six months on active duty with the US Army Reserves, I went to Los Angeles to attend school at the University of Southern California (USC) to hopefully play baseball. I never saw so many people of color in my life. Asian Americans, Hispanics, and African Americans were very visible in Los Angeles. The baseball dream really didn't pan out, but this began my *Rediscovery and Renaissance* into the Asian American culture. This LA experience of actually hanging out with a bunch of Japanese American youth was a whole new world for me. This, along with living a couple of years in Hawaii as a missionary for the Church of Jesus Christ of Latter-day Saints (Mormon), gave me an exposure to the Japanese American and Asian American culture and community that I had missed for most of my life while growing up in Utah.

It was a complete rebirth in that I developed pride in who I was rather than harboring the shame of the war because of how Japanese Americans were treated and how the Japanese enemies were depicted. We were of Japanese descent, but we were Americans even though some people looked upon us as the enemy. As I associated with other Asian Americans as a college student, I saw that there was a good community out there and I could fit into it.

We have true leaders within our community. Back in 1959 when Hawaii became a state and I was walking down Main Street in Hilo, Hawaii, as a Mormon missionary, I met a young one-armed Japanese American man campaigning for Congress. He had lost his right arm fighting for our freedoms in World War II as a member of the 100th Battalion/442nd Regimental Combat Team, a segregated unit of Japanese Americans in the United States Army from Hawaii and the mainland of the United States. It was Sen. Daniel Inouye's first campaign, and he became the first Japanese American in the United States House of Representatives and later became the first Asian American United States senator. He is now the most senior member of the US Senate and currently serves as President Pro-Tempore. He is actually third in line for the presidency of the United States, and he has a secret service detail assigned to him. Senator Inouye has now served over fifty years in Congress and has been a role model for many.

These experiences motivated me to major in Asian Studies (along with Economics) to learn the history, art, economics, and culture of my heritage. There were no *"Asian American Studies"* programs way back then as there are in colleges now. I found a lot to admire in Asian cultures and much which brought me to feel good about myself and my heritage. The values that my parents had instilled in our family began to make sense to me.

Some of you may have heard one of the slogans of the civil rights era, *"Black Is Beautiful,"* which was used to help African Americans feel pride in their heritage. I began to feel some of that pride in my own heritage and found that being of Asian heritage was okay.

I would like to say a few words about the organization which I represent, the Japanese American Citizens League or JACL. Formed in 1929 by young Japanese American leaders born in the United States of immigrant parents from Japan, the JACL is the oldest and largest Asian American civil and human rights organization in the nation. The JACL was organized because of the discrimination, prejudice, and racism faced by Japanese Americans on a regular basis. Japanese American college graduates with degrees were refused work in their chosen fields. There were many laws against Asian Americans, so these JACL leaders worked hard to get them reversed to make a better world for all of us.

The JACL continues its important work today and is open to any interested persons regardless of ethnic background. It may be of interest to this group to know that the JACL has a number of excellent scholarships available to college students who are members of the JACL and especially those who have given service while active in the organization. I encourage you to check it out. The JACL is always looking to grow its ranks and gain new members. Besides the national organization, the JACL has local chapters throughout the country which give opportunities for service, leadership, culture, social activity, and scholarships. The JACL is a good organization for any Asian American or other interested persons to join before, during, or after college.

The new engagement with the community which I was experiencing during my college days involved beginning to associate with Asian American organizations and actually becoming a leader in student activities. Although I had occasionally attended JACL social and athletic events with my older siblings when I was a child and received a JACL chapter scholarship as a youth in Utah, I now became more involved. At that time, I went more to hang out with new friends rather than for being part of any civil rights movement. The more I learned and participated in the JACL, however, the more committed I became to remain involved in trying to help others through the organization.

This is when I learned the reality about *camp*. During the war when I was a child, camp meant recreation of some sort. When people talked about the camps where Japanese Americans were taken and incarcerated during World War II, I did not have a real understanding of what it actually meant. It wasn't until college and afterward working in California that I understood the real meaning of *camp* to the Japanese American community during World War II. People seldom talked about those experiences and times.

Students did not often learn about it in school. I assume that many of you were surprised the first time you learned about the World War II incarceration of a group of people simply because of the color of their skin and the fact that they were of Japanese descent. The imprisonment of these innocent Japanese Americans was later attributed to racial discrimination, war hysteria, and a failure of political leadership. It is surprising even today that many people are still unaware and may have never heard of this dark period of our nation's history. For some of you, this may be the first time you have heard of it.

The era of the 1960s and 1970s in the San Francisco Bay Area where I then lived was the site of a lot of protest. This is when that generation of younger Japanese Americans fought for fairness alongside other protesters. The forced removal from their homes and the incarceration were wrong, and the government needed to apologize. Working with college students on a daily basis as a teacher, I was immersed in an atmosphere of protest and activism. The Japanese American community joined in on the party. Redress and an apology for the incarceration were the goals and demands of the JACL and other civic groups in our community. This is when I really learned what injustice was and how it impacted a total community which was innocent and imprisoned without due process.

The Asian American community broadened as newer immigrants came to this country. As a California State legislator and being one of only a few Asian faces, I was able to work with the new Korean communities in the late 1970s and early 1980s. When Saigon fell and refugees came to this country, I was there to officially greet them and welcome them to California. They were placed in a temporary camp of tents with less than ideal living conditions such as were the Japanese Americans during World War II, but I was able to show them a friendly face. I had the opportunity to meet people who were incarcerated in the district that I represented, people like Patty Hearst to advocate for her pardon and Wendy Yoshimura to assure that she would be treated fairly. You may not have heard of these people, but they were activists of that day.

We sponsored the first Asian American Student Association at the college where I taught. Later I hired Asian Americans on my legislative staff in the California State Assembly because we were so underrepresented at that time.

The critical part of an Asian American *Renaissance* is *rediscovering* or maybe discovering for the first time that you have a legacy of good and great things. I hope that it also brings with it the sense of responsibility to contribute to the community from where you have received so much, even your very existence and the opportunity to attend college and to be in attendance at this conference today. The Jeremy Lins of the world do not come around every day, but there are increasing examples of Asian Americans providing a pathway and role model for somebody else on his or her way.

Having been there to see first-hand the impact of Katrina on the Gulf Coast Asian American community, I had a great deal of pride when I saw the Vietnamese American community come back after the disasters and rebuild their neighborhoods with very little help from the government which had largely ignored their needs. They helped each other and rebuilt while other neighborhoods still were in shambles. The values of their Asian heritage spoke very loudly that they were not going to let a hurricane or an oil spill disaster keep them from attaining their version of the American Dream.

I think that watching the Japanese people respond and cope with the earthquake and tsunami disaster of a year ago has given young Japanese Americans new pride in their cultural heritage. Some have even had a desire to spend some time in Japan helping with the recovery efforts. I have also had the privilege of working closely with the relief efforts in Japan through the JACL and Direct Relief International partnership.

There is a current day parade of many Asian Americans who are showing and leading the way in many walks of life. Asian Americans have been and are members of Congress and Cabinet Secretaries. The political field is seeing more and more Asian Americans entering the fray from Connecticut where an Asian American is running for the US Senate, to California where Asian Americans are running for every level of public office, to Alaska where an Asian American represents Fairbanks in the State legislature, to Las Cruces, New Mexico, where there is an Asian American mayor. It is no longer just in Hawaii and California that we have elected officials of Asian background. We are seeing new political leaders from the Asian American community and other minority communities who are sitting *at the table* making an impact from school boards all the way up to working with and in the White House.

While the professions have been a favorite goal for parents of Asian Americans to set for their youth, we see emergence into the media and entertainment fields as well as other aspects of business and entrepreneurship. In World War II there were very few Asian American officers in the United States military.

Today there are a number of admirals and generals who are Asian American with a new crop of officers at the service academies.

And speaking of the military, the recent honoring of the World War II Japanese American veterans with a Congressional Gold Medal has been inspiring to the entire nation. These men were willing to rise up out of the American concentration camps in which they and their families were incarcerated and held prisoners to serve the democracy of which they hoped to be a part after the War. The stories of their courage in doing so and their heroic service to this country have filled many columns of newsprint throughout this country. These people who served bravely during World War II have been credited with making the world much better for Japanese Americans, Asian Americans, and all Americans in the ensuing years. They were, unknowingly at the time, part of the civil rights movement. This became part of this *Renaissance* for Asian Americans.

So where do we go from here? I hope that you are sufficiently comfortable in the skin in which you were born. I suspect you are because you are involved with ECAASU. I am confident that you are prepared to leave your mark in your community and the nation. Your involvement will take us one step closer to being perceived as equal. While we have made significant strides, there is still much to do. The *Revolution* has begun, but it must go on into the future.

There are those who continue to stereotype. There are those who cause pain by their bullying and harassment of innocent people. Just take a look at the tragedy of the Private Danny Chen case which we are battling today. The media needs more nudging to realize that Asian Americans are actually a real part of society and not exotic stereotypes that really do not exist.

War hysteria brings out the worst in society. It appears that we did not learn a real lesson from the constitutional mistakes of World War II against the Japanese Americans, and we are repeating them in the hysteria of 9-11. I was in the Oval Office in 1976 when President Gerald R. Ford rescinded Executive Order 9066, which gave the authority to the military in 1942 to round up innocent Japanese Americans and immigrants on the West Coast simply because of their heritage and physical appearance. Today we see Congress pass a law that allows the same kind of indefinite detention based on being a suspect because of your ethnic background, and the President has signed this into law.

We have come a long way, but there is a lot of work yet to be done. It seems that racism will always be with us in some form or another because of the ignorance and hatred of some in society. You, as young people, are our hope for the future. You need to be part of a continuing vigilance against the worst in human nature. By understanding who you are and how you came to be where you are, you have an obligation to maintain that legacy of those on whose shoulders we stand today. Our past leaders have sacrificed greatly for our sakes. Now it is your turn to stand out in the world. We cannot all be leaders, but we can all be good citizens and do our part.

Thank you for allowing me to share this time with you.

This speech was prepared as a keynote for an East Coast Asian American Student Union (ECAASU) Conference of college students held at Duke University on February 25, 2012. The theme of the conference was: "Rediscovery: Renaissance. Revolution." The J word referred to is the very derogatory term used for Japanese people during the war and since, which is the first three letters of the word Japanese. Those three letters should never be used to reference Japanese people or as an abbreviation for Japan or Japanese. A preferred abbreviation is JPN.

FROM CONCENTRATION CAMPS TO TODAY'S ISSUES CONNECTIONS OF HISTORY

Speaking to University Students
Asian American Student Group
Swarthmore College
Swarthmore, Pennsylvania, March 16, 2012

It is good to be here with you today on your beautiful campus to speak a little about the Japanese American experience of World War II and current issues in our community. Since Hiro Nishikawa and I are close to the same age, we both personally experienced World War II as very young children. Hiro has told you what life was like in the camps. I will talk with you primarily about what happened after the war ended.

For many years before the start of World War II, Asian Americans faced extreme discrimination and prejudice. The Japanese American Citizens League (JACL), which is the oldest and largest Asian American civil and human rights organization in the nation, was formed in 1929 by leaders within the Japanese American community. These were mostly people who were slightly older than college age. They were American citizens who had been born in America of immigrant parents from

Japan. Some were already doctors or lawyers, but it was difficult for many of their peers to gain meaningful employment in
their fields of study because of the prejudice they faced. The great
majority of Japanese immigrants and their families had settled on
the West Coast, mostly in California with some large groups also
in Washington and Oregon. These leaders felt the need to form a
national organization to advocate for civil rights for themselves,
their families, and their friends.

There were many laws against Asian Americans, and they
wanted to change those discriminatory laws. Japanese immigrants were not allowed to become naturalized citizens. They
were barred from owning land in California and some other
states. They could not marry outside their race. They were not
allowed to use public swimming pools except for the day before
the pool would be drained and cleaned. They were restricted in
where they could sit in movie theaters. Many of the laws which
were a result of the segregation of African Americans in the early
days were also used against those of Asian backgrounds.

The JACL was effective in working to eventually repeal and
change many of those laws (mostly years after the war's end).
However, no one was able to stop the evacuation and incarceration of innocent Japanese Americans during World War II. The
JACL tried to stop the evacuation but then they were told that
they should cooperate with the government. There was no choice
in the matter. The few Japanese Americans who were brave
enough to protest were arrested.

I was a child of Japanese immigrants, but I was born and raised
in Utah so the forced removal and incarceration was not something my family experienced because only the people from the
West Coast were directly affected. However, I remember relatives
coming to our home after they "voluntarily evacuated," as was at
first requested of the Japanese Americans by the United States
government. These cousins of my mother had lived in San Pedro,
near Los Angeles, and my parents were able to sign for them to

move inland to avoid being sent to the camps. My wife's family also did the same as they were living in Los Angeles where her father had a successful small business. Her mother was a Japanese American who had been born in Utah, and they had relatives who would sign for them to voluntarily evacuate. Her parents lost nearly everything they had, and her father never regained the economic well-being which he had when the war started.

The government had asked Japanese Americans to move inland ahead of the time when the forced removal was slated to occur, but most declined to do so. Many believed that their imprisonment in the rumored camps would not really become a reality, and they did not feel that it was economically possible. The immigrant parents thought their children born in America were safe because they were citizens. They did not expect that their own government would treat its citizens in that manner. The governors of the inland Western states had been summoned to meet in Salt Lake City where they were asked to accept people of Japanese ancestry into their states if they voluntarily left the West Coast. All the governors protested that they did not want them in their states except Gov. Ralph Carr, the Republican governor of Colorado, who stated that the Japanese people had done nothing wrong and should be allowed to live wherever they pleased. It was obviously not a popular position with his constituents, however, as he lost a subsequent bid for the Senate.

Governor Carr said the Japanese people would be welcome in Colorado, and he even hired Japanese Americans himself. A Japanese American family who moved to Colorado from California told of being stopped by a highway patrolman at the border as they entered the state. They were initially full of fear for what he would say to them, but the officer kindly welcomed them into Colorado.

It was not until many years later that I understood what the Japanese Americans went through during those difficult war years and even after that period of time. My own experience in Utah as a young child included discrimination and prejudice because I was a Japanese American and the United States was at war with Japan, but my family did not have to endure the hardship of being taken from our home. Especially those who were incarcerated in the illegal detention centers which are called American concentration camps suffered extreme hardships and difficulties which affected them throughout their entire lives. Although the young children and teenagers may have actually enjoyed some social parts of the camp experience, most have carried scars with them of the experience of being locked away behind barbed wire and watched over by armed guards. Many people blocked out the painful memories, and some never recovered from the ordeal.

The Japanese Americans found few friends after Japan bombed Pearl Harbor on December 7, 1941. Most of the Japanese Americans had never even been to Japan, but they were immediately looked upon as the enemy and as potential spies because of their physical features. They found little support although there was one group which notably spoke out for them. The American Friends or Quakers, who are important to Swarthmore, showed compassion and sympathy to the Japanese Americans. A few political leaders tried to speak up for their rights, but they were greatly outnumbered and voted down. Japanese Americans had faced prejudice and discrimination for many years, but it suddenly became highly escalated. Their lives were very difficult.

The JACL served as a liaison between the Japanese American community and the United States government during the early days of World War II. Mike Masaoka, a leader within the organization and the only administrative staff member at the time, suggested that the people should go along with the government's orders. To prove their loyalty to the United States, he also argued for the formation of the famous 442nd Regimental Combat Team in the US Army.

At the outset of the war, there were young men who were Japanese Americans born in this country who tried to enlist in the United States military. They were refused as they had been reclassified as enemy aliens or noncitizens. Although there were a few who were successful in joining some branches of the armed forces, most were denied until the government set up the segregated unit of Japanese Americans in the United States Army. They became the 442nd Regimental Combat Team, a group joined by the 100th Battalion which was comprised of Japanese Americans from Hawaii. The Japanese American young men in the camps were at first asked to volunteer, and about three thousand did. Others were drafted. The 442nd became the most highly decorated unit in the history of the United States military for its size and length of service. It was likely due largely to the inordinate number of casualties which they encountered while fighting in combat on the European fronts which resulted in numerous Purple Heart Awards. Some were given various military honors years later for their service, but it was relatively unusual at that time for these patriotic soldiers to receive many awards for their bravery and courage.

After the war had ended in 1945, President Harry S. Truman commended the 442nd Regimental Combat Team/100th Battalion for their outstanding service. He presented the seventh Presidential unit citation to them and said, "Not only have you fought the enemy, but you fought prejudice and you won. Keep up the good fight, and you will continue to win." In 1947, President Truman desegregated the military which had also had other segregated units including African American and Native American units.

Soon after the end of the war, the JACL renewed legislative efforts to secure the rights of Japanese Americans. In 1946, the JACL embarked on a campaign to repeal California's Alien Land Law, which prohibited all Japanese immigrants from purchasing and owning land in the state. In 1948, the JACL was a founding member of the Leadership Conference on Civil Rights. Also that year, the JACL succeeded in passage of the Evacuation

Claims Act, which was the first of a series of efforts to rectify the losses and injustices of the incarceration. In 1949, the JACL initiated efforts in the US Congress to gain the right of Japanese immigrants to become naturalized citizens of the United States which had been denied to them for over fifty years. The Walter-McCarren Act allowed for Japanese immigrants to become naturalized citizens in 1952.

During the late 1950s and the 1960s when I was in college, the civil rights movement began in earnest. Leaders within the minority communities started to speak out in order to gain civil and equal rights. Although slavery had long been abolished, much of the discrimination against African Americans and other minorities still remained. We know that some of it still exists even with all the strides which have been made.

In the early 1970s, the JACL began the effort to obtain redress for the Japanese Americans who were forcibly removed from their West Coast homes by the government during World War II. Although President Gerald R. Ford rescinded Executive Order 9066 in 1976, the redress effort was not progressing much up to that point. Executive Order 9066 had originally been signed by President Franklin D. Roosevelt on February 19, 1942. This order paved the way for the forced removal and incarceration of nearly one hundred and twenty thousand persons of Japanese descent, the majority who were citizens of the United States. The JACL wanted to redress those wrongs.

At the National JACL Convention in 1978 held in Salt Lake City, Utah, the JACL voted to seriously work toward redress and formed the National Committee for Redress. I had grown up in Utah, but I was living in California at the time and attended the Convention as an honored guest because I was then serving as a California State Assemblyman.

Over the course of the next twelve years, the Japanese American members of the United States House of Representatives at that time, Norman Mineta from San Jose and Bob Matsui from

Sacramento, worked hard for passage of the Redress Bill. There were two Japanese American United States senators, both from Hawaii, Senators Daniel Inouye and Spark Matsunaga, who also worked tirelessly to help the redress effort move forward. There was some support from other members of Congress, but it was a monumental job to get the majority of members of Congress to vote for the bill.

Senator Inouye suggested that a commission be set up to tell the stories of the Japanese American experiences so that their colleagues would fully understand the issue. Judge Bill Marutani of Philadelphia was the only Japanese American on the commission. The federal Commission on Wartime Relocation and Internment of Civilians (CWRIC) held hearings at various locations throughout the country at which Japanese Americans who had been incarcerated came forward to tell their stories, and leaders within the community testified to advocate for redress. After keeping it bottled up inside for decades, it was difficult for most to speak about the experiences of that period of time. Many had not spoken even to their families about the incarceration and their experiences.

The CWRIC later issued a report in which they determined that the incarceration of these innocent Japanese Americans had been the result of wartime hysteria, racism, and a lack of competent political leadership at the time. The evacuation and incarceration were clearly unjustified, unfair, and unnecessary.

The Civil Liberties Act of 1988, HR 442 also known as the Redress Bill, finally passed. Although he had opposed the monetary compensation in the bill for five years, President Ronald Reagan became convinced to sign the bill into law on August 10, 1988. Those who advocated for the legislation felt that it was necessary to have the money factor to be meaningful and have lasting consequences to prevent such a travesty of justice from happening again. Those Japanese Americans who had been forcibly removed from their West Coast homes who were still living on August 10, 1988, were awarded a monetary sum of $20,000 and they received a letter of apology from the President of the United States.

The Constitution had not protected these citizens, but an apology was received at long last. The JACL and others who had worked hard for this effort were anxious for the measure to pass in order to assure that no other citizens would ever have to suffer such an experience of unjust incarceration of innocent civilians as occurred during World War II against the Japanese Americans.

Many of those who received the apology and reparations expressed the regret that their immigrant parents were not alive to see the passage of the Civil Liberties Act of 1988 as it was felt that they were the ones who suffered the greatest harm from the mistreatment by the government. Most of the younger generation made the best of things and had attained some of their goals in life, but many of their parents never recovered from the experience of being locked away in the camps for years.

History is replete with discriminatory acts against Asian Americans. The 1882 Chinese Exclusion Act was signed on May 6, 1882, by President Chester A. Arthur. It was the first major law restricting immigration to the United States. At that time, native-born Americans blamed the Chinese workers for unemployment and declining wages. Chinese immigration was halted for ten years, and Chinese people were prohibited from becoming United States citizens. The law was extended in 1892 for another ten years before becoming permanent in 1902. The law was repealed in 1943 during World War II when China was an ally in the war against Imperial Japan. There is currently a bill before Congress to have an apology for the 1882 Chinese Exclusion Act. The JACL and other civil rights groups have joined with Chinese American groups to work for its passage.

As Japanese Americans started to see some economic success in America during the 1920s, they were looked upon by the majority community as a threat to their economic well-being.

Although Japanese American young people were graduating from college, they had a hard time finding employment in their field of study. They were told that no one would hire them. There was a lot of discrimination and prejudice which was hurdled at them on a regular basis, including from the newspapers. Yet they persevered.

The incarceration experience and the injustices done to Japanese Americans during World War II need to be talked about even today. It is a story which must be made known in order to prevent the same thing from happening again. There are many people who have never heard about these experiences. It is important that people understand that the Constitution must be upheld even during times of war.

Immediately after the events of 9-11 when terrorists attacked the United States by flying hijacked commercial jet airplanes into the World Trade Center in New York City and the Pentagon in Washington, DC, the JACL issued a press release to caution against targeting innocent American citizens who may happen to look like the enemy. There have been many instances of violence against American Muslims and others who have physical appearances which are similar to those of the terrorists. We must not condemn the innocent simply for their heritage or physical characteristics.

Today we see anti-immigrant sentiments surface in various parts of the country. There has even been talk by at least one politician suggesting that undocumented immigrants be rounded up and put into camps such as the Japanese Americans were during World War II. There are those who have not learned from the lessons of history.

We must be aware and ever vigilant in order to protect the civil rights of all people. I would admonish you as young people to remain involved and to be advocates for good and just causes. The community and the nation need committed people to carry the torch of freedom into the future. You can do a lot of good in the world.

Thank you.

———⊗———

Hiro Nishikawa, a leader in the Philadelphia JACL Chapter, invited Floyd Mori to join him in speaking to an Asian American student group at Swarthmore College in Pennsylvania. Hiro spoke of the World War II experience of Japanese Americans being forcibly removed from the West Coast and his family's experiences in particular. He was a young child just three years old when his family was uprooted from their home and sent to an assembly center at Salinas, California, where they were housed in animal stalls. They were living in Hollister, California, where they had resided for only one month before the war broke out. They previously lived in San Francisco where his father was a chef and where Hiro was born. They were later transported to the Gila River camp in Arizona where they lived in almost unbearable heat and undesirable living conditions. Each person was given a tag on which was written their family number. They became prisoners during the war and were held in an American concentration camp where they lived in crowded barracks. Floyd was born and raised in Utah so his family was not required to leave their home during the war. He spoke about the experiences of Japanese Americans after World War II and today's issues as related to the Japanese American experience of incarceration during World War II.

OUT OF CAMP AND STARTING OVER IN PHILADELPHIA

Information from a Newsletter
About Japanese Americans
in Philadelphia During World War II
March 26, 2012

Recently I had the privilege of speaking to a group of Asian American college students at Swarthmore College in Pennsylvania, eleven miles southwest of Philadelphia, where they have a beautiful sprawling 425-acre campus. Founded by the Religious Society of Friends (Quakers), Swarthmore is one of the nation's first co-educational colleges. Today, Swarthmore is non-sectarian, but it still reflects many of the traditions and values of the Quakers such as a commitment to the common good and preparation of future leaders. Swarthmore is a private school which is open to all. The Quakers were kind and helpful to Japanese Americans when they were being evacuated from their homes on the West Coast and incarcerated in American concentration camps during World War II.

Hiro Nishikawa, a leader of the JACL Philadelphia chapter and former JACL Eastern District Governor, invited me to speak along with him about the topic: From Concentration Camps to Today's Issues.

At the event, some materials were passed out which explained a little of the history and stories of the Japanese Americans who went to Philadelphia out of the camps during World War II. Some people were allowed to leave the camps if they were able to enter college or find employment in an area away from the West Coast. These Japanese Americans who were able to relocate to Philadelphia then had the task of starting over after their lives had been disrupted by the incarceration. They were wandering into unknown territory. One publication of days gone by was a newsletter put out in October 1943 by the American Friends Service Committee (Quakers), one of the few groups (or possibly the only such organization) which supported the Japanese Americans during that difficult period. Much of this information was gleaned from that newsletter.

Although most of the Japanese Americans and Japanese immigrants who were incarcerated had to stay in the ten concentration camps for the duration of the war, some of the people were allowed to leave the camps while the war was still in progress. If they could be accepted into a program to find jobs or go to school away from the West Coast and obtain a travel permit, they could receive permission to leave the imprisonment of the camps. It was an option for some former college students or those who had already graduated from college when the war broke out. Some couples took advantage of this opportunity.

The Philadelphia office of the War Relocation Authority was opened in July 1943. The territory covered by the office was Eastern Pennsylvania, Delaware, and Southern New Jersey. The officer in charge was Henry C. Patterson, who was a member of the Providence Friends Meeting. His wife, Mary Sullivan Patterson, was a volunteer worker in trying to find jobs and living quarters for Japanese Americans coming to the area from the camps.

The American Friends were planning to secure an adequate large house which could be used as a hostel for the Japanese

Americans. They had not been successful in finding anything suitable so they appealed to the community for assistance in finding temporary hospitality, a home, or a job for the uprooted people who were arriving in the Philadelphia area from various camps. These were largely former college students and young adults who would accept any kind of work to be able to escape the confinement of being held captive in the barbed wire camp enclosures in which they and their families were incarcerated.

In asking people to open their homes to these people, it was suggested that they could charge the former internees only a moderate sum, not more than a dollar a day which was the hostel rate, until they could find employment and start to earn money. The Friends asked people to welcome the Japanese Americans into their homes and said that such homes were urgently needed.

Many of these Japanese Americans (largely young women and couples because most of the young single men had joined the US Army or were drafted) were interested in working for their board and lodging in addition to holding daytime jobs. The Friends said that twenty-one hours a week should compensate families for a room and food. Although that amount of time might seem perhaps a little excessive, they did suggest that it would be unfair to require them to do too much heavy work or to place too much responsibility on them.

The Friends' newsletter stated: *"In these days of shortage of domestic labor, it seems probable that enough good homes can be found with considerate people who really have the welfare of these uprooted Americans at heart."*

There was a labor shortage because of the number of men who had gone off to fight in the war so it was not too difficult to place the Japanese Americans in hospitals, laboratories, dairies, printing establishments, factories, war plants, retail stores, mechanics' jobs, dry cleaning establishments, and the like. The office had many requests for singles and couples to work as domestics. Unskilled labor jobs were plentiful. The Japanese Americans were known, or considered, to be industrious so they were able to find work in those areas.

It was a more difficult task to find appropriate work for professionals. A Japanese American dentist with a family to support had an extremely hard time finding a job as a dentist. He had a successful dental practice in Seattle with predominantly non-Japanese patients before the war started. There was a shortage of dentists in the Philadelphia area at the time, but the Friends could not find work for him. He was doing volunteer dental service to groups within the American Friends, hoping that someone would hire him. The Friends were appealing for some dentist to give him the opportunity to be an assistant in a dental office, but placing him was very difficult. The Friends said that they were *"hoping that some dentist will have the courage to give this man the opportunity he should have as an assistant or that some group of Friends will want to sponsor him and his family until they can make a new start in the East."*

The Japanese American dentist had probably been quite fortunate to be able to practice dentistry in Seattle. Many college graduates, even in the professions, had found before the war that they were having great difficulty getting work in their field of study even after completing their college degree as people just simply would not hire or patronize them. It was not uncommon for college graduates to be doing menial labor rather than working in the areas in which they had obtained degrees. Professionals such as doctors, dentists, and lawyers often had only patients or clients of Japanese heritage.

Another of the Japanese American people who went to Philadelphia was a music teacher with a fine reputation. He had finally, after much difficulty, connected with one private and one public school where he was able to teach. The work came after long, hard, and painful effort with frequent rebuffs before anyone would hire him.

Young women who were secretaries started out for Philadelphia from the camps with high hopes. Others were students who hoped to enroll in school and help support themselves by finding work in addition to their studying. Many were anxious to try anything to get released from the imprisonment of the camps where they could see no progress in their lives. Education had always been extremely important to the Japanese immigrants who encouraged their children to attend college. The American Friends Service Committee and the National Japanese Student Relocation Council helped former college students get released from camp and return to college studies. The Student Relocation Council was formed by a group of leading educators who tried to make sure that the communities welcomed the Japanese American students after they found colleges willing to accept the students. They helped work out financial arrangements through jobs, financial aid, or grants. There was opposition to their efforts from various groups, including the American Legion and the University of Southern California where the president refused to send transcripts for the former students to other colleges because he said it would aid the enemy.

A Japanese American college student at that time reported that he felt welcome when he arrived at Swarthmore. He felt privileged to be selected for the program and was determined to do his best. He said they had to give American democracy another chance to overcome the racial prejudice which had caused the evacuation. Still, he wondered what would happen to the Japanese Americans after the war.

It had to be hard for these formerly incarcerated people who had been forced from their homes and stripped of their freedoms. Leaving the camps meant that they had to start over in a new area totally unfamiliar to them usually without their families or friends nearby. They did what they had to do. Members of the American Friends Service Committee were helpful and kind to them after the Japanese Americans had been persecuted by their neighbors, former friends, strangers, and their government. Although friends appeared to be few and far between for the Japanese Americans during the war, there were some such as members of the American Friends and other individuals who proved to be friends to this persecuted group of people during World War II.

KINDNESS, LUCK, AND TIMING

Speech Presented to an Employee
Group at American Association
of Retired Persons (AARP)
Washington, DC, May 18, 2012

Today I will be speaking about kindness, luck, and timing and how these factors have played an important part in my life. They are influences in all of our lives.

If you go to the city of Murray, Utah, right along I-15, south of Salt Lake City, you may pass the spot where I was born. In 1939, in the area where our home was located, it was the other side of the tracks. In that swampy, unwanted piece of land was the Mori farm where my life began. I was the fourth son and seventh child in a family which eventually had eight children. My parents were immigrants from Japan. I was among the youngest of the Japanese Americans who were the second generation children born in America of Japanese immigrant parents. Some of my Japanese American peers were the third generation born of American citizen parents with Japanese immigrant grandparents.

We lived there until 1942, which was a significant year for Japanese Americans. That was right after the start of World War II, when those of Japanese heritage living on the West Coast of the United States were required to evacuate. Before the forced removal from their homes and incarceration in America's concentration camps became a reality, the government asked the people of Japanese descent to voluntarily evacuate to inland states. It was necessary for them to have family or friends living inland who would sign for them to come, and they had to leave the West Coast by a specified date. Our family did not have to leave our home because we lived in Utah, but we had relatives from California who came to stay with us during that time. My wife's mother had been born in Utah and her family had relatives there as well, so they also took the option of the voluntary evacuation from Los Angeles to Utah.

My family had moved to another farm in Sandy, which is a little farther south. I was a young child at the time. I didn't understand what "camp" was and I wasn't sure exactly why the relatives had come, but I enjoyed having the chance to meet family members that I had not known before that time. They were cousins of my parents along with their families. I learned the value of family ties at that time.

As a small child, I was relatively oblivious of the true horrors of war which were raging around the world until my oldest brother who had joined the United States Army was returned home in a casket. He had been serving in the Military Intelligence Service and was in Japan during the occupation after the war had ended. We expected him to return home soon but not in the manner he did. He died in the crash of a US Army airplane in Japan. It was a terrible time for my family. I was six years old.

When I entered the first grade in 1945, there were no other minorities in the school besides my family. While there was some rejection from my classmates because I looked different than the rest of them and Japan had been at war with the United States, I did not accept it. I tried to fit in. The teachers were kind and helpful to me.

One day a girl in my first grade class passed out invitations to her birthday party. Everyone received one except me. On the day of the party the other children got off the school bus at her stop and went to her home. I rode the bus on up the road to my house. I am not sure what I told my family, but I had decided to go to the party. I walked the mile or so back down the road to her house. I knocked on the door. Her mother answered and invited me in to join the party. Although it was perhaps unkind to exclude one small boy, her kindness in welcoming me and not turning me away allowed me to have a good time at the birthday party.

I remember that there was some taunting, mostly by other students who were not in my own class who did not know me. My older sister had left a good impression so I was expected to be a good student. The teachers were kind in their dealings with me, and I was even chosen for the leading role in the school play where I played the part of a snowman. I felt lucky to have the teachers which I had.

In remembering the war, I recall that it did bring some shame to me. The Japanese people in the bomber planes were depicted as being terrible people. Their physical appearance was scary. The cartoons of the Japanese enemies made them out to be horrible looking creatures.

When I entered junior high school, I had to leave the relative comfort of the small elementary school where I had come to feel like I belonged. Going to junior high meant attending a larger school which was comprised of students from several elementary schools so it would mean having new classmates who were unknown to me. It was a scary prospect in some ways, but again I was able to find some kindness shown to me.

Coach Curtis nurtured me in basketball, and I was allowed as a seventh grader to play on the school team with the ninth graders. I had grown to my full stature by junior high so at that time I was tall compared to most of the kids my age. I was able to excel in basketball at school because of hard work and many hours of practice. The coach often put me up as an example to the rest of the team.

My family all worked in the fields during the spring, summer, and fall months. I was allowed, however, to play sports. I used baseball to escape some of the work in the fields. I turned out to be a pitcher who could throw a curve ball. Sports became my ticket to becoming one of the boys. Baseball became my sport of choice, and I was able to be All State in baseball during high school. I say this not to brag but to indicate that sometimes an outlet needs to be found to find acceptance in this world, and the kindness of others helps.

Right out of high school I joined the United States Army Reserves which meant going to six months of basic training at Fort Ord, near Monterey, California. I was the only Asian and was the smallest person in my unit. I received preferential treatment by Drill Sergeant Claybourne. He was from Texas, and I suspect that he knew of the 442nd Regimental Combat Team which was a segregated unit of Japanese Americans during World War II. They rescued the Lost Battalion which was a unit of Texans. The 442nd suffered 800 casualties during the rescue of the 200 Texans. I was at the top of the class in clerk typist school and was a top performer in PE because I had learned the value of hard work from my parents and my teachers over the years. The Sergeant's kindness and my good luck in having him as my leader helped me during that time.

When I finished my six months of active duty in the Army, I moved to the Los Angeles area where I entered college at USC. This opened my eyes to the Asian American community. I had seen few other Asians in Utah while growing up except at an occasional summer picnic, a sporting event of the Japanese American Citizens League (JACL) with my older brothers and sisters, or on a visit to Japantown in Salt Lake City to shop for

Japanese groceries. I developed Asian American friends in Los Angeles who accepted me and were kind.

A church mission to Hawaii further enlightened my understanding of the Asian American culture, and I was able to be surrounded by a number of people who were of Asian background. The shame I had previously felt about my Japanese heritage from my childhood turned to pride. I gained an appreciation for Asian and Pacific Islander Americans and the heritage we share. The people were especially kind to the missionaries.

My mentor in college was my professor, Richard Wirthlin, who later became the pollster and chief strategist for President Ronald Reagan. I had entered Brigham Young University (BYU) and had decided to major in Economics. Dr. Wirthlin gave me the opportunity to teach as a senior and as a graduate student. He awakened in me an interest in politics. He took some of us as his students on polling trips to various cities in Utah where we learned to glean information and opinions of others. Dr. Wirthlin was very kind and became a big influence in my life. Many years later we were able to do some work together in the international business arena along with Michael Silva, a friend and business partner we had in common.

My first full-time employment out of college was teaching Economics at Chabot College in Hayward, California. A recruiter had come to BYU to interview prospective instructors for the new college, and I considered myself very lucky to get that job. I tried to look at my students as my own kids although I was not that much older than they were. I was not an easy teacher and made the students work hard although I tried to be kind. I generally got good marks as a teacher and greatly enjoyed teaching. It is gratifying now that students will occasionally find me on Facebook or Google after all these years and contact me to thank me for being their teacher.

I always told my students that they needed to be good citizens. While teaching college students, an opportunity came up for me to run for the City Council of Pleasanton, California, which at that time was a city of about thirty thousand people in the early 1970s. I decided to practice what I preached and threw my hat into the ring on the last day of filing. It was all a matter of timing.

An editor of the local paper took a liking to me and did a story about me as a mayor and professor three years later. The California State Assemblyman, Carlos Bee, who represented the district in which I lived had just run for and successfully won another term in office. However, he was in ill health and passed away around Thanksgiving soon after having been reelected. I decided to run for the seat and won in the special election although I was a definite underdog in the field of fifteen candidates. I campaigned hard and knocked on many doors in the district. My brother-in-law, Ken Mano, became my campaign treasurer. Many of my fellow church members, political friends in Pleasanton, and my students campaigned for me, including James Rogan, who later became a California State Assemblyman, United States Congressman, and a Superior Court Judge in California. After winning the primary election, the State Democratic Party stepped in to help me. We were lucky to be victorious.

Being a State Assembly person was a full-time position so I resigned from my teaching job at Chabot College. Another Japanese American, Paul Bannai of Gardena, had just been elected in the November election so he had become the first Japanese American elected to the California State Assembly. We were the only Japanese Americans in the Assembly, and we had the privilege of serving together for six years. Again, it was due to the kindness of people around me, a bit of good luck, and timing which gave me these opportunities.

In politics, I had many good mentors and made good friends. I had become friends with Rep. Norman Mineta when he was mayor of San Jose and I was mayor of Pleasanton. He later became Secretary of Commerce under President Bill Clinton and Secretary of Transportation under President George W.

Bush. I first met Sen. Dianne Feinstein and Former Speaker of the House, Nancy Pelosi, during those days as well as having the opportunity to work with Gov. Jerry Brown. I had met President Ronald Reagan at his office when he was Governor of California, and I met President Jimmy Carter, and many other high-level government officials. While I was a missionary in Hawaii in 1959, I met Sen. Daniel K. Inouye when he was first campaigning for a seat in the US House of Representatives representing Hawaii after it became a state. Years later I had the privilege of becoming well acquainted with the senator and working closely with him on many issues of importance. All these people were kind to me over the years.

Being at the right place at the right time through luck and good fortune has given me experiences which I could not have imagined when I was a young child growing up on a farm in what was then rural Utah.

After leaving politics and returning to live in Utah, I spent over fifteen years working in international business helping companies establish themselves in Japan. I worked with Subway Sandwiches, Mrs. Fields Cookies, Pennzoil, Hitachi, Suntory, Mitsubishi, Sony, ITOCHU, and others. I explored entrepreneurship in the golf shaft business. Lee Trevino and J. C. Snead used our shafts so I was invited to take our products to the practice tee at the PGA Senior Tournaments (now called the Champions Tour). It was a privilege to chat with Arnold Palmer, Chi Chi Rodriquez, Gary Player, Sam Snead, and other pro golfers.

In 2005, I began work for the Japanese American Citizens League (JACL) as its director of public policy in Washington, DC Although I had planned to only stay for two years in the nation's capital, I became the national executive director of the JACL after the former director, John Tateishi, vacated the position after having given his notice and becoming ill. Now it has been seven years, and I am ready for a new phase in my life. I will be retiring from the position in the JACL on June 1, 2012.

As you look at where my life has taken me, there has been much kindness shown to me. From the early years of grade school with kind teachers and neighbors to later kindnesses from various important leaders, I could not have had the experiences which I have had without a good dose of kindness and good luck. Also, the timing was right to afford me these opportunities.

Where I had lost pride in who I was and in my heritage as a young child because of the mistreatment showered upon Japanese Americans, I was able to overcome those problems and discover the great value in my Asian American heritage. My parents and family had financial struggles for years. The community persecuted us because of World War II in which Japan was the enemy. Leaders within the JACL were instrumental in finding remedies for some of the prejudice and discrimination endured by the Japanese Americans for many years. Laws were changed, and certain rights were attained or restored with the right timing.

The type of discrimination and racism which was experienced by Japanese Americans during World War II, unfortunately, has not disappeared. Bruce Yamashita is a Japanese American lawyer in Washington, DC who grew up in Hawaii. In 1989 he went to Officer's Candidate School of the Marine Corps where he faced discrimination and harassment. He was finally able to win a lawsuit against the Marines. Danny Chen was a Chinese American who was born and raised in New York. His desire was to join the US Army and serve his country. He was nineteen years old when he was serving in Afghanistan where he was harassed and beaten by his fellow soldiers. He was six four so he might seem to not to be the type to be bullied, but he was quiet and shy. Being unable to take the ill treatment, he apparently shot himself in the head in 2011. Jeremy Lin has found great success in the NBA, but he has faced racist comments from sportscasters and others. It is not a perfect world, and there needs to be more kindness shown to others.

There is a lot of kindness, luck, and timing involved in everything that we do which allows us to accomplish anything in this life. We are all recipients of it. We need to work and do our part to find fairness in our economic and political system. We should show kindness to others. There is a lot we can do to make this a better world for those around us and those who come after us. Our work is not done. I am very grateful for those who have shown kindness to me and who have given me support and friendship throughout my life.

May you all find joy in your work and success in your future. Thank you.

———— ✺ ————

Floyd Mori was asked to be in an ad for AARP to be used in an advertising campaign in their outreach to the Asian American population. Permission was granted to use the ad which appears on page 41. Others who did similar AARP ads were Ginny Gong, former president of the board of OCA National, and Major General Antonio Taguba, US Army (Ret.), who authored the Taguba Report on abuse of detainees held at Abu Ghraib prison in Iraq and is now chairman of Pan Pacific American Leaders and Mentors (PPALM).

Other graduate student teachers in Economics at BYU who worked with Dr. Wirthlin at that time were David Hunter, Bruce Kimsey, Bob Parsons, and Gordon Wagner.

After winning the Democratic primary for the California State Assembly, the State Democratic Party had Paul Kinney and Dan Howle assist Floyd with the general election. Dan became Floyd's chief of staff in the Assembly and later a supporter of the JACL through Eli Lilly.

Floyd was involved in many business ventures and projects over the years with various business partners including Michael Silva, Chuck

Terakawa, Richard Wirthlin, Alan Smith, Logan Hunter, Steve Mori, Stephen Yagi, Jotaro Fujii, Junzo Nakata, and Yoshi Nakata, among others.

REMARKS AT MEMORIAL SERVICE FOR JAMES MURAKAMI

Speaking at the Funeral
Sebastapol, California, May 20, 2012

It is a privilege for me to represent the Japanese American Citizens League (JACL) at this memorial service for James Murakami, a past national president of the JACL and a personal friend. I would like to thank Margarette and the family for this honor to pay tribute to a great man.

Jim was a friend and a champion for the causes of the JACL. On behalf of the National JACL, I want to offer condolences to the family. We want the family to understand that Jim Murakami stood tall in the midst of giants, and he distinguished himself as a fearless crusader for the justice for all that we repeat each time we say the Pledge of Allegiance.

While we mourn Jim's passing, we celebrate his life and the commitment he displayed to the basic values imbedded in our great Constitution. He was not a loud orator but a relentless crusader for justice who made his influence known through a soft and kind manner. Others could not deny his convictions.

While I was associated with the JACL nearly all of my life because my older siblings always participated in the JACL activities while I was growing up in Utah, it was Jim who really got me acquainted with the vital mission of the JACL and introduced me to the inner workings of our important civil rights organization which was established in 1929.

Jim became the National JACL president in 1976, a year after I was elected to the California State Assembly.

As one of the first two Japanese Americans to serve in the Assembly, I was immediately immersed in issues of concern to the Japanese American community and the JACL. I attended the JACL convention when Jim was elected national president of the JACL. During the next two years, Jim tirelessly pursued and advocated for one of the major initiatives in the history of the JACL, the movement to seek redress for the Japanese Americans who were unjustly incarcerated in the American concentration camps during World War II.

Jim's home in Santa Rosa was not that far from the state capitol, and Jim visited my office in Sacramento on several occasions during his term as JACL president, working hard to further the work of the JACL. Jim was the organization leader when the JACL formally endorsed the redress concept and made important changes to what it had been doing to right a horrible wrong. This began a decade-long advocacy effort that finally won passage in Congress. This was HR 442 or the Civil Liberties Act of 1988 which was signed into law by then President of the United States, Ronald Reagan. Jim instilled in me a firm understanding of the injustice of the World War II detention camps. He was a key factor in engaging me in the Redress Movement. Jim played a very important role in the history of the JACL.

Next year will be the twenty-fifth anniversary of the signing of the redress legislation into law. Today, many look at this effort as the great example of the values within the Constitution that should protect individual rights, rights that were ignored by the government during World War II when Japanese Americans were forcibly removed from their West Coast homes. This past week the debates in Congress included many references to the mistake of incarcerating innocent Japanese Americans and the redress effort which implanted a lesson which our nation should never forget.

It was in large part Jim Murakami's work when he was national JACL president that assured that this legacy would continue on into the future. So as we celebrate Jim's life, let us remind the younger generations that we owe a huge debt of gratitude to Jim and the other leaders of his era. May we as family and friends work to make sure that legacy lives on and that the work of Jim Murakami remains as a beacon for generations. We are all blessed because of Jim's convictions for the right and more importantly the nation is better off for the work he and others of the community did.

I am a firm believer that we will see Jim in another existence and that he is continuing the work that he so ably did while he was here with us in this earthly life. He is a valiant son of God who has earned a coveted place of glory. We can be assured of that.

It was always good to see Jim as he regularly attended the National JACL Conventions. Jim had a happy demeanor, and he was always kind and friendly to me as he was to everyone. He will be greatly missed. It was a wonderful privilege to know him and to call him a friend.

To Margarette and the rest of Jim's family, thank you for sharing him with us.

James Murakami served as national JACL president from 1976 to 1978. He was born in Santa Rosa, California, and grew up in Sonoma County. After the attack on Pearl Harbor, his family was incarcerated in the Assembly Center at Merced and then in the camp at Amache, Colorado, for three years. Jim served in the United States military and later graduated from the University of California, Berkeley. He owned his own electrical/mechanical engineering business in Santa Rosa for over forty years. He and his wife of fifty-nine years, Margarette, have two children and four grandchildren. Jim passed away on April 28, 2012, and a memorial service was held at the Community Church in Sebastopol, California, on May 20, 2012. Floyd Mori was asked to speak at the funeral to represent the National JACL.

CWRIC HEARINGS

Commission on Wartime Relocation and
Internment of Civilians (CWRIC)
Los Angeles Hearings Held in August 1981
Testimonies of Japanese Americans
and others at the Hearings
This review of video tapes from the
hearings was done in August 2012

President Gerald R. Ford formally rescinded Executive Order 9066 on February 19, 1976, thirty-five years after it was issued by President Franklin D. Roosevelt on February 19, 1942. In Proclamation 4417, President Ford stated the following: *"We now know what we should have known then—not only was that evacuation wrong, but Japanese Americans were and are loyal Americans... I call upon the American people to affirm with me this American Promise—that we have learned from the tragedy of that long ago experience forever to treasure liberty and justice for each individual American, and resolve that this kind of action shall never again be repeated."*

President Jimmy Carter said the following on July 31, 1980, after signing legislation to create the Commission on Wartime Relocation and Internment of Civilians (CWRIC)], regarding the CWRIC hearings: *"It is not designed as a witch hunt. It is designed to expose clearly what has happened in that period of war in our nation when many loyal American citizens of Japanese ancestry were embarrassed during a crucial time in our nation's history. I don't believe anyone would doubt that injustices were done, and I don't think anyone would doubt that it is advisable now for us to have a clear understanding as Americans of this episode in the history of our country. ...We also want to prevent any recurrence of this abuse of the basic human rights of American citizens and also resident aliens who enjoy the privileges and protections of not only American law but of American principles and ideals."*

———— ❧ ————

On the very day that the Imperial Navy of Japan bombed Pearl Harbor in Hawaii early on Sunday, December 7, 1941, and soon thereafter, leaders within the Japanese American and Japanese immigrant population in various parts of the United States were immediately arrested and removed from their homes. Men in dark suits (FBI Agents) arrived at their places of residence or meeting places to take them away. Obviously, the FBI had been researching Japanese resident aliens along with Americans of Japanese descent who were leaders within their communities for some time before the outbreak of the war. Beginning on the day and night of December 7, government agents began to pound on the doors of certain individuals, searched homes, and took men away. This included owners of businesses, religious leaders such as Buddhist priests, civic organization leaders, Japanese language teachers, people who worked for Japanese-owned companies, and any others who were suspected of being capable of espionage.

These people (primarily men with families) were arrested and taken away without their families knowing where they were sometimes for months. Some were imprisoned for the duration of the war and did not see their families for years as they were held without due process simply because of the public opinion and prejudice of that time. Some were sent back to Japan. There was never a single case of espionage or sabotage among the Japanese Americans during World War II, and these innocent people were held without cause. When President Franklin D. Roosevelt signed Executive Order 9066 on February 19, 1942, giving authority to the military commander to remove any persons from a designated area, life changed drastically for Japanese Americans. Their quiet lives were immediately disrupted and damaged. The order was only used against Japanese American citizens and Japanese immigrants to forcibly remove them from their West Coast homes and incarcerate them in hastily constructed concentration camps in what were then desolate areas of the country. It was clearly racist as it was not used against Germans or Italians as it could have been. It was determined not to be necessary or possible to implement in Hawaii because of the large concentration of Japanese Americans who were an important part of the economy there and because men who might have been suspect had already been picked up.

A small number of people took the option of the "voluntary evacuation" to move to inland states, which was at first admonished by the government. Those people were required to have someone living inland to sign for them to come, and they needed to have the means to leave in a hurry. Some people moved to what was rumored to be a "safe zone" near Fresno, California, where they thought they would not be evacuated. However, the people were taken from that location as well and placed in the illegal detention centers. Many did not leave their homes early because they had no place to go and they did not believe that their government would actually treat its citizens in that manner although the rumors were rampant. When the American concentration camps became a reality, they had no choice (as many people testified at the hearings) but to go like lambs to the slaughter.

The Japanese American Citizens League (JACL) was the only national organization for Japanese Americans at the time of the war, having been established in 1929 to fight for civil rights because Japanese Americans and their immigrant parents were routinely discriminated against in the days prior to World War II. Although it was a relatively small organization which certainly not a majority of Japanese Americans had joined, the JACL leaders recommended that Japanese Americans should cooperate with the government. Most people had not believed that they would ever be sent to concentration camps, but they felt they had no recourse but to follow the military orders to leave when it did happen. Indeed, they were rounded up under armed guard. They were required to report at specified locations bringing with them only what they could carry. Some people testified at the hearings that in retrospect they wish they had protested the evacuation at the time as some few did.

There were four now famous cases where Japanese Americans tried to defy the orders of the government and to seek their constitutional rights. The courts upheld the evacuation order, but the convictions and decisions were reversed in the rulings in those cases many years later. These were courageous individuals who took a stand and suffered for it.

Gordon Hirabayashi was convicted for violating the curfew which was imposed on Japanese Americans. As a student at the University of Washington, he felt that the curfew violated his Fifth Amendment right of due process so he disobeyed the curfew which said that all persons of Japanese ancestry residing in certain areas must be within their place of residence from 8:00 p.m. until 6:00 a.m. He did not report for the bus that was to take him to his assigned camp so he was arrested.

Min Yasui was an attorney born in Hood River, Oregon, who was working in Chicago when the war broke out. He worked for the Japan Consulate there because he could not find work in Oregon as a lawyer after he had completed law school. He returned to Oregon where he decided to be a test case for the constitutionality of the evacuation order. He walked into a police station and asked them to arrest him for violating the curfew. Though his request was at first rejected and he was told to go home, he was later arrested and sent to prison. He was a second lieutenant in the US Army Reserves.

Fred Korematsu was living in the Bay Area when he refused to obey the order to leave his home and report to a camp. He had a Caucasian girl friend, and he did not want to leave. He was arrested and placed in jail in San Francisco. An ACLU attorney, Ernest Besig, approached Fred in jail to ask if he would be willing to use his case to test the legality of the evacuation although the ACLU argued that Besig should not fight this case because its leaders were close to President Roosevelt. Besig took the case in spite of this. They lost in the Court of Appeals and appealed to the US Supreme Court to challenge the constitutionality of the deportation order. The Supreme Court upheld the order excluding persons of Japanese ancestry from the West Coast zone during World War II. Korematsu was sent to the concentration camp at Topaz, Utah, where life was difficult for him.

Mitsuye Endo was working at the Department of Motor Vehicles in Sacramento, California, at the time of Pearl Harbor. She was forced to move to a camp which meant that she was summarily dismissed from her job without any hope of reinstatement. James Purcell, a civil rights lawyer in San Francisco, represented Endo although she had not been interested in the notoriety of being a test case. The original reason for her case was to regain her civil service job and not to challenge the evacuation. Purcell used the case to protest her illegal relocation and dismissal. He filed a writ of habeas corpus requesting that she be released from the camp so that she could challenge the terms of her dismissal. The government offered to release Endo outside of the West Coast rather than test the constitutionality of detention. Endo refused the offer and remained confined for another two years.

The US Supreme Court much later finally decreed that persons of Japanese ancestry could not be held in confinement without proof of their disloyalty and that the entire evacuation program was an example of an unconstitutional resort to racism.

There were others who indicated that they were not willing to fight for their country while they and their families were incarcerated. They were called the Resisters of Conscience. Because of the government's reaction to their courage in trying to seek freedom, many of the Resisters were sent to the Tule Lake camp which supposedly held the troublemakers. Some of the leaders who resisted the draft were placed in federal prison. They endured pain and suffering for years within the Japanese American community although they had received a pardon from President Harry S. Truman when the war ended. President Truman recognized their principled stand for justice. With a ceremony in San Francisco in 2002, the JACL apologized to the Resisters for the treatment they received from the JACL community.

The War Relocation Authority (WRA) was formed on March 18, 1942, by Executive Order 9102. The director was Milton S. Eisenhower, who disapproved of the idea of the camps and served in the position only until July 1942. He wrote to his former boss before an April 1942 meeting, *"When the war is over and we consider calmly this unprecedented migration of one hundred twenty thousand people, we as Americans are going to regret the unavoidable injustices that we may have done."* He pushed President Roosevelt to issue a public statement in support of the loyal Japanese Americans, to raise wages that incarcerated Japanese Americans were being paid, and to petition the US Congress to create programs for postwar rehabilitation, none of which seem to have been done.

The next director of the WRA for the duration of the war was Dillon S. Myer, who took over after Eisenhower reportedly *"got sick of the job."* Myer's oral history reports that he asked Eisenhower if he should accept the job to which Eisenhower replied, *"Yes, if you can do the job and sleep at night,"* which Eisenhower said he could not do. Myer decided that he could do it and sleep at night so he became the director. He was an unlikely choice as he was a farm boy from the Midwest who knew nothing about Japanese Americans or about running such an agency. He defended the work of the WRA and said that camp conditions were not as bad as reported. He claimed in a 1942 film entitled *Japanese Relocation,* which was produced by the Office of War Information, that the Japanese *"cheerfully"* participated in the relocation process.

Myer was awarded the nation's Medal of Merit in 1946 by President Truman at which time Harold L. Ickes, the secretary of the interior, commended Myer for setting a precedent *"for equitable treatment of dislocated minorities,"* a statement with which most Japanese Americans would disagree. He stayed in the job until 1946 and was later commissioner of the Bureau of Indian Affairs.

There were some few people and groups which spoke out during World War II against the mass removal of Japanese Americans from the West Coast. The American Friends Service Committee or Quakers showed early and continued support for Japanese Americans.

A US Navy lieutenant commander, K. D. Ringle, issued a report dated December 20, 1941, in which he said that the large majority of Japanese people are at least passively loyal to the United States. He said that there might possibly be three percent or three thousand five hundred of the Japanese population in the United States who could be suspect, but those were already in custody. He suggested that it should be seen as an individual problem instead of mass evacuation which was certainly a racist issue and clearly only because of their physical characteristics.

James Rowe of the Justice Department has said that he and others fought desperately and unsuccessfully against the planned incarceration.

Francis Biddle, Attorney General, opposed the evacuation but later gave in to *"political expediency"* and eventually supported the policy for which he said he was haunted for years afterward. J. Edgar Hoover, the Director of the FBI, is said to have been neutral and to not show support for the mass evacuation.

Unfortunately, many people supported the forced removal of the people of Japanese descent from the West Coast. Chief Justice Earl Warren, who had been the California State Attorney General, spoke out in favor of the mass evacuation, an act which he later said he deeply regretted. The Hearst and McClatchy newspapers were clearly racist against the Japanese. Journalists and respected intellectuals joined in the demand for the forced incarceration of Japanese Americans. A majority of politicians were for it as were most of the general public. Hatred toward the Japanese Americans was widespread and openly exhibited in the printed word and in the actions of Americans.

There could be found almost no support for the Japanese Americans at that period of time so the American concentration camps became a reality. It was a dark period of history during which people of Japanese heritage suffered greatly because of the injustices inflicted upon them. There were severe economic consequences caused by irreparable losses of property. The humiliation and shame of being uprooted from their homes and treated like criminals have stayed with many throughout their entire lives. They have suffered untold sorrow accompanied by physical and mental distress. There have been feelings of fear and apprehension which have continued. All types of medical problems have been the result of the camp experience. The psychological problems are numerous. Denial and depression are common results of their repressed memories. There were a number of people who died in the camps or shortly after being released. There is at least one instance of a person being shot and killed by one of the guards who may have thought he was trying to escape. Babies died or became ill because of inadequate medical care.

The trauma and difficulties continue to this day. Some people testified at the hearings that they still feel like second-class citizens. The same or similar experiences are common to thousands and thousands of people who were forced to suffer the fate of the evacuation and incarceration. All Japanese Americans were treated as second class citizens and were classified as non-citizens or enemy aliens, presumably until the formation of the segregated unit of Japanese Americans in the US Army when the young men were asked to volunteer for service. The 442nd Regimental Combat Team of Japanese Americans from the mainland combined with the 100th Infantry Battalion of Japanese Americans from Hawaii to become the most highly decorated unit for its size and length of service in the history of the United States Army. They suffered unusually high casualties with many Purple Heart Awards being earned because of injuries or death.

At the war's end, those who were incarcerated left the camps mostly with no money, no job, no friends, no home to which to return, no prospects for housing, and little hope for the future. Generations of Japanese Americans are still suffering the effects of the events and experiences inflicted upon them during World War II when the Constitution did not protect them. Basically, no one was able to escape unscarred, including those Japanese Americans who were not incarcerated but who faced prejudice and discrimination in the outside world.

The JACL had been seeking redress since 1970 at the urging of some of its leaders, notably an activist by the name of Edison Uno, a university professor in San Francisco who had been imprisoned at Crystal City, Texas, during the war. Although some progress had been made, such as the rescinding of Executive Order 9066 by President Gerald R. Ford on February 19, 1976, the redress effort had not moved forward as was hoped and anticipated. The first effort in Congress did not get out of committee.

The very beginnings of the Redress Movement may have come during the war when a group called the Heart Mountain Fair Play Committee demanded some type of restitution for their incarceration. The JACL, with the work of Mike Masaoka, tried to gain some compensation over the years for those whose lives were so severely disrupted. The Japanese American Evacuation Claims Act of 1948 gave some extremely small token payments for property and money lost, which in no way came anywhere close to being fair payment for damages. People were advised to take the minuscule payments as this was thought to likely be their only chance for any compensation at all.

After the JACL voted at its 1978 National Convention to earnestly seek redress with monetary compensation for those who were incarcerated in the American concentration camps during World War II, a long struggle began. It was known that Congress would never simply issue an apology or provide reparations to the Japanese Americans affected by the mass evacuation without a person or group of people pushing for it. It would take a huge effort on the part of many leaders and ordinary people.

Other groups besides the JACL were also involved. Sen. Daniel Inouye (D-HI), who had been a member of the 442nd Regimental Combat Team/100th Infantry Battalion during World War II, recommended that a commission to study the issue should be formed to hear the actual stories which could ultimately convince Congress to back the redress effort.

President Jimmy Carter signed Public Law 96-317 on July 31, 1980, which formed the Commission on Wartime Relocation and Internment of Civilians (CWRIC). The CWRIC was charged with studying the mass removal and incarceration of Japanese Americans during World War II and to recommend an appropriate remedy.

The nine member CWRIC consisted of: chair, Washington, DC lawyer Joan Z. Bernstein; vice chair, Rep. Daniel E. Lungren (R-CA); Hugh Mitchell, former US senator; Dr. Arthur Flemming, chair of the US Commission on Civil Rights; Arthur J. Goldberg, former Supreme Court Justice; Judge William Marutani, a Japanese American on the Philadelphia Court of Common Pleas; former US senator Edward Brooke; former congressman and priest, Robert Drinan; and Ishmael V. Gromoff, a Russian Orthodox priest. The executive director of the CWRIC was Paul Bannai.

The CWRIC in the end issued a report and declared that the evacuation of Japanese Americans was the result of wartime hysteria, racism, and the lack of competent political leadership at the time of the war. The recommendation of the CWRIC was to seek an apology from the President of the United States and Congress and called for individual payments of $20,000 to the approximately 60,000 former internees who were living by the cutoff date to be determined. Their report came after eighteen months of research after the hearings were completed. The report was published under the title of *Personal Justice Denied* and dated June 16, 1983.

[Five years later President Ronald Reagan signed the Redress Bill into law as The Civil Liberties Act of 1988. It was later decided to also include those who had "voluntarily evacuated" as recipients of the redress effort. The cutoff date was set at August 10, 1988, the date that President Reagan signed the bill.]

The CWRIC held hearings in ten locations throughout the country. The first was held in Washington, DC. The second set of hearings was in Los Angeles, California. Some of the other locations were San Francisco, Seattle, Anchorage, Chicago, and New York.

A steering committee of four community groups met on January 30, 1981, to coordinate efforts for the hearings in Los Angeles. The groups were the National Coalition for Redress/ Reparations (NCRR), the Japanese American Citizens League (JACL), the Japanese American Bar Association (JABA), and the State Bar Subcommittee on Redress/Reparations. Although the groups had different priorities, they were all concerned with the issue of seeking redress.

Not all those who testified were for the redress and reparations for Japanese Americans. S. I. Hayakawa, was a Republican United

States Senator from California who was a Japanese American. He had been born in Canada and was an English professor who had served as president of San Francisco State University. He testified that Asian Americans had suffered racial discrimination for one hundred years, but he strongly opposed the request by Japanese Americans for monetary reparations for their incarceration. He stated that some people enjoyed the camps, and it could have been worse. He called it a three-year vacation when they had the time to do things they could not do if they were living ordinary lives where they had to work everyday. Many, who later testified, including elected officials, disagreed strongly with Senator Hayakawa and criticized his views.

Lillian Baker, a white woman very opposed to redress and obviously full of hatred, was present with a female associate to object to the redress issue. A letter she read was from Dillon Myer, the WRA director during the war, in which he defended the conditions in the camps and said he never knew of anyone being shot in a camp (which people testified did happen). He was actually old and perhaps dying at the time of the hearings when he purportedly wrote the letter. The woman had previously insisted in newspaper accounts that the evacuation did not happen and that Japanese Americans did not deserve redress. Later the two women caused trouble at the hearing when they tried to grab papers away from a witness who was testifying. They were ejected from the hearing to the cheers of the audience.

Some of the elected officials who spoke in support of the Redress Movement and who expressed disagreement with Senator Hayakawa were: Barbara Marumoto, state representative in Hawaii; Mayor Tom Bradley of the City of Los Angeles; Edmund Edelson, chair of the board of supervisors of Los Angeles County; Mike Antonovich of the board of supervisors of Los Angeles County; and Mas Fukai, who was a Gardena city councilman who is a Japanese American who had been incarcerated during World War II.

Many Japanese Americans who testified before the CWRIC expressed thankfulness for the opportunity to tell their stories although it was emotionally difficult for most of them. These people for the large part had not even told their families of their experiences of World War II. The CWRIC members, early in the hearings, acknowledged that the forced evacuation and incarceration were definitely wrong, and they asked for recommendations as to what remedies should be recommended to Congress.

Most who testified suggested individual monetary reparations of $25,000, but others mentioned sums of $50,000, $100,000 and $1,000,000 to compensate for the huge losses incurred by Japanese Americans who lost basically everything when they were rejected by their own country and forced to leave their homes and nearly everything they owned. Most had to start over, and many were never able to recover financially. It was stated that $25,000 would equate to $2,500 for the time of the war. Although no amount of monetary compensation could ever right the grievous wrongs which were committed against Japanese Americans by their own country, monetary reparations were stated as an absolute necessity in order to ensure that such an act would never be permitted to be repeated against any other people in the United States. Some other suggestions were to create libraries, community centers, or trust funds to provide scholarships, grants, and legal funds.

Studies have indicated that the financial losses to the Japanese American community were in the billions in 1981 dollars. Some of those incarcerated lost valuable property, and everyone lost their livelihood. They could not earn money, and earning power was destroyed. Although many of the older first generation Japanese immigrant men were established and enjoying some measure of financial success when they were stripped of their freedom, most could never regain their previous economic stature even though some were still relatively young when they got out of camp. Many were broken in spirit and in health. Starting over was extremely difficult.

Specialists in the mental health field, doctors, social workers, lawyers, elected officials, and other community leaders testified about the effects which were suffered by the Japanese Americans during World War II. Many spoke of people who are still intimidated and of the continuing racism that exists even to this day. Those who had been incarcerated and testified represented all Japanese Americans, many of whom are still unable to speak about the experience without breaking down emotionally.

Commissioner Goldberg stated that the evacuation of Japanese Americans is absolutely unthinkable and unconscionable because the Constitution should protect citizens and resident aliens alike, and that no person should be deprived of life, liberty, and property without due process of law. He said that no one can dispute that the evacuation took place and that it was done because the Japanese Americans faced discrimination due to prejudice and looking different physically from the mainstream population. He stated that there can be no argument that the mass evacuation happened because of racism, and he said it was a profound mistake which should never happen again.

Commissioner Goldberg went on to say that war does not excuse the violation of basic constitutional rights which happened during World War II when loyal American citizens were rounded up and imprisoned behind barbed wire with sentries posted and housed in barracks not suitable for human habitation. He also stated that hostility was great after the war and that he has seen even at those hearings in Los Angeles that racial tensions still exist.

The personal stories of the mass evacuation were poignant and heart wrenching. The suffering was universal. Someone mentioned that they never did "get out" of camp even after they left. Those experiences are affecting their lives everyday.

One man who testified said that he and his father were picked up in the middle of the night. When they woke him up after banging loudly on the door, they said something like, "We have a young one here." Nevertheless, he was taken on a train to an unknown area and ended up in a prison in Montana. He said that they received good food on the train ride, and he was pleased with the steak which was served to him. The older men who had been arrested with him said that they suspected that they were being fed well because it was going to be their last meal ever in this life. They fully expected to be on their way to their death without any due process.

Because there was a travel restriction placed on Japanese Americans whereby they were only allowed to travel within five miles of their homes without permission, many found it difficult to run their businesses. Indeed, those who did have businesses with Caucasian customers found that their clientele immediately ceased patronizing them. Their bank accounts were frozen. The financial hardships were immense and cannot be measured.

Many who testified talked of losing personal property, farm equipment, furniture, and other items which they had left with trusted neighbors or friends. A few came back from the camps to find their property intact, but most found that their possessions had been stolen or ruined. Some were told that their property was destroyed in fires of the barns or buildings where they were being stored. The Japanese Americans had no way of knowing if that were true or not. Some suspected that the items were stolen and sold by the people who then used the fire as a cover up.

Many people used the term "vultures" to describe those who came ready to pounce because they knew the Japanese Americans were required to dispose of their possessions within two weeks or less. Acquaintances and strangers alike, knowing their plight, came to their doors asking to buy cheaply or to take away their items for free. The Japanese Americans received pennies on the dollar if even that much. One man said that he had a new tractor which they had just purchased for $750 which they sold for a mere $75. The Japanese Americans had no recourse and had to take the offers or simply leave their possessions. People told them that they could accept the low price or the person would come back later and take it for free after they were gone.

Although there were alien land laws in California which prevented Japanese immigrants from owning land, some did have property because they had either bought it earlier or had purchased it in the names of their adult children born in America. By that time some of the Japanese Americans were old enough to have become established enough to own homes. Those who did own land, farms, homes, or businesses often left them in the care of so-called friends who had agreed to pay the mortgage and the taxes. Many found after the war that they had lost the land due to nonpayment of the required payments. Some people had rented out their homes and were supposed to receive the rent as income while incarcerated, but they never saw any money and lost the property. Some few fortunate Japanese Americans came back to find their property well cared for by kind neighbors and ready for their return.

People spoke of the primitive living conditions of the camps where whole families lived in one room with no partitions and no running water. There was no privacy. The weather was unbearable with extreme heat in the summer and severe cold in the winter with dust storms a common occurrence throughout the warmer months. There were community latrines. Distasteful food was served in community mess halls. Those who had jobs worked for extremely low wages. Family life disintegrated. They tried to make the best of a very bad situation, but life was difficult and stressful.

Women and men who had been children or teenagers while in camp testified of how they thought they had fun in camp where they had few responsibilities, but in later years they could see the lingering effects of having been locked up with sentries holding rifles guarding them. In retrospect, they can see that there were devastating remains of the incarceration which may have been repressed. The lives of the young were adversely affected by the camp experience, but the older generation suffered even more.

Although Japanese Americans and Japanese resident aliens who had been incarcerated in the American concentration camps had been reluctant to speak about those experiences to even their families for almost forty years, many came forward at the hearings to speak before the CWRIC to tell their personal stories. They told of hardship and suffering. Their stories were poignant and heart wrenching.

———— ✦ ————

This review contains just a portion of the information and the background of the Japanese American experience of incarceration during World War II taken from video tapes of some of the testimonies given at the CWRIC hearing held in Los Angeles.

There was no logical reason for the Japanese Americans and Japanese immigrants to be evacuated and incarcerated.

Lt. Gen. John DeWitt in offering his justification said the following in 1942 about the people of Japanese heritage: "... There are indications that these were organized and ready for concerted action at a favorable opportunity. The very fact that no sabotage has taken place to date is a disturbing and confirming indication that such action will be taken." [It never happened.]

Milton Eisenhower described the evacuation to the camps as "an inhuman mistake."

Francis Biddle later said of the matter: "The program was ill-advised, unnecessary, and unnecessarily cruel."

Justice Tom C. Clark stated: "Looking back on it today the evacuation was, of course, a mistake."

HATE CRIMES PRESS CONFERENCE

Testimony at Press Conference
Held after the Senate Hate Crimes Hearing
Washington, DC, September 19, 2012

When my father immigrated to this country over one hundred years ago, it was in the midst of a total lack of knowledge and understanding of Asian culture, Asian religion, and Asian values. The next three decades turned this lack of understanding into hate and bigotry. There were language barriers and cultural differences that society in general did not take time to investigate. Japanese families were relegated to basically the other side of the tracks and not allowed to participate fully in the American communities in which they lived.

The war hysteria of Pearl Harbor caused the unthinkable. American citizens were persecuted. Fathers were picked up by the FBI and separated from their families. Within months, around one hundred twenty thousand people of Japanese descent were herded up and put into assembly or detention centers. They were later to be placed in one of ten of what could be called today, illegal detention centers or concentration camps on American soil. This happened only because they were of Japanese ancestry and nobody understood who they were nor did anyone want to know for what they stood. It is considered to be one of the most egregious crimes against our sacred Constitution.

The miraculous occurrence that happened some forty-six years later is that our nation recognized this mistake. Through advocacy efforts of the Japanese American Citizens League (JACL), other Japanese American organizations, a large coalition of civil rights organizations, numerous individuals, and finally support from Congress, the government apologized for this grave abuse of constitutional rights. This redress effort could not have been accomplished without the tireless efforts of the four Japanese American members of Congress at that time (Senators Daniel Inouye and Spark Matsunaga of Hawaii and Reps. Norman Mineta and Robert Matsui of California).

One of the main reasons for seeking redress was to assure that such neglect of basic constitutional and human rights would not happen again to any other innocent citizen. It was to be a simple lesson in history. We recognized it was wrong then, and it is wrong now.

The evacuation and incarceration of Japanese Americans occurred because we allowed uninformed hate to flourish into violence and hysteria against a community that had to prove that they are as loyal as any American. Their skin color, their religion, what they ate, or their heritage did not lessen their love of this country nor their effectiveness as productive and enlightened citizens. Their values were honorable, and their motivation to get ahead was no different than someone who happened to emigrate from the other side of the earth.

I applaud this Senate hearing and Senator Durbin for maintaining this focus on the hopelessness of hate. Hate has no place in today's American society. Unfortunately, it continues to exist. We cannot allow the repeat of grave mistakes of the past. May we strive to gain understanding and respect for the values and culture of all who have chosen America as their land of opportunity.

Thank you.

———⚹⚹⚹———

Floyd Mori was National Executive Director Emeritus of the JACL when he was asked to speak at this press conference.

EPILOGUE

Thank you for taking the time to read about the Japanese American story, particularly as it pertains to the World War II experience when persons of Japanese heritage, most of them United States citizens, suffered untold hardship from their evacuation and incarceration in America's concentration camps. These innocent people who were living on the West Coast of the United States had done nothing wrong. The forced evacuation was totally unnecessary.

Most of the *Issei* (first generation immigrants from Japan) left this world years ago. They are likely the ones who suffered the greatest as they lost their livelihoods and self esteem, many to never regain them. Many of the *Nisei* (second generation born in this country of immigrant parents from Japan) were young adults or teenagers during their incarceration, and they are sharing their stories to some extent. Some of the younger *Nisei* and the *Sansei* (third generation children of American citizens) who were alive during World War II were children during that time.

The main purpose in telling about these experiences is to ensure that no one will ever have to endure such injustice as the Japanese Americans of that period were made to go through because the Constitution did not protect these innocent people.

This book contains repetition because the speeches were presented to different groups of people. As stated earlier, the speeches were all presented in public settings and the articles were previously printed in media outlets.

If you already knew the story, thank you for being willing to read this book to be reminded. Please share the history of Japanese Americans. This information was gleaned from years of research, experience, study, and listening. The facts of the incarceration may be substantiated by scholarly books or the Internet.